Train Seats and Hostel Beds
A Backpacker's Journey Across Europe

Nathan Rastatter

Honey Bea Publishing
2019

First Printing: 2019

1st Edition.

ISBN: 9781082702532

Honey Bea Publishing
honeybeapublishing@gmail.com

To Samie

Contents

Acknowledgements   ix

Introduction   1

Chapter 1: The Low Countries   4

Chapter 2: France   58

Chapter 3: Spain   100

Chapter 4: Italy   178

Chapter 5: Central Europe   252

Chapter 6: Germany   314

Chapter 7: Epilogue   372

Acknowledgements

I would like to thank Samie for supporting me through the three years it took to write this book. I would especially like to thank her for listening as I read this book, every word of it, out loud to her.

I would also like to thank Chloe, for being our friend, for going on this trip with us, and for posting so many pictures on Facebook. I used those photos extensively as I wrote this book. Of all people, I hope you will read and enjoy this book.

Lastly, thank you, whoever you are, for picking up this book. Whether you are a friend, a family member, or perhaps even a total stranger (especially if you are a total stranger) I thank you for getting this far and hope you enjoy it.

Introduction

I had the distinct pleasure of spending five weeks exploring Europe in the spring of 2014, while I was studying abroad in Leicester, England. I had opted to study abroad, in part, after reading a collection of amateur travel stories I came across in my local library. The rawness of the stories captivated me. The book was not like the polished travel guides I was familiar with, but was instead something much more engaging. I could actually picture myself in the shoes of the various authors as they explored Spanish hostels, Norman beaches and German discos.

As I travelled Europe, I jotted down notes and memories in a small black notebook. I had no intention of doing anything with the notebook, except to read it from time to time and relive the memories.

But, two years after I returned home, I started to transcribe the book into a Word document. As I typed up my notes, I began to add more details from the trip. The book soon grew exponentially in length. From the forty pages I handwrote, this volume emerged.

I began to tell people I was writing this book and several expressed interest in reading it. Thus, what began as a simple keepsake for only myself, is now a fully published book.

It is my intent that perhaps somebody like me will find this book and flip through it. I hope that they will be inspired to travel as well. Since returning from the travels described here, I have barely stopped moving. I owe a huge debt to that random, amateur book I accidently found, for it helped put me on the path I am on today. If my book could inspire just one person, I would count my work on this book to be worth it.

Enjoy,
Nate

Chapter 1: The Low Countries

Leicester, Day Zero: 27th of March.

The rain poured down on the afternoon I planned to leave this cold English city. The drops splashed onto my head and shoulders, chilling me to the bone. My waterproof jacket didn't offer much protection, being as soaked as it was. The overcast sky made the red brick buildings look even more gloomy than usual. My scruffy hair was perpetually damp.

The rain meant it was another typical day in the East Midlands of England. Despite the weather, I had grown to love the United Kingdom. I had been studying abroad in Leicester for several months. Classes had been significantly more challenging than in my home school of Kent State University. Outside of class, which only met three days a week, I had been traveling extensively. I had not grown up travelling, and before I came here, I had barely even ever left northeast Ohio. So, while I enjoyed exploring the English countryside and small towns, I was yearning for a new, more exotic adventure.

The University of Leicester was shutting down for the Easter holiday. Unlike in America, the school shuttered for an astounding five-weeks. Most of my British classmates planned to retreat to their homes in Nottingham or Sheffield to work on their final papers, but us foreigners were on our own.

I entered my student house, ran up the weathered wooden stairs and bounded into my room. I had already packed the night before. I only had two things in the dorm, my big red Osprey backpack and a set of wheeled luggage. I strapped my pack on and grabbed my suitcase. As I struggled to haul it out of my room, my ever-present, problem roommate briefly looked up from his incessant FIFA video gaming and gave a weak half-wave.

"Good knowing you," he said, as the white wooden door to our shared room swung shut.

"Well," I said, "I'm coming back in a few weeks," but the door had already closed in my face. My roommate gave no sign that he had heard me. We did not have the best relationship.

I rolled my suitcase down the stairs and out of the grand front entrance. The house had once been an elegant old manor but had been utterly abused over the years by dumb kids. One could almost see its former opulence, beneath the initials scratched into every open surface, the scuff marks and the deep stench left by years of only male students.

I dragged my suitcase over the ever-damp lawn to the street. I paused for the green buses to pass by. The buses were extra-long with two carriages. These buses were much more ubiquitous than the semi-mythical red double-decker Americans often picture.

I checked the road for traffic before crossing. By now I was well accustomed to vehicles on the 'wrong' side of the road. I strode between two massive hedgerows to the dorms across the street. Their heavy wooden doors were propped open. This place had once been a majestic mansion owned by a gentleman whose ancestors had crossed the English Channel with William the Conqueror.

The doorway led into a cavernous dining hall. Students filled it during the school session, but it now stood empty. It could fit a few hundred students, but it was always noticably quieter than American cafeterias.

There was a small storage room at the far end of the hall, guarded by a janitor. The room wasn't normally used, but the school allowed international students to store their luggage during the break in it. It was only open for a few hours today, and would not be unlocked until the first day of class after the holiday.

I shoved my wheeled luggage into an empty corner and stepped away. In my backpack, I possessed one pair of basketball shorts, five pairs of underwear, five cotton t-shirts, two flannels, and one black beanie. Besides these clothes, I also had my trusty red Nalgene water bottle, my tiny Asus laptop, one pair of cheap plastic sandals, some toiletry supplies, a quick-dry towel, and a small fleece blanket. I was wearing my socks, underwear, one additional flannel, my only pair of jeans and my second-hand vintage leather jacket. This would be all I carried for the next five weeks.

Back outside the storage room, I saw my friend Chloe struggling with her heavy suitcase. Standing at five feet eleven inches, her naturally pale skin was flushed from exertion and accentuated by her flaming red hair that stretched past her waist. Chloe was a friend of my girlfriend from Ohio, but we had gotten to know each other this semester. We were in the same dining hall and shared most of our classes.

We greeted each other as she stowed her belongings. Like me, she was just bringing an Osprey pack, although hers was a vibrant purple color.

"I decided to leave my laptop," she said, breathing heavily. I nodded. Between her, Samie and I, we had nine full-length academic papers to write. It was going to be challenging just using my laptop and Sam's tablet, but Chloe's computer was too new and expensive to schlep around Europe.

We were in the midst of small talk when my girlfriend, Samie, entered the hall. Her shoulder length brown hair, done in a neat ponytail, dripped with rainwater. She was smaller in stature than Chloe and I and was a more experienced traveler. Samie had cut her teeth backpacking along the Salmon River in Idaho and had been to Greece and Turkey the year prior.

Samie stored her bags alongside ours, adjusted her Deuter backpack and joined us. We were all set.

We left the hall and walked across town to our friend Oksana's apartment. The rain had let up a little bit, but in England it could return at any moment. Oksana had chosen to live in the student apartments instead of the dorms.

Waiting patiently outside her apartment complex, Oksana beamed at us when we arrived. Her smile spread across her face, complimenting her light brown skin and jet-black hair. Her backpack was a small school bag, unlike the large framed packs that we had.

Oksana would be joining us only for the first leg of the trip before returning to Leicester to meet a friend visiting from America. She had grown up in a military family and spent nearly her whole life in Europe and Ukraine. She was a seasoned traveler, and the four of us had been inseparable since the start of our semester.

We initially met Oksana moments after our plane had landed in London in January. On the first weekend in England, she had joined the three of us on an impromptu trip to York. Since then, we had gone exploring with her every weekend. We were all stoked about our upcoming tour across Europe.

The four of us walked to a nearby bus stop. As we waited the rain picked back up. As we stood getting wet, the bus did not arrive on time. Minutes ticked by. The bus was soon fifteen minutes behind schedule. We started to get nervous because our train was departing in a half-hour.

The bus finally pulled up twenty minutes late. We got on, relieved that we would make it to the train station in time. The bus pulled away.

Then, as soon we started to move, we immediately were stuck in standstill traffic. I looked out the window. I could still see the bloody bus stop and Oksana's apartment behind it. Panic blossomed in my chest. If we missed our train to London, we might miss our bus to Amsterdam, throwing our whole trip off.

I looked at the girls. We were thinking the same thing.

"Excuse me," Oksana tapped the bus driver on the shoulder. "Can you open the doors and let us out?"

The bus driver, like a lot of people in Leicester, was East Indian. He smiled in understanding and opened the door. We quickly thanked him and got off the bus.

Back on the sidewalk, we broke into a run. The train station was a mile and half way. We ran the whole length. We ran past the University campus, past the posh Lansdowne pub, past hole-in-the-wall curry houses, all the way to the station.

We jumped over puddles, ran haphazardly through intersections, and sprinted past puzzled pedestrians. The station came into view, and we dashed inside. Barely breaking our sprint, we whipped out our train tickets, fed them to the machine and ran to our platform. The train was already there and we boarded without a moment to spare.

Drenched but relieved, we stowed our bags in the racks above us and settled in. The inside of the carriage was cozy and warm, and only half full. It took several moments for us to catch our breath. Over the loudspeaker, the conductor was giving the usual information.

"Thank you for riding British Rail," he began. He began to stumbled over his words. "We are London going, ah, I mean departing London – oh bloody hell." He abruptly stopped talking, and the whole carriage erupted in laughter. The English rarely made sounds in public, so it was almost shocking to hear them laugh so openly.

Our train soon arrived in London. Having spent some time in London before, we headed right to our destination without pause. The Megabus depot was only a few blocks away. It was dark now, and still rainy as we walked. We were in the heart of bustling London. I caught only the briefest glimpse of the city before we found the station.

We were taking a Megabus to our first stop of Amsterdam. We located our bus within the massive depot and waited around until it was time to board. I bought a terrible tasting sandwich from a vending machine for dinner. We had had our final classes that morning, so I was tired from an already full day.

They let us on the bus around ten. Sam sat with me while Chloe and Oksana shared a seat behind us. Samie and I settled in for the overnight ride by watching the first episode of *Game of Thrones*, in what was about to become a years-long obsession.

After two episodes and some sleep, we were jerked awake when the bus suddenly screeched to a halt. I sleepily looked around and saw some people exiting the bus.

"There had been an accident ahead," the driver said, "three dead." A few people gasped.

More people got off the bus. The seats were small and uncomfortable, so soon enough we got off as well.

Outside the bus, an eerie heavy mist shrouded the motorway. In either direction there stretched endless snaking headlights. It was deathly quiet despite the many people who were standing around smoking cigarettes and talking in hushed tones.

After a while, the driver called us back to the bus, at which point he threw the vehicle into reverse and drove backwards a couple of miles to a car park.

At the car park, I fell back into a fitful sleep. I woke only once, in a dreamlike state, to see white marble cliffs rising out of the ground and disappearing into the inky black night. The White Cliffs of Dover couldn't keep me up, and I fell back asleep.

I awoke again to Sam shaking me as everybody was standing up.

"This is the border crossing," the driver explained. "The Frenchies will wave you over when they are ready."

He continued, deadpan, "Don't look them in the eye."

Sam and I looked at each other. Was he joking? We had no time to decide, as we filed out of the bus and into a small chilly building. Inside, the room was utterly bare except for two desks, each with a French soldier behind it. Nobody spoke as we formed two lines.

The French soldiers worked quickly. They would wave somebody over, glance at their passport, stamp it and wave to the next person. They looked tired and indifferent. They stamped my passport and I was soon back on the bus.

I woke up again in the depths of the cross-Channel ferry. I was too tired to think. We exited the bus and filed towards the stairwells. We trudged up the cold winding stairs, seeing level after level of endless rows of vehicles. There was a mass of people around me, but everybody was hushed. After what felt like twenty floors I passed a window. Looking out, I saw the gray water bobbing at eye level, and I suddenly shivered as I realized how deep underwater I just was.

The stairwell opened out to what looked like an American shopping mall. There were fast food joints, coffee shops, and duty-free stores. People were sleeping on chairs, on the tiled floor, and on uncomfortable couches. Groups of people were huddled around scarce outlets, charging their phones. Some people rushed to buy beer or wine from the fast food counters. Burger King advertised a combo meal with Heineken as the drink option.

As the girls claimed a couch, I walked around, in a daze, past the shops and sleeping people. The scene was too bizarre for me to merely sleep through it.

I walked through a big doorway and unexpectedly found myself on the back deck of the ship. I found a secluded corner to watch the lights of Dover disappear into the night. It was two in the morning. I watched the lights shrink and vanish into the thick fog. I looked down to watch the waves of the English

Channel lap against the ship. I watched the waves blissfully. I hadn't seen the water very much since I had left my home in Cleveland. I missed it.

I reflected on my life's journey in the frigid Channel air and felt sanguine about where my life had been so recently and where I was now. I was traveling across the damn English Channel in the dead of night. I never would have expected this. I felt at peace.

About a half hour or so later, I found my way back to the girls and promptly fell asleep in an uncomfortable love seat. I don't remember boarding the bus back in the bowels of the ship.

I awoke later, and my tired eyes saw the blue morning sky over Calais. I looked out the window and saw a fenced-in refugee camp. Inside the camp, ragged African men stared listlessly at our passing bus. Ramshackle huts, their homes, were haphazardly laid out behind them. The men stared at us without emotion. It was the infamous Calais Jungle, where refugees from Africa, the Middle East, and Afghanistan would wait for the slim chance that they might be granted asylum into the UK.

Just six months later, over a hundred refugees would scale this very fence and charge the kind of ferry we had taken. The crews used fire hoses to stop them from getting onto the ships.

As I watched them watching me, I had no idea that this was just the start of one of the most significant humanitarian disasters in modern times. The steady flow of refugees had not yet turned into a flood.

I fell back asleep, and next time I woke it was because the driver had stopped.

"All out for Amsterdam," he called.

Amsterdam, Day One: 28th of March.

The bus deposited us in an empty car park, seemingly in the middle of nowhere. The other passengers and I stumbled off the bus. Shaking my head to clear my mind, I took note of my surroundings.

The sky was bright blue with only a few wispy white clouds. We stood in a big asphalt lot, with a wire fence and a highway beyond it. Loads of cars were driving by. I looked down the road and saw a skyline in the hazy distance. I turned around and looked the other way and saw another skyline.

One of these must be Amsterdam, I figured. Following the milling crowd, we got our bags out from under the bus and walked away from the wire fence to the concrete platform everybody was gathering around.

There was a large wooden sign with a laminated map printed on it. The map was apparently showing all the tram routes in the greater Amsterdam area. We were too tired to make sense of it.

We did not know where we were or where we were going. People crowded around us, also looking at the map, also confused by it.

When the next tram pulled into the platform, I briefly wondered why I never planned our next step after the bus ride. The tram doors slid open. Inside of the car, was a man in a uniform sitting in a glass booth.

Samie, taking the initiative, asked where the tram was headed.

"Centraal Station," the man replied, sounding annoyed. Since we weren't sure where to go, we decide to go to Centraal Station.

We handed the man some euros. Walking away from the ticket man, we looked around for an empty spot to sit. There were no open seats.

The tram was packed full of our fellow Megabus travelers. We squeezed ourselves into the far end of the last car, slid off our backpacks and stood around them protectively. I looked quietly out of the window as we passed suburbs, shops, and apartment buildings. My first time in a genuinely foreign land looked remarkably like suburban Ohio.

Reaching our stop at Centraal Station, we stepped into the station. It swarmed like a beehive as people hurried from one end of the station to the next. Slightly overwhelmed, we followed exit signs to leave the sprawling complex.

As we searched for the exit, we passed by a row of the ever-ubiquitous currency exchange counters. Oksana halted and asked us, sounding a little embarrassed, if we thought the exchange booths could break a bill.

"I'm sure they can," I said.

"Well," she responded, "it's a big bill."

Oksana looked around, a little nervously, and withdrew a note from her purse. My jaw dropped when I saw the five hundred euro note. I did not know that bills could go that high.

Oksana walked over to the counter and was back within moments. The tellers had broken it without issue.

While Oksana did this, Chloe, Sam and I withdrew euros from an ATM. Withdrawing money always incurred at least one fee from our banks and another from the host ATM, so we always withdrew enough cash to last a week or so.

We stowed our money in our wallets and purses and finally exited the station. Outside we saw our first view of Amsterdam. We stood at the end of a large brick plaza. It was full of people but big enough as to not feel crowded. We saw a few pleasant 19th-century townhouses and buildings made of red stone. We saw a church dome or two, heard the cries of seagulls, and the low hum of boats and cars moving around the city. There are no skyscrapers here.

Centraal Station sat on the northern end of the city, perched on the sea. We walked away from the water, towards the town, directionless and unsure where to go.

We walked between apartments and stores. The red brick buildings were lined with green trees and bike racks packed so full I wondered how anybody managed to retrieve them. I noticed the buildings weren't very tall. They only rose up a few stories. It felt like a large suburban center rather than a sprawling metropolis.

We walked over dainty canal bridges, crowded squares and passed coffee shops emitting the unmistakable odor of marijuana. As we walked down the crowded streets next to the canals, we spied a familiar green and white mermaid logo. In the U.K. we had come to heavily rely on the free wifi at Starbucks. We bought some much-needed coffee, used the toilet and pulled up directions to where we were staying.

Although the girls had smartphones, I only had a cheap flip phone. As they looked up the directions, I studied the Dutch Starbucks menu.

The menu was easy enough to translate. The word drinks was *Draken*, coffee was *Koffie* and milk was *Melk*. I was relieved Dutch wasn't nearly as indecipherable as I feared it would be.

The girls found out that our bostel (boat-hostel) was only a little bit away. We made our way over, found the dock and strolled up the promenade to our ship, *The Christina*. We were excited as we climb the plank (the gangway?) up to the deck of the boat.

On the deck, we felt the ship sway gently below us. We walked across the deck to a hatch. The doors of it were wide open. Inside was a wooden ladder leading down into the boat.

Down the ladder, we found ourselves in a lovely wood paneled room with a few tables, chairs, and a beat-up computer. There was a laminated world map hung up on the far wall. Most of it, including Northeast Ohio, was already well tacked.

A man in the back of the room wearing a captain's hat, with short-cropped blonde hair, weather-beaten skin, and a broad smile greeted us in accented English.

"Welcome to the Christina!" he excitedly said, in a vaguely Eastern European accent. "You must be the four for Nathan!"

I smiled back, surprised that he knew my name. I had booked and paid the deposit online, but I had never been greeted so warmly at a hostel before.

He pulled out a big logbook and crossed our name off a list. We paid the remaining balance in cash and got a short tour. The place was tiny but full of character.

"This is the deck," the captain said, gesturing up towards where we had come from. "There are no drugs allowed on this boat, but marijuana can be smoked up there."

He pointed towards the refrigerator across the room. "There is beer in there, please leave one euro per can."

He told us this was where breakfast was served and then led us into a narrow hallway.

"This is your room," he said as he unlocked a door with a big number three on it. The room consisted of a bare light bulb, a round window, and four bunks. There were only a few feet of space above the bunks. *Wow*, I thought to myself, *this is an actual boat.*

As we squeezed into the room, the man pointed further down the hallway.

"Toilets are there, men on right, women on left, and shower room in the middle. I stay in captains room next to breakfast area if you need me."

With that, he handed us some maps of the city and told us to let him know if we needed suggestions for things to do. We thanked him sincerely. He left us to in our tiny room.

There was not space enough for the four of us to stand at once, so instead, we took shifts as we entered or exited the room. Once we got settled, Chloe, Samie and I left to explore Amsterdam. Oksana opted to nap.

Soon, we were walking down beautiful canals, past trees thick with green leaves, feeling the cool breeze off the sea, and basking in the peaceful vibes of the city. It was a pleasant sixty degrees and sunny, a welcome change from the U.K.

After walking for a while, we sat on the sunny side of a canal basking in the beautiful sun rays. We kicked off our shoes and watched as boats full of tourists glided down the scenic canals.

It was blissful as we sat with our backs leaning on one of the hundreds of stone bridges. The three of us laughed, and joked, and people-watched.

A few hours quickly flew by, and so we went to check on Oksana. We passed through the Red Light District on our way back. The neighborhood looked regal, and it was just as peaceful as the rest of the city. The only difference was that the front of the buildings were broken up by glass windows where scantily clad women sat on stools and looked out at us.

While it was somewhat of a shock to see prostitutes right out in the open, I was more surprised at how bored they looked. They sat naked or nearly naked, with their legs crossed, eyes and fingers glued to their smartphones, just like anybody else my age would. A few of the prostitutes half-heartedly waved at us, but they knew we weren't buying.

Past the Red Light District, Chloe and I found a giant wooden clog painted bright yellow with pink flowers. We immediately jumped in the shoe and insisted Sam take our photo. Sam, mortified, pretended not to know us.

We picked up some sandwich supplies at a nearby grocery store. It was a tiny storefront built out of a metal shipping container. I was delighted to find I could read the labels on the meats and cheeses with my rudimentary German skills.

As I paid for some cheese, bread, and meat, the woman at the counter spoke to me in Dutch. I nodded, smiled and handed my euros over.

"*Dank je wel,*" I said, trying to make an effort at the language. The lady smiled, made change, and spoke a bit back. I pretended to understand and walked away, triumphant about my first ever interaction in a different language.

We joined Oksana sitting on the deck and made sandwiches together. As we ate, we acknowledged the inevitable. We had to check out a coffee shop. After all, we couldn't come to Amsterdam and not smoke some weed.

After eating, we went to the only coffee shop that I knew of. Earlier that day I had seen a proper businesswoman light up a monster blunt in the window, so I figured it would be as good as any shop.

It only took us a minute to get there. Outside the shop, we hesitated for a moment. Chloe and Sam had never even smoked before. Amsterdam was a hell of a place to start. Summoning our courage, we drew our breath and in.

We were immediately swallowed up by a crowd of people. The room itself was the size a large studio apartment, with maybe eight tables with four seats each. Almost every single seat was full. There was a wooden bar facing the street where even more people were perched. The room was thick with smoke, and we had to shout over reggae music.

Sam and Chloe pounced on a table some people were just vacating while Oksana and I went up to the counter at the back of the shop.

There was a mob of people in front of the counter. Two bearded men were working like mad behind the bar. They were tossing out joints, bags of weed and taking money. There was no menu, so I held up my index finger and mimed smoking a joint. Within milliseconds I was tossed one.

"How much?" I yelled a few times before I finally caught the attention of one of the men. I feel I could have easily walked away without paying.

The man flashed his fingers, and I handed over the two euros and fifty cents he had mimed. Oksana and I pushed our way back to the table.

I set the joint down on the table and the four of us looked at each other.

"Well let's smoke then," Oksana said, letting out a nervous laugh, breaking the tension.

"Do you have your lighter?" I asked her. Oksana smoked cigarettes occasionally, so she usually had a lighter on her.

"Shit," Oksana said quietly as she searched through her little purse. "I left it in the boat. I wasn't thinking because I was so tired."

Since none of us had a lighter, we had to borrow one. Seeing as everybody in the room was smoking, I didn't think it would be hard to find one.

I turned to the table next to me, where two bearded Middle Eastern-looking men sat, eyes red with lazy smiles on their faces.

"Can I borrow your lighter?" I asked while miming flicking a lighter. The men did not change expression nor even acknowledge me. I continued to imitate, and their eyes slowly began to focus on me. Not only was there a language barrier here but these guys were epically stoned.

I eventually got my message across and finally, the man reached into his coat and handed me a lighter.

"I'll give it right back!" I said and he just laughed.

I sparked up the joint and took a deep inhale. I blew out a big cloud of smoke and passed it to Oksana. It was a professionally rolled cone joint, thick as a cigar. I immediately felt baked. I watched Chloe and Sam start to cough as they exhaled the smoke.

The tiny café was so full of people and thick smoke that it quickly began to feel claustrophobic. We took a few hits each and then set the joint down on the ashtray, all of us coughing heavily.

Wordlessly, we stood up to leave. We were all coughing too much to smoke more. Oksana deftly stubbed out the remaining half of the joint and stuck it in her purse.

We stepped outside and I physically felt the sunlight hit me. I felt blissful in the afternoon sun with the blue skies above and the gently blowing breeze. I saw people strolling around and smelled marijuana smoke wafting out of the open door behind me.

I looked to my left and saw an old Catholic church next to me, and a restaurant next to it that was topped by, bizarrely, a mini-Statue of Liberty. *Amsterdam*, I thought, *is the best city ever.*

Then, I started to freak out. As we began to walk up the street, panic engulfed me. Looking at the street signs written in Dutch, I realized how much more foreign Amsterdam was from England. The realization of being in a genuinely foreign country for the first time in my life hit me like a ton of bricks.

I thought about how we were alone on this strange new continent for a full month with no support system. We had only our clothes and our backpacks. A small part of my mind was able to enjoy the surreal feeling of being stoned in a strange, beautiful city but feelings of anxiety were overwhelming me.

As I freaked out about my situation I accidentally bumped into a dirty homeless man who immediately cursed and started to follow us, yelling and shaking his fist.

I kept walking, partially to avoid trouble but mainly because I was stoned as shit. Being in Europe and the UK had given me a sense of security I didn't feel in the US. Perhaps it was foolish, but I always felt safe even in large cities like Amsterdam. In Cleveland, this kind of altercation would be much more worrisome, since the person could have a gun. Here I felt ok just walking away. He followed us for a while, shaking his fist at us, but eventually Oksana turned to give him a withering icy stare. The man stopped bothering us.

We came across an Arabic kebab shop. The incident had not helped my state of mind. We stepped inside the dingy restaurant and took a seat in the back. It should have been familiar because we had eaten at many kebab shops in England, but this one filled me with a sense of stoned dread.

We ordered. The plate of food I received looked disgusting. I had ordered a big fried piece of meat, but I could barely eat. My stomach churned as I picked at my food. Nausea overwhelmed me.

Looking around instead of eating, I watched two little girls come out and hug the legs of the cook. He reached down, shifted the spatula to his other hand, and patted their heads. The familial scene was comforting. My stomach loosened a little, and I choked down some of the food. I had eaten almost nothing the entire day. I was too stoned to talk.

We left the restaurant and trekked back to the docks. We climbed up the plank to the deck, nodded hello to some backpackers smoking weed and descended down the ladder.

I grabbed my travel journal from my bunk and headed into the common room just up the hallway. There, Chloe was Facetiming her partner, while Oksana was listening to Bon Iver on the boat's speakers. Sam was writing in a journal of her own. Before sitting down, I opened the refrigerator and grabbed one of the small cans of Heineken.

Writing and sipping the beer, I thought it tasted better than at home. It may have been placebo, but the booze always tasted better where it was made. Looking up from my journal I saw Sam looking thoughtfully into the distance as she wrote her own story. I wondered what her story was like, and how we could never have the same perspective no matter how close our relationship got. We would always be separate people. *I am definitely still a little stoned* I realized.

After I wrote for a while, I pulled out my other notebook where I kept all the hostel bookings, train, and plane information. As I looked at all the numbers and costs, I finally formed an official budget. I had a total budget of twenty-five hundred dollars or just over two thousand-one hundred euros. I took a solid guesstimate on our transport and lodging costs. I knew we were going to take at least one flight and that we might be taking a sleeper train from Spain to Italy. Sleeper trains were not included on our Euro rail-passes and were going to be hideously expensive.

Once I subtracted those costs, I divided my remaining money by the total number of days and reached a daily budget of precisely thirty-six euros. I would have thirty-six euros to spend each day on food, museums, tours, and souvenirs. This was forty-three US dollars. I knew it was going to be tight, but I was disheartened by my conclusion.

Perhaps seeing my sad look, Sam came over and asked if I would like to take a walk with her. We often took night walks in England, and both figured this would be a welcome break from the others.

Sam and I started to walk down the pier, but we only reached the end of the dock. It was too cold and we were too tired. I called it a night and went to the room. I climbed on the top bunk and settled in. The ceiling was only two feet or so from my body, so the bed felt uncomfortably like a coffin. The boat rocked gently as I quickly fell asleep.

Amsterdam, Day Two: 29thof March.

I had slept like a rock. Yawning as I awoke, I attempted to do a morning stretch, only to have my knuckles knock against the hull of the ship. I couldn't even extend them past my head.

The one redeeming feature was the fresh air coming in from the tiny round window in the room.

Getting out of our bunks and dressing one at a time, we exited the room and headed up the short hallway to the common room. Waiting for us was a fantastic breakfast of sliced meats, several kinds of cheese, orange juice and coffee. The spread was very generous and I took full advantage of it. With my daily budget now firmly planted in my mind, I was determined not to spend one more Euro-cent than I had to.

After gorging myself, I went back down the hallway, past our room and into the male bathroom. It had been at least a full twenty-four hours since I had gone last.

Now perhaps I should have realized before I sat down that this toilet was a bit different from what I was used to. I had urinated a few times already but had not looked very carefully at it. There was no bowl in this toilet. Instead, there was a flat ovular plate, sloping slightingly forward, and emptying into a small hole located at the very front of the contraption.

In retrospect, I suppose I should have perched over the tiny hole, and sat in a very uncomfortable position, to do my business. But, I did not. I sat on it like a normal toilet.

The smell that soon filled the room did not bother me. In England, I had already long since gotten used to the minimal amounts of water in toilet bowls. While the smells were certainly stronger, I appreciated the far greater water efficiency. When I returned home to the States I would have minor culture shock the first few times I used the toilets, surprised at how full of water they were.

So, having long since gotten used to these natural smells, I was initially unperturbed. I finished my business, wiped up, and reached behind me to flush. I heard the flushing noise as I stood up to buckle my pants. I turned to look out of the small window that was directly above the toilet. This was when I noticed things were not going as planned.

Looking down at the toilet I could see the water flowing from the rim, like normal. I couldn't believe my eyes when I saw the water was just streaming around the pile of waste. The pile was not budging one bit as the extremely low-pressure water glided around it.

I immediately flushed the toilet again. Then I did so a third time. No result except for the same trickle of water that accomplished absolutely nothing.

I began to panic. There was no way I could leave this mess there. I looked at the roll of toilet paper and contemplated my options. I considered wrapping my hands in toilet paper and pushing it down the hole.

The smell was becoming oppressive. The bathroom was tiny, barely big enough to even let me stand up fully. I hadn't eaten very healthy in the last twenty-four hours, which had made the pile of shit even worse. I desperately looked around the bathroom for something to help me.

I found a large toilet brush stashed behind the seat. I looked at the brush. I looked my shit. I knew what I had to do.

I tentatively poked the pile with the brush. It slid forward a little bit. Gagging from the smell, I pushed the pile of poop into the small and inconveniently located toilet hole. Proud of my victory, I flushed the toilet several more times to rid the bowl of any evidence. I tried to wash the brush off as good as possible in the clean toilet water but was only partially successful. The color of the brush told me I was not the first to have used it for this purpose.

I decided to chalk up this frankly disgusting episode as just another cultural experience, another difference between my home and Europe. I washed my hands intensely and then stepped into the hallway. Looking around quickly I saw the female bathroom door open and nobody around. I glanced in the other bathroom.

The toilet was normal.

For the rest of the time on the boat, I used the female bathroom.

I went up the deck to meet the girls, eager to get this behind me and start our day. We stood on the gently bobbing deck and looked out at the city skyline. The air was crisp and chilly, cold enough that we wore jackets. The mid-morning sun did little to warm us, but it did feel quite refreshing. At least it wasn't raining.

After hanging out on the deck for a while, snapping selfies of our group, we were off. We went westward into the city, toward Anne Frank's house. Having all grown up reading her diary in school, this was not something we wanted to miss in our short time in Amsterdam.

The half-hour walk was beautiful. Every tree-lined canal was peaceful and welcoming. The city was quiet and subdued this morning, and we did not walk near any of the bars or coffee shops. A few bicycles whizzed by.

We turned onto a lovely cobblestone square in front of a church. A long line of people gently zigzagged around the square. From the map we were given by our bostel owner, we were still a block away from Anne's house. The line extended around the corner and out of sight. We figured this must be the line for the house and joined it.

Judging from how slow the line moved, we knew we were going to be in it for a while. We took turns popping into the inevitable tourist shops located around us. I browsed for postcards and found one easy enough. I had been collecting these from every city I went to.

I also saw several flags with an interesting design. It was a deep red color, with a thick black band running through the middle of it. In the band were three white X's. The design looked like a bottle of booze from a cartoon. It was not the Dutch flag. I wondered if the design was a tongue-in-cheek reference to the reputation of Amsterdam.

Walking back to where the girls were, I tucked my postcard into Sam's purse. Later I would stuff them into the back of my travel journal, hoping they wouldn't get crinkled or bent.

As the line shuffled forward, we stopped in front of a storefront that sold sweets.

"Chupa Chups!" Samie exclaimed. "My stepdad used to buy these for us for special occasions. They are so good!"

It was too tempting to pass up and we each bought some of the flavored suckers for a few Euro-cents.

The mood in line was fairly jovial as people chatted in a multitude of languages. But, as the people in line grew nearer to the house they got quieter and quieter until we stepped through the door. Inside, everybody was deathly silent.

The bottom floors of the house were somewhat unremarkable. Signs told the story of the Franks. The apartment was empty. The Franks, of course, had not lived in this part of the building, which had been a factory, but instead had dwelt in a tiny hidden apartment in the attic.

The signs, written in several languages, described the life of the Franks before the war. They had lived comfortably. We were surprised to learn that Anne Frank's name is actually pronounced 'Anna Franc,' with an annunciated 'a' sound in Anne and a soft 'c' in Frank. All Americans pronounce her name incorrectly.

Before long we were climbing the stairs into the actual hidden apartment. It was sobering. Nobody said a word. The mood was somber as we filed through the empty rooms, the wooden floor gently creaking beneath our feet. After the war, Anne Frank's father had sought to preserve the place exactly as he had found it. The Germans had emptied it out when they seized the family and empty it remained all these years later.

A small child began to cry and was quickly shushed by parents unwilling to break the spell of silence.

We looked into the room Anne had slept in, and where she had written her diary. It was small, and I suppose it would have felt smaller with beds and furniture in it. She had never been able to leave these rooms from the moment they went into hiding.

In her room, I saw the window Anne would have looked out of as she wrote her book. How could somebody be so hopeful in such a situation?

"Think of all the beauty left around you and be happy."

I saw a leafy courtyard through the window. The trees swayed in the slight breeze. I felt that strange aura of hope she wrote about. It sent shivers down my spine. I felt genuinely touched in Anne's room.

Leaving the secret apartment we continued the tour as it led into another building. We learned the fates of the family and the postwar life of Anne's father. He worked tirelessly to preserve the memory of his family and spread the message of joy Anne had written about. Then, in a case of glass, I was shocked to see the actual diary of Anne Frank. This was the very diary she wrote with her own hand.

It was strange because nearly every American has read this powerful book but I never really pictured it as being a real document. Yet here they stood, open to select passages written in her beautiful cursive Dutch. I marveled at the diaries.

Near the exit of the museum, there was a large forum with videos playing. The videos were asking in-depth and controversial questions about how best to combat racism and war in this world. The people in the videos openly discussed questions of immigrants and refugees, topics not always easy to talk about. People around us were engaging in conversations with each other, affected no doubt by the compelling atmosphere of the museum.

Stepping out into the street, I looked across the canal to the beauty of the city around us. It had been a powerful experience.

Needing a break from the heaviness, we decided to go to Vondel Park. We didn't know much about the park, except that it was a big green space on our map. We had packed lunch when we left the boat, and agreed lunch in the park would be nice.

It was a short walk, and the closer we got, the more the crowds grew. As we entered the park, there was a crush of people around us. People were sitting in every inch of free grass. They were sitting on the rocks, on trees, and on the broad gravel paths. There was a small pond thronged with people around it.

Seizing a spot as a young family stood up to leave, we swooped in and spread out our blanket to eat Nutella sandwiches and oranges. This would be a standard lunch for the entire trip. Looking around at the big park completely covered in people, I realized we were in Amsterdam's version of Central Park.

Being comfortable in crowds, I didn't mind the experience, but I could tell Sam hated it. I would not mind living in a big city like this, but I couldn't help but think she was going to have a nervous breakdown from these great unending crowds and the concrete jungles we would be spending our whole trip in. I saw her looking around forlornly, her mouth set in a grimace and twitching a little.

We finished our sandwiches and then meandered up the canals, along the busy tourist routes. We pass enormous museums, tourists on canal boats and the occasional coffee shop.

We ended up off the beaten path, to places where there were no people about and the English on signs gave way to Dutch. This part of the city was much less busy than the downtown area and was much more reflective of how average inhabitants lived. This was the orderly, peaceful Netherlands I had pictured.

We came across a group of metal statues commemorating the Dutch uprising against the Spanish in the 16th century. There were twenty or thirty statues depicting a crowd of men in period clothing carrying muskets and swords. The sculptures were realistic; each one was different and had unique features. I later find out it was a representation of a famous Rembrandt painting, *De Nachtwacht*.

As we continued to wander and take in the hustle and bustle of the city, we unexpectedly stumbled across the famous IAMSTERDAM sign. Located in front of the Dutch Imperial Museum, these were big red and white letters, seven or eight feet high. Highly iconic, although unknown to me, we immediately ran over and had fun climbing on them with the other tourists. I was struck by the fact that everybody was smiling and happy. Apparently climbing on big letters is universally enjoyed. It's always the little things that please people the most. We took plenty of pictures of each other as the sun set behind us.

"Jump down, I'll catch you," Chloe called to me, her arms outstretched. I was on top of one of the letters.

"Chloe, I will crush you if I do that," I said.

Undeterred, Chloe called out to Sam.

"Sam, jump down to me! I'll catch you."

Samie, although smaller than me, was also rightfully fearful of crushing Chloe's petite body.

"Chloe, it's ok. I can get down myself."

After having our fun climbing on the letters, we walked into a local bar. The building was a few stories tall and leaning drunkenly over the canal next to it. We sat on the patio overlooking a statue of the philosopher Spinoza.

In high school, I took an excellent philosophy class led by the venerable Mr. Esakov. It was his last year teaching, as he was retiring after decades of work. A passionate cigarette smoker, he used to love smoking with students in the break room. When that became illegal, he moved to a classroom with a fire door and would often step outside to smoke, inviting smokers who were of age with him. The school eventually banned students from smoking, but Mr. Esakov would still pop out to smoke. Finally, near the time I entered high school, the faculty prohibited all cigarette smoking from all staff. This being the last straw, Mr. Esakov retired.

So, being his last class, he jumped into the philosophy passionately, challenging us with advanced concepts and ideas. He would continually ask us to interpret famous works, ask us what we thought, and encouraged our responses. Spinoza was one of his favorites. Mr. Esakov infected me with an appreciation for philosophy and its impacts on our culture.

Travelers can be a snobbish lot, and in recent years Europe has gotten a bad rap. Why go to Europe, they ask, when you can travel to Southeast Asia, India or Africa. Why stay in stuffy Western cities, when you can ride across the open savannas of South Africa, hike the beautiful Nepalese mountain ranges, and get lost in dirty Bangkok alleyways?

Europe speaks to me because of the closeness of Western history here. In this square, where we were drinking Jupiter beer, I was in the area where Spinoza penned his idea that society should be a place where freedom of thought is encouraged. He would argue, from this spot, that religious leaders should not restrict the people in thought or action.

Although I certainly respect the beauty and diversity of other places, and love traveling to those more exotic locales, Europe is the birthplace of my culture and society. The idea of freedom of thought is so fundamental to Western culture that we forget it even exists, or much less that it was a revolutionary idea. In the birthplace of the Enlightenment, I gained a new respect for the people who shaped my culture. To me, this is what Europe offers that other places do not.

We went back to the bostel for dinner. There, we ate a simple meal of bread, meat, and cheese in the cozy dining room.

During the meal, Sam and I bickered between ourselves. It felt like we had been nipping at each other for weeks. It had been particularly bad when the two of us had gone to Dublin a few weeks ago. Instead of having a wonderful time to ourselves in the Irish capital, we fought constantly with few moments of peace. I began to fear that our relationship, less than a year old, would not survive our journey. I had been through the slow death of a relationship before and was not eager to repeat it.

Finishing dinner, we decided to check out the Red Light District. It was evening, and we were sure the area would be much different from yesterday afternoon. We cleaned up our dining area and got ready. I zipped up my black leather jacket to keep out the cold and perhaps look a little tougher.

The District, or *De Wallen* in Dutch, was close to our bostel. The closer we got, the thicker the crowds grew. There was a palpable energy in the air as the mass of people all headed in one direction. The nervous energy grew as we started to hear music thumping from the District. The rush of voices and street noise gathered and strengthened.

We passed an empty cathedral bathed in red light, a striking contrast to the black sky above. The crowd was getting rowdier with each step. People were drinking in the streets. I smelled marijuana and cigarette smoke. As we walked in front of the church, it's bell rang out. It was a low deep metallic sound that repeated several times.

"It feels like something fucking crazy is about to happen" Oksana shouted over the crowd. The feeling was ominous.

The bell rung one last time, and suddenly we were in the Red Light District, swallowed by crowds and noise. There were American bikers, giggling tourists, Japanese businessmen and drug dealers offering us cocaine. Mounted police strode down the streets, and I saw more than one person who looked dangerously inebriated with glassy eyes and a hollow stare. And, of course, every building had women in their red-lit windows.

The bored texting ladies were gone, replaced by gyrating young women wearing lingerie. They would gesture at people who walked too close or looked too long. A few motioned to us to come closer but they mostly focused on the young single men. Sometimes the windows would swing open, and a man would hop in, an eager look on his face. A red curtain would slide down as soon as the prostitute closed the window behind him. Later, we would see the curtain lifted, the young man would step out of the window, and quickly disappear into the crowd, never to be seen again.

We were far from the only wide-eyed tourists wandering around, content just to witness such a scene. There were overflowing bars, with buildings full of hookers on each side. There were rough looking men in leather vests and tattooed arms laughing wildly, groups of bachelor parties stumbling and spilling their beers on the streets and neon signs flashing all around us.

"This is like New York," Oksana yelled over the din of the crowd. Samie had a look of terror in her eyes, overwhelmed by the people and noise. We peeled off from the throng, down a quieter side street. Like most tourist areas, the Red Light District ended abruptly. Walk one or two streets over, and suddenly there are no more noises or lights, just sleepy quiet streets and the low hum of the city around you.

We passed Anne Frank's house, now closed. We walked over endless bridges, up and down romantic streets softly lit by streetlights. Everything outside the city center was long since closed.

But then, we passed a small playground. Chloe and Samie immediately jumped into the playground, messing around on the seesaw. They were not letting the night go to waste. I walked around them as they played. The playground was located on a divider between two streets. They built the playground at an intersection, something uncommon where I was from. I felt a bit strange here, in this deserted city, at the edge of a playground hidden beneath a thick canopy of leaves.

Our walk taken two hours. Eager to buy some weed before the night was over, Oksana and I decided to pick some up on our way back through the District. *Surely, we could find a shop there*, I thought.

Pushing our way through the crowds, we again passed in front of the red-lit windows where prostitutes danced and sold themselves. Although officially regulated, it was a common fact that a lot of these girls were from Eastern Europe, and had not exactly wanted this as their career.

Although nominally representing a progressive 'my body my choice' ethos, in reality, a lot of these women had been tricked into coming, having been promised legitimate work and good pay. As we passed through the bacchanalia once more, the loud, sharp drunken laughs, the way the men stared so hungrily at the women, the sheer overconsumption started to bother me. I was not digging this place.

Working our way through the main thoroughfare, we kept our eyes peeled for coffee shops.

"You see any?" I shouted to Oksana, who shook her head.

"No! You'd think there would be more here," she replied.

Finally, we came across a store covered in psychedelic paintings of bulldogs and celebrities.

"Let's try here," Oksana suggested, and I agreed. We climbed the few steps and entered the joint, while Chloe and Sam waited outside.

The shop turned out to be the original coffee shop from the 1970's, an era when was still illegal. There were neat little displays on the walls of hidden stashboxes and devices used to warn the patrons of police raids. The interior was packed full, and as Oksana and I walked around, we couldn't find where they sold the weed. Seeing a neon sign shaped like an arrow and reading 'Basement,' we followed it down a flight of stairs.

There we found a small space with a few beat-up couches and a small black bar with a huge muscular man behind it. We walked up after the only other patron left. We asked for pre-rolled joints. The budtender grunted and showed us a menu without speaking.

Scanning the menu, Oksana asked the man, "Do you only sell joints in packs of four?"

The man grunted again and nodded. Oksana looked at me, and we decided to leave. We were leaving tomorrow and didn't want to be bringing weed into other countries.

"Did you get it?" Chloe and Sam asked in unison when we met them outside.

"No, we didn't," Oksana said and explained the situation.

Going forward, we came across another coffee shop, only to find that it closed.

"Cocaine?" a young man asked me as we walk past the shuttered shop.

I threw my hands up in frustration. We were in the heart of the Red Light District where people were jumping into hooker-booths and offering us cocaine, but we couldn't find a damn place to buy weed.

Finally, on the next street over, Oksana and I walked into another coffee shop. Here, finally, they sold pre-rolled joints. Asking what we wanted, the worker showed us a list of about ten options. Eager just to go back to the boat Oksana and I quickly settled on a joint of White Widow.

We emerged, triumphant, back outside. Although we were tired from walking, we stopped to buy some waffles.

Waffles in Europe are a sugary snack, not a breakfast food. We had learned this much from England, where they are often sold in packages and covered with powdered sugar. In Amsterdam, they were covered in chocolate and fruits and were simply amazing

We gobbled them up, sitting on the curb with our feet in the road as we watched men stumble down the narrow streets, incoherently drunk and high. More than one person looked pretty rough, so we were alert as the revelry unfolded around us. Although Amsterdam is a safe city, I couldn't quite bring myself to relax, not this late at night and with so many people so far in the bag.

It was around midnight when we finally made it back to the boat. We went to the dining room and grabbed some Heinekens from the refrigerator, tossing our one Euro coins into the wicker basket.

Heinekens in hand, we climbed back up the ladder to the deck. We sat in cold metal chairs around a small table. Oksana, having grabbed her lighter, lit up the joint. This time, smoking was much more enjoyable. As we passed it around, coughing, I reflected again how strange it was to see Sam and Chloe smoke at all, much less smoke on a boat in Amsterdam at midnight.

Of all the times to smoke for the first time, these two get to say they did it on a deck of a boat in a foreign country at midnight. That's super cool. My first time was under a freeway overpass in Cleveland, next to where homeless men slept.

"You look like a thug," Samie told me as I took a hit. I was wearing my leather jacket and my favorite winter hat, a black and grey beanie. I didn't think I looked like a thug.

Changing the topic, I try to talk about how cold the air was.

"It feels like a cold blanket," I said, "like instead of making you warm, it's a blanket that you makes you colder." The girls stared at me in disbelief for a moment before erupting in laughter.

"A cold blanket?!" they laughed, "what you are talking about Nate? You sound crazy!" The doubled over in laughter.

You know those moments where you say something that people take as a joke, but you did not mean it as one? This was one of those moments.

"Cold blanket!" they say to each other and crack up again. This will become a phrase they will taunt me with for the rest of the trip. The phrase 'cold blanket' had made a lot more sense in my head before I said it out loud.

As we smoked more, I got a little too high again and had a bit of a freakout. My paranoia from yesterday returned, only slightly weaker than before. I started to feel very uncomfortable and cold on the deck, so I went back down the ladder into the warm common room.

I sat down at the small wooden table we had eaten dinner at. The girls joined me shortly after. Zoning in and out I looked over to see Sam and Chloe bickering with each other. Tension filled the room.

Oksana walked over to the communal computer and started to play some soothing Bon Iver. I did not know if she was playing it for her enjoyment or to calm us down, but it helped the situation. I started to relax and enjoy the experience.

I was finally getting my anxiety under control when Oksana perked up and asked if anybody wanted to go to the deck and finish the little bit of the joint we had left up there. To her dismay, none of us did. I had had more than my share for tonight. I was exhausted and stressed out and just wanted to go to bed.

It was funny because we had only been traveling for two days. Each weekend we went somewhere for three or four days, so this shouldn't have felt any different, but it did. I kept thinking about how long our journey was and how utterly we were on our own. My mind raced in circles. Would I even have enough money to cover my expenses? I had barely ever left Cleveland before I moved to England.

Getting ready for bed a little bit later I sat perched on a wooden ladder facing the doors to the bathrooms. The boat was silent as Oksana and Chloe had already showered and gone to bed. I was waiting for Sam to leave the female bathroom, you know, because of my last time using the men's room.

I sat in the dimly lit hallway, illuminated by a weak blue light. Samie exited the bathroom and was surprised to see me.

"Hey," I said softly, "where are you going, young lady?" I slowly stood up from the ladder.

"Why, to my room," she said playing along, speaking softly as well, as she entered my embrace. My arms closed around her. The embrace felt warm and safe. Wordlessly we kissed in this dark hallway in the small stinky boat in Amsterdam and all the unsaid and pent-up feelings of sorrow and happiness, joy and frustration were felt and exchanged all at once. The kiss went on for a long time. Gently and lovingly stroking each other's hair, we pulled away slowly, each one unwilling to break the moment.

All of our unsaid feelings were said without speaking a word. As I brushed my teeth and went to bed, I felt like everything was going to be ok.

Bruges, Day Three: 30th of March.

I awoke to find the morning sun still weak, meaning it must have been early. Checking my phone, I saw the time was improbably early. I felt drained, like I had got no sleep last night. On top of staying up so late, we soon learned Daylight Savings had taken effect last night, taking away another desperately needed hour of sleep.

We headed to the main cabin to eat our fantastic breakfast one more time. We thanked the captain for having such a cool place, and he seemed genuinely happy to hear we enjoyed it. Stepping onto the deck I pulled my leather jacket out of my backpack. The spring air still had a bite to it.

As we walked down the gangplank, I looked one more time at the *Christina*. The mid-morning sunlight sparkled off the murky blue water that extended past the pier all the way to the North Sea. The air felt fresh, with the last vestiges of winter in retreat. After a few pictures of the boat to remind me of my time here, we went to the train station to leave Amsterdam.

We arrived at Centraal Station. It was just before eleven and we were not sure how to activate our Eurail passes. Our train didn't leave until twelve thirty, but we didn't know how long the process would take.

Passing the weed shop from the first day, I reflected that we did not meet a single Dutch person in Amsterdam. My Dutch friend from England had told me that most Dutch people are embarrassed of Amsterdam and the fact that everybody thinks only of weed and whores when they think of the Netherlands.

This made me think of all the times I have told people I am American and they say to me that they have visited the US. When I ask them where they have visited, the inevitable response is always "New York City!"

"Do you live there?" they ask. Their disappointment then follows, as I do not, in fact, live in New York City.

We entered the sprawling train station and located a Eurail office. We waited in line with a bunch of other scruffy travelers until it was our turn to go up to the counter. Once there, a friendly Dutch woman simply wrote our passport numbers on the pass and stamped it with the date.

The pass itself looked like a folded train ticket, about the size of a standard envelope. The top of it had lines for the holder's name, passport number, and other details. Underneath, were thirty or so blank lines where the holder was supposed to write in the destination and departure time. Theoretically, a ticket inspector will verify the information and stamp the pass, but in practice, this rarely happened.

The woman at the counter explained this to us and then even handed us a printed schedule for the next leg of our trip to Bruges. Thanking her, we took our now active passes and found our platform.

Our train pulled in and we hopped aboard. The seats were comfortable and we stowed our bags in the racks above us. The ride to Bruges was a short three hours with two transfers. The first stop was Antwerp.

The train was modern and comfortable, as good as any in England. I watched the Dutch countryside slide by, passing towering windmills, small villages and fields of poppies. The countryside was idyllic. Sometimes the stereotypical images of countries are accurate, and I can confirm the Dutch countryside looked exactly as I had pictured it. I later spoke with some of my study abroad friends back in England, and a few went on long bicycle trips through the countryside, taking breaks in the shadows of the windmills and napping in the sunny poppy fields.

The ticket inspector came around and we proudly handed him our brand new rail passes. He smiled bemusedly and stamped the passes.

We crossed the border to Belgium as I wrote in my journal. I alternated writing with sightseeing. I enjoy train travel, as one gets to see so much more of the countryside than in an airplane. There is something romantic about trains that other forms of travel don't have.

Our train neared Antwerp. We had a bit of layover there. Departing the train at a leisurely pace, we walked off the platform and into the station. Inside it was another behemoth station. I looked up at the ceiling and saw there were several stories above us.

"How are there other floors?" I asked incredulously. The ceiling was all glass and steel beams, like a steampunk cathedral. Looking to my left I saw a huge window overlooking the city. It gave the station a feeling of being at the dawn of the Industrial Revolution when glass, steel, concrete and steam power were the wave of the future.

We spotted a giant electronic board listing the trains coming and going. Usually these signs in trains stations were pretty small, but this one was as big as ones in major airports. Scanning it, we found the train we needed and made our way over to the platform. We made sure to use the bathrooms. In England, we learned train station bathrooms were often better and more pleasant than lavatories on the train itself.

As we waited for the train to arrive, Oksana bought some French fries or *pommes frites,* and we helped her finish them. This slow pace of travel wasn't too bad.

We soon heard the train whistle and got on board. We walked past the reservation cars until we reached our spot. Our Eurail passes meant we had to sit in the unreserved section. This posed no problem at the moment, but it did mean that if a train were full, we would have no choice but to wait for the next train. We boarded the train towards Ghent.

Holding up the schedule, Chloe told us that we would have fifteen minutes to change trains at Ghent.

"No problem," Oksana said, shrugging. "We've done that a million times in the U.K."

Sam and I agreed, and we sat back in our seats, not worried in the least.

As we got a little nearer to Ghent, a voice came over the loudspeaker. They were speaking in a language we couldn't understand. The voice then switched to accented English, "Our train is running late to Gent-Sint-Pieters. We will be arriving ten minutes later than scheduled so please plan accordingly."

Shit! Ten minutes late? I looked over to Chloe. She had a panicked look on her face.

"We have five minutes to change trains," she stated. I felt a nervous pinch in my stomach.

We had initially planned to have four nights in Amsterdam. However, a few weeks before our trip we watched the classic film *In Bruges* while drinking wine and eating cheese. Fascinated with the city after the quirky movie, we had cut Amsterdam in half to fit in two nights in Bruges. Missing this train would deprive us of a big chunk of our limited time in Bruges.

We passed the second last stop before Ghent. Without speaking, we stood up and grabbed our stuff. We moved to the sliding doors.

Typically, the vast majority of people will stay in their seats until the train stops. It is not common to see more than one or two people standing near the doors of the cabin, but already a small crowd had formed. We squeezed into the car, aware that all four of us had obnoxiously large backpacks on. Usually we would do the polite thing, and unstrap our packs, keeping them between our legs to let people pass us more easily.

But now, we stood with our packs firmly strapped on. We even buckled the front straps, something I rarely did. More people crowded in. Soon folks were spilling into the other compartments. The tension was palpable as the train slowed down. I felt everybody around me tense up. The train seemed to be taking forever to stop entirely. I felt like a paratrooper getting ready to jump into battle.

Finally, the train ground to a halt. Everybody looked up at the small red light above the door. We were holding our breath. *Ding.*

The red light changed to green and the doors slid open.

The crowd pushed into us as everybody tried to leave the train at once. True Europeans, the exiting was a mixture of panic and politeness as people tried not to be too aggressive.

Next thing I know, we were outside and running. There was a big group of people around us, and we ran into the station. Luckily, it was much smaller than in Antwerp. The lot of us dashed into the station, and there was a strange feeling of solidarity with these strangers.

"This way!" Chloe yelled at us, pointing down a hallway, "I see the sign!" Without breaking our run, we split from the main group and dashed up the hallway. Only a few people from our last train ran with us.

Pushing past old ladies and other travelers we ran down onto the platform. Seeing our train, we sprinted towards it, our packs slamming into our kidneys and lower backs.

The train let out a shriek and did that slight jerk forward. We ran desperately down the cars tugging on the doors.

"They are all locked!" I shouted as we keep running.

"Go further down," Sam yelled back. "To the unreserved cars!"

If we lose the train right there, I'd never forgiven myself, I thought.

Finally, we came to an open door. There stood a conductor in a double-breasted suit and cap, laughing openly at the sight of us.

"*Willkommen,*" he said holding the door for us, smiling jovially. He sported a thick mustache on his upper lip, the living stereotype of the old-timey European train conductor. We clambered onboard and the man closed the door just as the train pulled away. We stood there panting in the compartment, red in the face and trying to catch our breath.

"That was.... close" Sam said between heavy breaths. We nodded. We were no strangers to tight layovers, but this had been the closest. We looked at each other and started to laugh uncontrollably. The whole spectacle had been ridiculous. Our trip was like a movie we were living in.

In the next cabin over, we snagged some open seats. These were not individual seats like in England and the Netherlands but rather two bench seats facing each other with a small foldout table between them. The large glass window would not open, but there was a smaller window, only about a foot tall, on top of it, which could. We slid it open to let some fresh air into the stifling cabin.

We could tell it was an old train. Tall wooden walls framed each group of benches, giving each four seats a decent amount of privacy. Across the aisle from us sat a group of German businessmen reading newspapers and speaking quietly. The car was otherwise empty.

When I took off my pack, I instinctively looked up for the wire racks to put my stuff. There was none. This truly must have been an old train. We put our bags between our legs and got comfortable the best we could for the remaining half hour ride to Bruges.

Pulling into Bruges, or *Brugge*, we left the small station and looked out over a road and some trees.

"Where is the city?" I asked aloud. Sam pulled out her smartphone and brought up the map she had downloaded last night. We followed the map and walked into the city, crossing over a river.

These rivers, alongside long-gone walls, had made Bruges easily defensible during its heyday in the Late Medieval/Renaissance period. The city, located just a short river trip south from the North Sea, had been an economic and cultural powerhouse for hundreds of years, only to finally fade as Antwerp and Amsterdam rose. The city was practically abandoned for many decades, with no industry to speak of. This was why the town was spared from widespread destruction during the wars of the 20th century and was still well preserved.

To get to our hostel, we had to walk across the entire city. It only took a half hour as we skirted around the city center. The town was far smaller than Amsterdam. The overcast sky added to the gloomy medieval feel of the city. We walked along narrow stone streets underneath medieval awnings adorned with statues of the Virgin Mary. We quietly took in the sights as we made our way to St. Christopher's Hostel.

Arriving at the hostel, we immediately saw that the reception was in a bar. Bad sign. I did not have any interest in staying at the infamous European party hostels. Judging by the grungy longhairs swilling beer as we signed in, I figured we might be stuck in one.

I never understood the crowds of people who drink their way across Europe or Southeast Asia. Especially in a town like Bruges, where so much incredible history was so easily accessible, why people prefer to sit and drink with other travelers is beyond me. Incidentally, I found these people can often be the snobbiest of travelers.

Well at least the four of us have our own room, I thought. Four is an excellent number to travel with because four-person dorms are the best balance between budget and privacy. With four you can buy out the whole room for a reasonable price and not have to worry about other people. Although it's easy to meet people in hostels, the girls and I preferred a quiet place to relax after a long day.

Once we paid, we climbed the flight of stairs in the back of the bar to our room. Located far from the bar, we would have no issue with noise. The room was sparse but clean, with two spacious bunk beds, a sink and a window. The window opened over an alley, but if we leaned out and craned our necks there was a decent view of the city.

We claimed our bunks and then checked out the bathroom situation down the hall. We quickly found out the place had no showers, only one working toilet, and naturally, no toilet paper. Great. It turned out that the showers and toilets were in the building next door. For sixteen euros a night, though, we couldn't complain.

We left our stuff in the room as we went to explore. We walked by touristy shops, various canals, and onto the main square. The town was beautiful, and the square was stunning. A few of the buildings looked as if they had been transported straight from the Middle Ages, which I suppose they had been. I had often pictured Europe as looking like this, but countless wars, revolutions, and industrialization have erased most of its medieval past.

In Bruges the buildings were still quaint. The architecture was interesting. A lot of buildings had a front façade that comes to a point, like a step pyramid or half-timbered house. The buildings weren't exactly colorful, as each was a different shade of gray, red or brown. The oldest buildings were imposing Gothic ones, turned black with age. The streets were mercifully quiet.

We ate dinner outside on the central plaza in full view of the grand clock tower, the cobblestone roads and the horse-drawn carriages trotting by. I ordered a plate of mussels while Oksana went for snails. I tried one, and it was fantastic. It tasted like a gooier salty mussel. Having forgot our water bottles, we ordered some water for the table. When we got the bill, we were shocked to find out that the water cost an astounding six-euro a bottle.

We went back to the hostel to rest for a little bit as the sun set. For our evening we decided to take it easy and just walk around, soaking up the magic of the city. Bruges was small enough we didn't need to use a map. We gauged where we were from the clock tower. It was centrally located and rose high above the rest of the town.

Every corner we turned brought us in front of cool medieval buildings, towering stone churches, statues of warriors on horseback and picturesque little streets lit by streetlamps. Most of the time we were the only people around, adding to the feeling of awe.

We walked to the far end of the city, just over the rivers and hung out in front of a large fountain. The fountain had several statues in it, including naked women with birds perched on their shoulders and pillars of differing heights. Other figures were of men in historical dress and a half-submerged mermaid.

Returning inside the city limits we found ourselves sitting in a garden courtyard, the four of us squeezed onto a wooden bench, under a canopy of ivy. A stray cat jumped up with us, and we began to pet it. It was surreal to be sitting in an empty courtyard in Bruges petting this black cat. It was one of those little moments that stuck with me.

We were delighted later when we left the garden, and the cat followed us for quite some time. It would disappear from our view only to come running back out of some dark alley, rub against our legs and then run off again.

We came to a little corner where there hung a map of the city made out of lace, overlooking a stone bridge covered in ivy. A small wooden boat hid half in the shadows under the bridge, and the St. Salvatore Church was lit up in the background.

It looked like a postcard come to life. So often sights in real life can be disappointing. So many pictures and videos only show the most idealized version of a place and none of the crap that inevitably surrounds it. This city didn't have that.

Later we walked up a cobblestone street to get some of that famed Belgium beer. We came to a bar that had outside seating on a small patio overlooking a similar view of darkened canals, creeping ivy, and gently lit medieval homes.

Soon we were sipping Leffe Blonde out of glass goblets on the patio. It was warmer here than in Amsterdam and just so damn peaceful. I enjoyed the wheat beer, until I later found out it was the Flemish version of Budweiser. Years later I would kick myself for missing the opportunity to drink some of the rare high-end brews that the country is so famous for.

Happy with our day, we enjoyed the quiet walk back to the hostel. Unfortunately, as we got closer, we started to hear blasting music. Exactly how I feared it would be, the loud thumping music was coming directly from the bar/hostel we were staying at. Walking inside, we were surprised to find the interior lit only by candles. We assumed it was just some gimmick in the medieval spirit of the town until we got to our room and flicked the switch on. No light. The power was out.

Chloe and Oksana left to go to the showers across the alley. Sam and I brushed our teeth in the dark, our room lit only by a nearby streetlight coming through our window. When Chloe and Oksana came back, I slid on my sandals, grabbed my quick drying towel, and multipurpose soap to take a shower. It felt strange to walk through a bar holding these items.

Across the street, I walked into where the shower stalls were. I was surprised to see some female travelers leaving as I entered. I double-checked the area, but these showers were not gender separated. There were four or five toilet stalls, and the same number of private shower stalls, with ten or so sinks across from them. Although pretty empty, it felt a little weird to have males and females coming and going. I showered quickly, just happy that the water was hot, and the lights were on.

If walking through a bar with a towel and soap felt odd, then walking through it with a wet hair and a damp towel felt even stranger. I climbed the stairs to our room, climbed up to my top bunk and fell asleep; happy it had been a good day.

Bruges, Day Four: 31th of March.

We woke up after sleeping in far too long for our only full day in Bruges. Doing two nights per city was going to be exhausting.

Going to the bar for breakfast I was disappointed by the offerings. It consisted of a roll, cereal and orange juice. I couldn't even get a damn coffee. The only memorable part of the meal was when I looked over to where they had put the candles the night before, and I saw the biggest hunk of melted wax I had ever seen in my life. It must have been a solid five pounds of melted candle wax.

After 'breakfast' we checked out the Church of Holy Blood for some touristy sightseeing. The midmorning walk was just as magical as last night had been. A gentle mist clung to the canals.

Unlike most churches, this one was built into a corner space on a square, like a storefront in a medieval strip mall. Delicate stonework, small gilded statues of knights and oddly tiny glass windows decorated the building. Just outside the gated entryway was a snarling lion grasping a painted shield in its paws.

The church had been around since the Crusades when returning knights brought back a vial of Jesus's blood from Jerusalem. We had to climb tightly winding stone stairs, like the ones you see in movies.

Getting to the primary church part, I was blown away by the magnificent stained glass and woodcarvings. The outside of the church was pretty small, so I had no idea there would be a big open space inside. In addition to the sublime stained glass, vivid colors covered the interoir and designs covered the walls.

Magnificent frescos of Jesus and the Apostles greeted me from behind the altar.

Seeing some wooden folding chairs set up in the nave we took a seat, along with a small crowd of maybe twenty other people. Just as we sat down, we found ourselves at the start of a religious service.

We were told to stand and cross ourselves, and we did. An old lady in robes came out and said an introduction in five languages. She did so without so much as a breath between tongues, no doubt having given this speech before. She told us we were here to venerate the blood of our Lord and Savior Jesus Christ. We were to form a line, come up one at a time and kneel at the small altar where the blood of Jesus sat.

The small crowd started to form a line. Oksana quietly stepped away from the service, telling us later she had no desire to be roped into a religious ceremony. As the line inched forward, I looked up to see the mid-morning sunbeams casting a spectacular show on the walls, colored by the stained glass.

Suddenly I was at the altar. The old lady in her white robes nodded at me, and I bent my knees. I quickly prayed while trying to get a good look at the relic. Inside a box of gold and folds of velvet sat the blood. It was a cork soaked in rust-colored fluid inside an ancient glass bottle, spotted and dirty from the long centuries. I prayed for good travels, and when I stepped away, I felt light and happy, with a weight lifted off my shoulders.

Although not particularly religious I was moved by the ceremony. Praying there, at a relic where so many people have prayed before me, it didn't matter if it wasn't real Jesus blood or that it had been stolen during a holy war. To me it is the fact that for a thousand years people have come here, to this very spot, to relieve themselves of their burdens, to cry in sorrow and pain, to ask for happiness and love, and to thank God for joy and peace. If nothing else, I was honored to have taken part in an ancient ritual so many people had done before me. How different it must have been for the crowds of people over the centuries. And yet, how similar in so many ways. I felt a deep connection to humanity there.

Feeling good, we exited the church and meandered around the city. Just over a little bridge, we saw people lining up for a boat tour.

"That sounds fun," Oksana said to me. I nodded. A boat tour sounded cool. Turning to Chloe and Sam, we agreed to go on the tour. We bought tickets from a small booth. The tour was about to leave, and we had snagged the last spots.

Soon we were gliding gracefully along the canals, seeing how the houses were built to face the water, not the street. When we went under bridges, we had to duck our heads.

The guide spoke poor English and seemed incredibly bored. He was in his late fifties, and probably did not wish to spend his time this way. Regardless, the town was still beautiful to see. Passing by one building we shared a laugh when we saw a dog lazing in an open window.

"This is what you call a dog's life," the guide said in his thick, silly sounding accent. We were excited because this dog, in the same pose, is featured in the opening credits of *In Bruges*. Some New Belgium beer labels have depictions of the buildings with the pointy roofs. Sometimes when I see this back in the States, I am transported back to Bruges, if only for a half second.

The tour wrapped up abruptly as we pulled back into the dock. The 'dock' was just a few wooden planks. The guide, suddenly breaking out of his bored routine, became a gentleman helping us out of the boat one at a time.

"It is customary to tip the guide one or two euro," the guide told us as he pulls us off the boat. "It is tradition."

In the name of tradition, not because he was in any way a good guide, I handed the man a Euro coin. A few weeks later, while on a long train journey across Austria, I will be reading Sam's Kindle. Her mom had bought her a copy of *Rick Steve's Europe*. While reading about Bruges I find out that this is not, in fact, a tradition, but just a cheap way for lazy guides to make more cash. In reality, they are paid quite well already by EU subsidies.

Leaving the tour, we stumbled across a small craft fair with a couple of booths set up. People were selling tasteful jewellery from these booths. I seriously ate into my daily budget by buying my sister a necklace.

As Sam paid for some souvenirs of her own, Oksana, Chloe and I discussed getting lunch. It was creeping past noon, and the meager breakfast had not done much for us. We put our new presents away and went into the first food shop we saw.

It was a small, homey looking place, with a menu written in chalk on a blackboard that gave it a vaguely hipster feel. The inside was modern, with a few wooden tables in the back of the room. There was a case of pastries and sandwiches, and an extensive coffee list. A shop like this wouldn't be out of place in any hip American neighborhood. It was somewhat jarring to be in a place like this and to see a medieval city through the window.

After ordering a sandwich, I decided to buy a shot of espresso. Espresso had tempted me for months, seeing it on menus all over the place. Sandwich in hand, I took my shot and sat down at a table. I downed it as if it was a shot of liquor.

I immediately regretted the decision. The pain was incredible. *There is no way I did that right,* I thought to myself through the burning in my mouth. I chugged water from my red Nalgene in a vain attempt to alleviate my tongue.

Two years later I found out this was, in fact, not the right way to drink espresso shots. I asked an Italian friend if it's ok to down the burning hot shot and he looked at me quizzically.

"No of course not, that's insane," he said finally. "You sip it."

Because I was nursing my tongue and mouth, I didn't notice the commotion when the girls sat down next to me. Sam had been gesturing at her throat.

"I am having an allergic reaction" she spoke in a low, urgent voice. "I need pop right now."

Samie was allergic to pine nuts, a common ingredient in pesto. The sandwich had a fine layer of that stuff in it. Samie stood up and went back to the counter. Thankfully, the allergy was non-fatal but would cause intense pain and nausea the rest of the day. For some reason, soda had a calming effect on the allergy, but only if drank immediately.

I watched as Samie located a cooler next to the door and swiftly grab a can of coke from it. She turned around to pay for it, but in the meantime, a man had gotten in line. He was taking his time deciding on a sandwich.

My tongue continued to burn as I watched Samie rub her throat and glare daggers at the back of this man. He was gesturing at the different sandwiches and having an engaging conversation with the man behind the counter. Samie looked back at us, and then, as if to say 'fuck it' she cracked open the can of coke and drained it entirely.

I turned back to my sandwich. I bit into it, but I could not taste a thing. I sighed and ate the tasteless food, just happy to fill my belly. Sam came back to us, saying she felt better, but that she would meet us outside when we were done. We finished eating, walked outside and found her up the street, leaning on a bridge and looking green.

"I think I am ok," she said shakily. For our sake, Sam did not want to stop us from doing our touristy activities. We began to slowly start walking around again, hoping Sam would feel better.

I stopped into a tourist shop to buy a Belgian flag. I had decided to purchase a flag from each country in addition to a postcard from every city. In the Netherlands, I searched long and hard for a flag before giving up and purchasing a magnet facsimile of the Dutch flag. Some countries are not very patriotic.

In Belgium, however, I was lucky enough to come across this souvenir shop that sold antiques, footballs, and flags. It was an odd mix. I looked for a small flag but they only sold ones that were about a foot across and nearly as tall. I stood outside and proudly displayed my oversized flag for a picture. As I held it some people laughed, as they went by, no doubt impressed by my size.

Samie, meanwhile, was not feeling good.

"I'm just gonna head back to the hostel," she informed us, "I think I just need to sleep it off," she spoke quietly.

"We'll walk you back, Sam," Chloe said.

"Yeah, Sam, of course," Oksana agreed.

We made our way back the hostel. Along the way, we kept an eye out for a pharmacy. Benadryl also helped Sam's reaction. To our dismay, we could not find a pharmacy. This was partly due to the fact that English signs here were not as common as in Amsterdam. We also did not yet realize that the neon green flashing cross was the universal European marker for a pharmacy. Like most things common to the rest of Europe, the British had refused to adopt it, so we were unaware of it.

We went back to our room in the hostel, and once inside Chloe and Oksana immediately went back out to scour the streets for the drugs. Samie had just laid down, ready to sleep off the rest of the reaction, when they came back rushing into the room with two packages. They told us they had found a drugstore just across the street but the pharmacist had spoken no English. Chloe and Oksana had to mime having an allergic reaction until the druggist picked up what they meant. The pharmacist then sold them two packages.

I looked at the packages. They were written entirely in French or Flemish, or some other language none of us spoke. Bravely, Samie opened the packages and swallowed the pills with water. It took more guts than I would have had.

It turned out the druggist was right. Sam's reaction soon calmed and now she only felt exhausted. Crisis adverted, Sam needed to rest.

I stayed with her as Chloe and Oksana went off to climb the bell tower. Lying in bed with Samie, it was warm with soft golden sunlight and a gentle breeze rolling through the open window. The quiet sounds of the street drifted in, with ancient stone buildings and tiled roofs just barely visible from our bed.

It is moments like this that are every bit as part of the European experience as seeing the historic sights. Travel isn't always meant to be easy. I often pictured travelling as one uninterrupted adventure from one exotic locale to the next but the reality is more gritty, dirty and unplanned. It is in these precious moments, lying in bed in the warm afternoon light when I would feel most grateful for this trip.

A few hours passed like this and eventually, Oksana and Chloe returned to us.

"How was the clock tower?" I asked them.

"It was rubbish," Chloe said.

"It was all windy stairs," Oksana added. "I'm not being funny."

I smiled. This leg of the journey had been an endless loop of us repeating lines from *In Bruges*.

I wanted to get out and see more of Bruges before we departed for Paris tomorrow. Sam was still recovering so the girls stayed in the room as I left on my own.

I strolled over to the clock tower, trying to get in, but I missed closing by just a few minutes. They had already strung the chain back over the entrance of the tower.

A little disappointed, I sat in the middle of the square on the steps of some monument. A few other travelers lounged there too. Some were reading beat-up paperbacks, while some were just looking around like I was.

I sat there, appreciating this foreign land. I saw solo backpackers, groups of teenagers, old Flemish ladies and couples riding in horse-drawn carriages. The square was quiet and calm, the plaza being large enough to hold all these people comfortably. The sense of traveling in a foreign place really hit me as I sat on the cobblestone under the beautiful blue sky. I was living my dream.

I flashed back to when I was twelve or thirteen. I remember telling my mom that I was going to backpack Europe. I remember reading books in the darker days of my recent years, dreaming of being far away from all the bullshit that was going on. I remember being trapped in my suburban hometown and thinking, *one day I'll blink and wake up far far away. One day I'll finally get out of here.*

Well, it looks like I made good on that, I thought, sitting there on those steps in this medieval city in Belgium. I nodded to myself. *Yeah. I made it.*

That evening we went to the supermarket for dinner. We picked up some sausage, cheese, fruit and chips. We ate it sitting in a circle on the floor of our hostel room. We were laughing and joking, cutting the meat and cheese with pocket knives and drinking from our water bottles. We laughed about our previous travels, about the power being out yesterday, and about our poor mans dinner.

Our lovely dinner finished, we decided to go and have a beer while walking around. We couldn't help but take advantage of the liberal open container laws. We left the hostel as the sun sank low in the sky.

On the way to buy the drinks, Oksana and Chloe bought some infamous Belgian waffles. I didn't know Belgian waffles were actually a real thing in Belgium. These waffles were steaming hot and covered in chocolate.

"This is so awesome!" Oksana said excitedly as she pulled a toothpick flag out of her waffle. It was a tiny flag of Belgium.

Waffles in hand, we found a small liquor store and bought a few bottles of beer. We walked back to that scenic little corner with the lace map. The sun set as we sat on benches and drank dark Trappist beer. We talked and enjoyed the view of the boat half hidden underneath the bridge, the ivy climbing the stone walls, and the belfry tower behind that.

I realized that the tension that had been subtly there since leaving Leicester was finally gone. Maybe it was Sam getting sick or perhaps it was because we finally spent some time apart from each other, but either way we were back to travelling like we did in the U.K., as four great friends.

I studied Chloe for a minute, with her pale white skin and flaming red hair, her red lips spread wide in a grin. I looked over to Oksana as she grasped her beer bottle with her slender perfect fingers, her long black hair swept by the light wind. I saw Samie with her arms comfortably in her jacket pockets, and her brown eyes alight with joy. I felt so happy to be here with my friends.

Finishing our beers, we walked down the winding cobblestone streets, under the streetlights, past gold shops and chocolate stores, over fairytale canals, and into stone and ivy courtyards and alleyways. Like it has been said before, this town was like a fairytale.

We got back to the hostel before it got too late. I climbed into bed and Chloe turned the lights off. Not quite ready for sleep I pulled out my tiny little laptop and put my headphones in. I had downloaded *In Bruges* for this exact occasion before we left England. Although I fell asleep before it finished it was awesome seeing the things in the movie that I had just seen a few hours ago.

If there is ever a time to watch *In Bruges* I would recommend doing it in Bruges.

Boat+Hostel = Bostel

Chapter 2: France

Paris, Day Five: 1st of April.

We packed in the grey dawn, walked down the stairs, tossed our keys onto the reception desk and hit the road. Our train left at nine, so we had to skip breakfast, with no time even for a quick coffee. We passed through the streets, taking in the city one last time.

A lot of travelers prefer to see many places quickly, rather than seeing fewer places for longer. There are pros and cons to each style of travel, but I certainly wished we had had more time in Bruges.

Reaching the station just before nine, we thankfully had enough time to buy some coffee at the vending machines. I bought a black coffee for one euro while we waited for the train.

The train ride was six hours and only changed one time. At the change in Brussels, called *Bruxelles* in the native language, I had enough time to leave the station and have a look around. I walked outside and a scruffy looking man in a leather jacket holding a beer approached me. It was eleven in the morning.

"Money?" he said in accented English, "Cigarettes?"

I shook my head and quickly walked back into the station. My mistake for leaving. Never leave the station.

Back on the train I looked up French phrases in a travel guide and wrote them phonetically in my journal.

Je ne coprends pas – Zhuh nuh comprend pah.

Je vous en prie – Zhuh vouz ahn pree.

I figured in countries where nobody speaks the language, like in the Netherlands, it would be easy to find English speakers. However, I knew there were entire countries of

Francophones, so I was expecting more difficulty with the language barrier. I felt like having some basic phrases would help me communicate.

Oui, s'il vous plait! (wee, seel voo play)

With Paris only an hour or two away, we sat alone. Looking around from our spot in the middle of the car, there were easily seventy or eighty seats, all empty. I looked out the window and watched the tiny French towns nestled in the wooded hills and hedgerows pass by.

So many of these towns were just a cluster of ten or twelve buildings centered around an ancient stone church. Around the towns were endless fields and gently rolling hills. It was early springtime, so the fields were covered in wildflowers instead of crops. The towns looked exactly as they did in all the movies and video games about the Second World War. I couldn't believe how beautiful it was.

I had known that Europe has a population over twice the size of America. As such, I had always pictured Europe as a series of endlessly sprawling cities and suburbs. However, in moments like this, I would be struck by how much of Europe was rural. I had never even considered that Europe had rural spaces.

As we drew nearer to Paris, two black men quietly entered the car and sat in the far back. We thought nothing of it. Soon after, a ticket inspector entered from the opposite end. He came over and stamped our rail passes. He smiled at our efforts at French greetings, happy we were making an effort.

"Bon voyage," he said and stepped away.

Pleased with ourselves, we settled back into our seats and returned to looking out the window. Then, we heard French being spoken between the inspector and the black men behind us. We thought nothing of it.

Suddenly, yelling erupted. I turned to see the inspector pointing his finger at the men and shouting. One of the black men stood up angrily and before I could even blink, six armed policemen and women entered the carriage from both ends. Some held automatic weapons. I sat back down.

"I guess somebody didn't have a ticket," I said to the girls.

The police surrounded the men for the rest of the ride. We arrived at the Gare-du-Nord train station. The gigantic station was bustling with activity. On the walk from the platform to the station, I glanced behind me. I briefly locked eyes with one of the ticketless men. He and his friend were in the middle of a police phalanx, unhandcuffed but downcast. They looked defeated, while the police strutted proudly.

A lot of left-leaning Americans imagine Europe as some kind of liberal paradise, a place with few guns, free healthcare and no problems. While in England, I had quickly discovered there was just as much epidemic racism and hatred as back home. It was different than in the US only in the fact that it was mostly religious, not racial.

In both England and Europe, the main 'other' group is Muslim folks. Coming from the particularly racially segregated city of Cleveland, I recognized the patterns instantly. I saw the glaring differences between the Islamic and non-Islamic parts of town. I saw how non-Muslims looked at the women with hijabs and bearded brown men. I could tell when I was in the Muslim part of town from its lack of integration with the rest of the city.

This was compounded by the rising tide of immigrants and refugees. During our trip, the floodgates of refugees from Africa and the Middle East were just starting to break open. Perhaps as a liberal American, well used to the lens of racial violence and oppression, I was reading too much into this arrest. But I just couldn't shake the image of the proud, heavily armed French police leading the two black men, obviously African from their accents, away. Any American who thinks Europe doesn't have problems is either ignorant or deluded.

From the station, we hopped on the metro and rode across the city to our hostel. Along the entire route we constantly had to fend off beggars, some with missing eyes or arms accosting us for change. I could tell the Parisian subway was going to be adventurous. We soon reached our stop and made our way to the hostel.

The building looked very Parisian, as it was made of handsome tan bricks with large airy windows. The buildings around the hostel had those iconic gray paneled rooves, home to cozy apartments with a small window or two overlooking the street. Flags of all nations flew in the hostel windows and across the street, unexpectedly, sat a Mexican restaurant.

Entering the hostel, I was surprised to recognize some friends from England standing in line, Bill and Bailey. Bill was a skinny quiet kid. He always seemed so happy to be out of his native Kansas. Bailey was an outgoing girl with wavy brown hair who hailed from Missouri. They were sharing their European adventure together, two small-town Americans taking in the wonders of Europe.

I'd known them tangentially for a few months but Chloe was fairly close with them. We greeted each other and stood in line for reception. I am not the best at small talk and neither was Bill. Once we said hello to each other, we stood there in awkward silence, unsure what to say next.

I would ask a question, Bill would give me a one-word answer, and then the silence would return. I overheard Chloe and Bailey having an animated conversation a few feet away, making the contrast between Bill and I even more awkward and uncomfortable.

Finally, the lady behind the counter waved me over. I bid Bill goodbye. Check in was a breeze and we lucked out when the lady upgraded us from an eight-bed dorm to a private four-person room for free. Tourist season was not yet in full swing so there was a lot of empty space. When we got to the room after climbing up a few floors, we were even happier to find that we had an ensuite bathroom with a shower. No sharing with strangers for us.

The room had a giant window overlooking the street, which gave us a nice view of the quiet residential neighborhood. Inside the bathroom, there was a big double window with shutters that let in wonderful amounts of natural light. The international flags fluttered outside of both windows. The room had hardwood floors, plain white walls, and a high ceiling. It was sparse but comfortable.

We opened the windows to let in some fresh breeze. The weather was perfect. It was warm enough to be refreshing and comfortable, while the hint of a chill required a light jacket. It was perfect for exploring a new city. Not too hot, not too cold. Back in Ohio, it was still snowing.

Connected to the wifi, I pulled up Facebook messenger on my laptop. I had been communicating with a different good friend of mine, Maxime, who had also just arrived in Paris. Max was Quebecois and an all-around great person. Classically handsome with a square jaw, jet-black hair and a perennial five o'clock shadow, Maxime had a heart of gold. Maxime spoke English with a heavy Quebecois accent.

Until I met Mac, I had never pictured Quebec to actually be, well, French. I figured since they had been part of Canada for three-hundred years that their native language had long since died. Sure, I figured they might have some vestigial food or some slang words but surely they were essentially English speaking Canadians. Instead, upon hearing Maxime speak a single word, I immediately realize how wrong I had been. From Maxime, and two other Quebecois I met in England, I came to realize the deep heritage of these people. They were fiercely proud of their language, not even learning English until later in life.

I was really looking forward to seeing him. We had plans to meet in front of the Notre Dame at seven and it was already quarter to five. No problem I thought, as we got ready to leave and start our trek back across the city.

My plan to meet Max became complicated when Chloe mentioned that even more mutual friends, Allison and Nerada were also staying at our hostel. I couldn't believe the coincidence until she reminded me that they had planned to go to Disneyland Paris the next day. Because I wasn't going, obviously, I had totally forgotten about it. Suddenly, we had to wrangle up these extra four or five travelers and try to get food together with Max.

I went outside and began to pace impatiently in the street as the situation grew into a confused clusterfuck. Some of folks would join us outside, only to run back in to shower or grab stuff from their rooms. The clock ticked past five as I waited and waited. I was impatient because I didn't know most of these people very well, while I considered Max to be a really good friend. I was getting irate, tapping my foot annoyingly and behaving like a spoiled child.

"Chloe, we have to leave now," I said to her as we neared five thirty. We had been standing outside for forty minutes and I was not going to ditch my friend. I had been unsubtly putting pressure on Chloe to get her friends in gear.

"Uh," Chloe stalled, looking back at the hostel. "I don't know," she said uncertainly, "I don't want to ditch these guys."

I was hungry, bored, and almost late for an appointment. Lateness is my pet peeve and I am notoriously hangry.

"You have to decide now!" I said, beginning to walk away. Chloe went white-faced in a moment of panic. Chloe is the type of individual who absolutely hates being put on the spot. She can be really indecisive, especially when it comes to picking between friends. A loyal person, she does not like being forced to choose. My patience having worn thin, I did this solely to push her buttons. Spending all day every day with somebody isn't always healthy, as my behavior was showing.

"Fine," she said coldly, "see you later," and walked back into the hostel. Two years later I will apologize for my actions in a bar back home, but at the time I was eager just to walk away.

Knowing this incident would mean trouble in the future Oksana, Sam and I left the hostel. We talked among ourselves as we walked, and hoped Chloe would not be too mad at us later.

We stopped by an ATM to withdraw another weeks' worth of cash. I preferred not to have much cash at any one time but at times like this, I had no choice. Although I had a money belt with me, I hadn't used it since we arrived in London four months ago. I never really felt like I needed it. Instead, I just kept my wallet in my front pocket with my hand habitually over it. Like most horror stories about travel, anything I had heard about pickpockets was totally overblown.

The corner where the ATM was located was ridiculously beautiful. Tall, sleek 19th century buildings surrounded us. All had magnificently detailed facades. Iron wrought balconies gently protruded from shuttered windows. Every building seemed to be white or light tan, and there was none of the dull urban greyness so common in other big cities. Light and color popped out all around.

We walked past charming little shops full of fresh fruit and vegetables. The weights, written in kilograms, meant nothing to me. Sometimes the little storefronts were set up in the tiny alleys between buildings.

I hadn't really eaten all day and I was starting to get dizzy from hunger when, to my delight, we approached a Subway. When traveling, I often relied on Subway to be consistently cheap, filling and reliable. I'd like to have at least try to hunt down some local food, but I was in a time crunch and feeling faint from the lack of food.

Entering the Subway, I saw it to be the exact same as Ohio or England, or anywhere else. On the menu I saw the same offerings, as usual, only written in French. I was amused to see they sold croissants. When it comes to Subway I am a creature of habit and only eat the Spicy Italian. It was pretty easy to find what I was looking for. The *Spicy Italien* sounded about right.

"*Bonjuer,*" I said hesitatingly, greeting the worker. "*Parlez-vous Anglais?*"

The young man with black hair and olive skins gave me a wide smile and nodded.

"A little," he said with a French accent. I began to order my sandwich. As the worker slid the bread down the counter, I took some time to try and learn some French.

"Lettuce," I said pointing at it.

"Lettuce?" I repeated with a questioning tone. Soon the young man caught on and repeated the word back in French.

"*Laitue,*" he said slowly. I smiled and nodded.

"*Laitue*".

The young man indulged me for the rest of the ingredients. I soon added *oignons rouges, tomates, concombres,* and *poivrons.*

"*Merci,*" I said to him as I handed over a couple of euros. I was feeling pretty good about myself. Trying French was working out great.

Subs in hand, we looked up at the cloudless blue sky between the buildings to see the Eiffel Tower beckoning us. Sometimes the Tower would disappear behind some apartments, and we would kind of forget it was there. Then our attention would swing to more immediate issues like ignoring the drunks and gypsies demanding spare change, or avoiding getting run over while crossing the street.

Our attention would drift to the sidewalk cafes where people sat sipping small espressos or nursing a glass of red wine. We'd smell whiffs of pastries and fresh bread, and maybe hear some strains of music over the incessant din of traffic. Then, we'd turn down another tree-lined boulevard and suddenly the Tower would appear out of nowhere, startling us with its elegant glory. It would hit us hard. *Wow, we are in Paris. We are actually in Paris.*

As we walked, the three of discussed the places that we really enjoyed.

"York is so cool," Sam said, "the crooked medieval streets and the walls that surround the city. It's so cute and compact, I felt like I was living in a dream when I was there."

"I really liked York," I responded animatedly. "Man, I am really digging Paris though."

Oksana was quiet for a moment before she spoke.

"Going to high school in Kiev was really cool. There was a lot of awesome people there and it was a really nice city." She looked up at the sky and continued.

"Me and my friends would hang out in the main square. It's weird to see it all barricaded and destroyed now."

Oksana was referring the rolling disaster unfolding in Ukraine. Two months previously massive protests had rocked the city, and ultimately ended up ousting the pro-Russian government. The success had come after violent riots and sit-ins, not least of all in the main square Oksana was referring to.

Then, only a few weeks ago, Vladimir Putin responded by forcibly annexing the Crimean Peninsula from Ukraine. For the first time in my life, Russia and the West seemed to be on a violent collision course, as the EU and NATO vigorously denounced this action. Was there going to be a war? This was compounded for me by knowing Oksana and hearing about her personal connection to it.

Oksana had grown up all over the world it seemed. Born in Belorussia after the collapse of the Soviet Union she was raised by a single mother. While Oksana was still very young, her mother married an American diplomat. Together the three of them moved across the world depending on her stepfather's job. Eventually joined by younger sisters, Oksana had spent years in Oklahoma, southern Germany, and Washington DC, before spending her teenage years in Kiev and Ukraine.

Oksana was a well-travelled and worldly person. She would tell us about how her grandmother was currently a high profile dissenter in Belorussia. Belorussia had never ended its Orwellian dictatorship after the Soviet Union collapsed. Instead, it had doubled down with it. Ranked as one of the least free countries in the world, the dictator did not lightly tolerate dissenters like Oksana's grandmother.

Her stories highlighted a world most of us in the West are comfortably isolated from. I always appreciated how Oksana would expand my worldview. She never did it in a boastful or bragging kind of way. It was always in quieter moments, like this.

Before the conversation could get darker, the three us turned another corner and suddenly spilled out onto the Champs de Mars. The Champs de Mars, or Mars Garden, was a park that sat directly in front of the Eiffel Tower.

We hurried on the footpaths through the trees. The sudden change from a busy street and towering apartments to foot traffic and trees was made more dramatic by the gigantic *Tour Eiffel* looming above.

Walking quickly, we passed the Tower up close. In a hurry to meet Max on time we could not spare a moment to stop walking. We craned our necks as we passed it.

"Guys I'm having a moment," Sam said as her voice rose with excitement. She had a giant grin on her face. I did too. We were struck by its beauty, magnificence and especially by its size. Most landmarks are slightly disappointing in this regard. The Tower of London is quaint and small and the White House looks like a generic plantation house. But damn, the Eiffel Tower was awe-inspiring.

We did not have much time to admire it for now, as we had to hurry on our way to the Notre Dame. On the map, the Eiffel Tower and the Notre Dame looked pretty close. So, we had decided to swing by the Tower on our way to the cathedral. No big deal right?

The walk to the Tower took a whole hour. Along the way we realized these landmarks were not close to each other in the slightest. Checking the distance on Sam's phone we realized the Notre Dame was another hour away by foot. *Damn*, I thought to myself, *it's going to be tight making it on time.* Public transit was definitely not an option due to our limited budget.

I abhor lateness in myself and others. It pisses me off to no end if somebody is not where they are supposed to be when they say they would. The fact that we might be late created a knot in my stomach.

We walked briskly along a busy road overlooking the Seine. Most of the famous landmarks in Paris straddle the banks of the river. Looking at our map I was surprised to learn that the Notre Dame is on an island in the middle of the Seine.

As we neared the Museé d'Orsay, it was already a quarter to seven. *Shit*, I thought to myself. I knew I couldn't be late so I made the impulsive decision to run the last two miles to the Cathedral.

"Umm ok..." the girls told me when I told them as much. They looked at me like I was crazy, but for me, I had no choice. I sprinted away.

I ran and ran. I ran past the shaded riverside, past the iconic green stalls. I ran past the old Frenchmen and women selling everything from antique books to model cars. I ran past them as they were just opening their green stalls, or closing them back up for the evening.

I ran past bridges where lovers were writing their names on padlocks and throwing the keys into the river. I ran past an unexpected statue of Thomas Jefferson. I ran past the first bridge to the island and onwards to the second.

Panting, I ran across the bridge, passing Asian tourists taking selfies and dodging gypsies holding up gold rings I just 'dropped'.

I was not in running shape. I was very used to walking a lot, but running was just not something my body was prepared for. I gasped for air.

On the island, I could not stop to admire the sun setting over the Seine, casting a brilliant orange hue on the buildings. I tore past restaurants and jumped around more tourists.

Finally, I sped around one last corner and the buildings gave way to the large plaza in front of the Notre Dame. Scanning the international crowd, I saw a black-haired young man sitting on a short stone pillar gazing contemplatively at the beautiful church.

"*Bonjour Max,*" I said reaching my hand out to shake his, before doubling over.

"Good to see you Nate," Max replied in his heavily accented English.

"Are you ok?" he asked as I gulped in air, my face beet red. It was ten past seven.

"Sorry for being late Max. I need to get some water," I gasped out these words and then stumbled over to one of the ubiquitous tourist stalls found in every major European city.

I bought a bottle of water from a rude Frenchmen for an insane price of four euros. He looked at me with unhidden contempt as I forked over my money.

I downed the water and then refilled it from a public drinking fountain nearby. Coming back to Max I asked him how long he would have waited for us if I hadn't come, thinking he say ten or fifteen minutes.

"Oh, I don't know," he replied, "probably until ten or eleven." I groaned and then laughed. I hadn't needed to run at all. Oksana and Sam strolled up to us a while later. They looked very relaxed. They told me about the cool stuff I was too busy running to see.

The four of us hung out in the shadow of the Notre Dame as the sun set. From the decorative portals around the doors to the circular stained glass, to the ornate double towers it was a truly a masterpiece of architecture. I was happy to be soaking in this sight surrounded by my friends on this beautiful evening in Paris. I was in Paris!

Our American accents and voices must have been really loud because right in the middle of a conversation a sunburnt older man wearing a straw hat interrupted us.

"Hey, where are you guys from?" The man asked excitedly.

"Uh, Ohio," Sam and I said, uncertain of this man's intentions.

"Ohio?!" The man exclaimed. "No way! We're from San Francisco!"

He gestured at his wife who was similarly decked out with a camera around her neck and straw hat on her greying hair.

"Oh. San Francisco?" Sam said, not really sure how to respond.

"Yeah what are the chances?" The man exclaimed loudly, smiling genuinely. His wife beamed at us.

Thankfully, before we could respond, the man and his wife turned away and walked off. We were standing in front of one of the biggest tourist attractions in the world, not to mention that San Francisco and Ohio are on opposite ends of our continent. The changes were quite high.

After that encounter, we decided get some food. We went north, crossing the Seine again, this time on the bridge Pont D'Arcole. Back in 1830 revolutionaries stormed across this bridge during a three day revolution which ended with the king being deposed and fleeing Paris.

We stopped in front of a massive medieval building. It was very ornate with marble statues and floor to ceiling windows. This was the Hotel de Ville, the old city hall of Paris. So much history happened here it was hard to imagine. The French Revolution had started here with the lynching of a royal official. Maximilien Robespierre directed the Reign of Terror from here. When his own downfall eventually came, he tried unsuccessfully to escape the guillotine by shooting himself in the face and jumping from one of those big windows.

The three day revolution in 1830 ended here when Marquis de Lafayette wrapped the new king in the tricolor flag, thus granting him legitimacy in the eyes of the people. Later, in 1871, communist rebels of the Paris Commune burnt the building to the ground rather than surrender. In 1944 Charles de Gaulle, with fighting still ongoing, declared Paris liberated from the Germans from one of the balconies I was now looking at. It was incredible, but all I could think about was food.

Oksana, Sam, and I were far too hungry to be picky about where we wanted to eat. As soon we came across a little street full of restaurants we walked into the first one we saw. Having Max with us made everything much easier. He went up to the host and dealt with him solely in French.

The waiter led us to our table. I felt like the staff respected him for speaking French natively.

"*Je suis Québécois,*" Max said to our waiter, a Parisian man in his late thirties.

He smiled at us and asks "*Oh, Vous parlez tous français?*"

Max shook his head. "*Non, ils sont américains*"

"*Américains? Pffffh*"

The waiter waved his hands sarcastically and walked off.

When the he came back, we ordered drinks and asked questions about the menu via Max. Having a personal translator was awesome. As we ordered glasses of red wine, the waiter set down bread. We had heard that in Europe bread with dinner was a scam. They set down the bread, you eat it unknowingly, and then the restaurant charges some outrageous price for it. We prodded Max to ask the waiter if the bread was free.

He does and the waiter exclaimed something loud in French, picked up a fork and yelled something else then picked up a knife and yelled more. Max chuckled heartily.

"Well," Max chuckled again, "he says we are not thieving Italians here where each fork and knife costs five euros to pick up." Delighted, we shared the delicious French bread.

Scanning the menu, I noted everything was pretty expensive. By default, I pick on a small salad with rabbit for a very affordable six euro, a *petite salade*. It was the only cheap item.

The waiters were silly and uncaring, which was exactly how I expected them to be. They teased Oksana by giving her the wine glass then pulling it away and laughing. I laughed along with them, but Oksana just glared at them with a deathly look.

She was not amused by their antics. "I didn't come here to play games."

When my salad came, it consisted of lettuce, rabbit, green beans, apples and a vinaigrette. It was delicious. I'd never tasted rabbit before but it was tender and gamey, with crispy skin. We ate slowly, sipped our wine and took in our sidewalk view of Paris. The moment was exactly what I wanted from this city. I was extremely content.

Afterwards, we wandered a bit along the streets in the 3rd *arrondissement*, or district. It was home to an older, more preserved part of Paris. We passed cute little shops and beautiful churches. I thought about being in third grade and reading a children's book about Descartes falling into the Seine. Now there I was walking along the same streets he had wandered and where he had come up with his ideas that shook the world.

The neighborhoods were spilling over with crowds of people. We would occasionally turn a corner and see French anti-terror patrols. They were in full uniform carrying their intimating assault rifles. They looked very serious and we gave them a wide berth. America has a reputation for militarized police, but we certainly don't have army units patrolling New York on a regular basis.

We eventually wound up back at the Notre Dame. Because it was later at night, the plaza was nearly empty. We sat on the low-slung stone walls and kept talking, all the while enjoying the lit up church and the giant equestrian statue of Charlemagne. I was hesitant to end the night but it was getting late and it had been a full day.

Saying goodbye to Max, we walked to the metro station that was adjacent to the Notre Dame. Just inside the entrance, we parted ways, him heading north and us heading south. We rode the metro back to the hostel, climbed the stairs to our room and collapsed, exhausted and happy into our beds.

Paris, Day Six: 2nd of April.

I was lying on my side when I opened my eyes. I stretched slowly, enjoying the sunlight streaming through the open windows, gently reflecting on the white ceiling. I rolled out of my bottom bunk and pulled on some pants. I brushed my teeth while looking out of the six-foot-tall window. The crisp air was invigorating as it came through the narrow window.

I greeted Oksana and Samie, and then we headed down the windy wooden staircase to breakfast.

Breakfast in a new hostel is kind of like roulette. It's exciting because you might win big like in Amsterdam, but you might get screwed like in Bruges. The staircase emptied out into a landing. Turn right and we would head past the desk to the street. Turn left and we would step into a pleasant dining area, with long wooden benches and tables, like we might find at a campground.

Everything was clean, and the room was similarly light and airy. The area was fairly large, with room for eighty people or so. Although not totally full, the room was bustling with young people eating, talking, and planning out their Parisian adventures. I didn't see any of the telltale signs of anybody being hungover, presumably because it was still too early for those folks to get out of bed yet. They probably only crawled into their bunks a few hours previously.

The food was located in a corner away from the tables and the stairs. It was guarded by a frazzled middle-aged cook screaming, *"Un croissant per person! Un croissant per person!"* to anyone daring to take two, or god forbid three light pastries.

Stepping around her, I joined the line for the small buffet. I took one of everything that was offered. The woman made damn sure I did not take two.

Unfortunately for me, one of everything turned out to be only a single croissant, a roll of bread, some jam and a cup of coffee. I sat down with my spread and sighed. The croissant was amazing. It was light, fluffy and buttery. It melted in my mouth. But, a single tasty croissant did little to fortify me for miles of walking.

When I was done eating I looked at my empty plate. I looked back at the pile of croissants. Then, I made eye contact with the cook.

"Un croissant per person!"

I went back to the room to finish getting ready. Chloe had left before any of us had woke, for the metro ride to Disneyland alone took over an hour. Oksana was going to fly solo today, so Samie and I could have a day to ourselves.

We stepped out in the sunny street and trekked to the Eiffel Tower, taking the same route as yesterday. The journey got off on the wrong foot as we immediately began to bicker, both of us tired and stressed from the last week. By now we were excellent multitaskers, so we bickered while simultaneously sightseeing and turning away beggars who approached us.

We passed corner cafes overflowing with people, drinking coffee and lazily watching us. We admired the wide-open sidewalks, the small birch trees that were everywhere and the gentle hustle and bustle of a typical Parisian morning. This was what I had always pictured when I thought of Paris and I had not expected it to actually exist.

By the time we reached the *Tour Eiffel* forty-five minutes later, we had gotten the stress out and were walking hand in hand. It can be hard to travel as a couple and not have time alone.

As the Tower came into view, we marveled at it again. We walked along the south bank of the Seine and were approaching the Tower from the back, so there were few people around us. We stepped from the pavement to the gravel pathways that went through the lush urban forest that rings around the Tower. At this junction, we had to move around French police hauling a group of protesting gypsies into vans.

I had heard a lot about the gypsies, of course, but they never seemed too prevalent in England. In Paris, I saw the olive-skinned women in colorful skirts and headscarves all over the place, usually in groups of four or five. I didn't know why these gypsies were getting thrown in the police wagons, but I certainly didn't hang around and find out.

Sam and I found a bench in the shadow of the Tower and enjoyed the brisk spring air. It was so surreal and lovely to be sitting directly in front of one of the most famous monuments in the world. We took pictures and cuddled, drinking it in.

Soon, we wanted to actually go up the Tower. It was still early and there were only a few people milling about so the line was quite short. Getting in line directly under the Tower, we looked at our options. There were a variety of packages to choose from, and naturally we picked the cheapest, most basic one.

Tickets in hand, we went through the security check, and then excitedly walked towards the iron stairs. Samie stepped one single foot on the first stair and then hesitated for a moment.

Suddenly, a big red tomato dropped right in front of her face and splat on the ground. We both looked up right away but there were a thousand winding stairs and a ton of people on them, making it impossible to see who threw it. Had Samie not paused it would have hit her square on the head. We both laughed at the absolute absurdity of the situation.

Laughing all the way, we climbed the stairs. It was definitely strange being inside the monument. It was a behemoth structure with spindly metal arms going everywhere. The stairs themselves, also iron, were surrounded by metal mesh, added later to stop people from falling off the stairs.

We reached the second level and admired the views. They were incredible. I saw distant 'downtowns' with clusters of tall buildings off in several directions. In order to preserve the Napoleonic grandeur, the geographic city center lacked any huge modern buildings. It was stunning to think each of these little clusters of skyscrapers in the distance were probably as big as Cleveland.

I looked over the green boulevards and man-made ponds of the Champs de Mars. It contrasted with the gray Seine and the endless buildings that stretched out of view. We walked around the viewing deck contently. We could have paid more to go further up, but we were happy with our cheap view.

We eventually descended back down to the front of the Tower. We happily wandered around, taking the most touristy pictures we could.

It was now approaching eleven and the tour buses were cranking out full loads of people every few minutes. The grounds were filling up. We were constantly approached by one of three characters.

The first was a group of gypsy girls would thrust 'petitions' at us. If you signed them, they would pickpocket you, or snap a bogus friendship bracelet on your arm and demand money for it. We easily avoided them by shaking our heads and saying *"Non."*

The second group was made of Sudanese men selling tiny replications of the Tower. They waved around big metal rings holding hundreds of these models. These guys weren't too pushy and I didn't mind them. I would see them continuously throughout the city.

The third, and most annoying, were the thousands of tourists swarming all over. They would thrust their expensive cameras at me and ask us to photograph them in front of the Tower. I played photographer for several international couples before I started refusing.

Although we had spent a couple hours there, the Tower never lost its magic. But, since we had limited time, we had to see more of Paris. For our next stop, we planned another long trek to the Louvre.

We started walking as the sun beat down on us. We walked near the Seine, which was hot and surrounded by loud traffic. I was starting to get faint from hunger and the sun.

Stopping in front of the Pont Alexandre III Bridge, I needed to sit for a moment. My seat was underneath a gold-plated angel perched atop a marble column.

I was so hungry that my vision swam in front of me for a moment. I needed to eat. Sam looked at me with concern in her eyes.

"I just need some food," I said.

I was parched, having finished my Nalgene an hour ago. Getting back up was a bit of a struggle but we continued our walk past the beautiful bridges that spanned the river.

Not far past the bridge, we walked down a ramp off the busy street in order to be level with the Seine. It was wonderful how just a few meters below the main streets almost all the noise from the traffic was gone. A few boats quietly floated by, and we spotted a little building where food was sold.

We bought two cheese sandwiches from the stand. It was the only sandwich we could afford and thankfully they were tasty. We idly watched kids play on a playground overlooking the river.

After finishing our food and resting a bit, we stood up again and continued towards the Louvre. Near the museum, we walked over the famous Pont du Arts, the bridge of locks.

On this bridge couples write their names on golden padlocks, fix them to the metal grates and throw the keys into the Seine. The ubiquitous green stalls along the river sold padlocks, keys and sharpies.

We do not join in with the tradition. We quickly decided that throwing shit into the river didn't really fit with our ethics. Later we found out that Parisians hate this act and periodically remove the locks. They even dredge the riverbed to recover the castaway keys. There are literally tons of metal keys taken out every year.

Nonetheless, the sight of a thousand steel padlocks sparkling in the sun was quite a sight.

Crossing the bridge, we walked around the outside of the museum. The façade was constructed in the sweeping grand style found in the other buildings in Paris. This was once the royal palace and the exterior was built in the 17th century, not long before King Louis XIV moved the royal quarters to Versailles. The stone was dark brown with soot and age.

We walked with the steadily growing stream of people towards the entrance of the building. Soon we were walking under an archway, passing by a man hawking bottles of water those little Eiffel Tower models. Over the crowd of people, I saw the famous glass pyramid in the stone courtyard of the museum.

The pyramid was very cool in real life. Its strikingly modern tone contrasted greatly with the old stone palace around it. We sat on the edge of a fountain and watched the people hustle and bustle, before joining the long snaking line to get in ourselves.

During our long wait in the line, I couldn't help but keep looking at the magnificent pyramid. Truthfully though, I found it smaller than I expected.

As we passed through security, we entered the pyramid and looked over an interior balcony. An enormous space sprawled out beneath us. There were huge tunnels leading off in every direction, each undoubtedly filled with more precious artwork than we could hope to see. I heard every kind of language imaginable. I was awed at the sight.

Sam and I walked towards one of the many ticket booths that awaited us after a short escalator ride down to the main floor. We saw on the booth that the price of admission was twelve euros. That was almost half our daily budget.

The attendant at the booth warily waved us over. He was a young man, probably no older than us.

"Do you speak English?" Sam asked him. He nodded.

"Is there a student discount?"

"Yes, it is free for students in the EU," he responded, in perfect English.

Sam smiled and pulled out her University of Leicester student card. She handed it to him as I frantically searched my wallet for my identity card.

He inspected it and then turned expectantly towards me. I searched through my wallet and pockets again, cursing myself for presumably leaving it at the hostel.

"Twelve euros," the man repeated to me.

"I go to school with her," I said. "I lost my ID"

"It's twelve euros without an EU student ID," the young man said in a bored voice.

"I swear I'm not lying," I said. I gave no sign of being willing to pay twelve euros.

"He does," Sam chimed in. "He goes to school with me."

The young man in the museum uniform looked at us with a tired expression and sighed audibly.

"Fine just go," he finally said, waving his hand dismissively. Elated we move away from the booth and headed into one of the many tunnels at random.

We had not gotten very far when the magnitude of the place sunk in. As we passed hallway after hallway, each with rooms upon rooms within them, we realized we couldn't even see a tiny fraction of the museum. We looked around for a map but couldn't find any place to get them. We backtracked to the entrance where the booth was.

"I think the maps are in the booth," Sam said.

"I think so," I replied.

We both looked down the hallway to where the poor young man was sitting in the booth.

"Do you want to ask him?" Sam asked me.

"Hell no, I barely got into this place," I answered.

Defeated, we turned back around. As we climbed up a stairwell Sam shouted out in joy.

"Look, babe, a map!" She pointed at a map lying on the ground on the landing of the stairwell.

Dodging the mass of humanity climbing up and down the stairwell, I grabbed the crumpled map. It was entirely in Japanese and there was a large muddy footprint in the middle of it. It would fit our needs nicely.

A few of the more famous pieces were marked by tiny black and white facsimiles. Using it as our guide, we located the *Mona Lisa*. Once we figured out which floor and building it lived in, we made a beeline for it.

The hallways grew even more crowded as we got closer. Soon we pushed into a large exhibition room. On the far wall hung the Mona Lisa. Given the mass of people around us, I could only see the top half of the painting. It was instantly recognizable.

The Mona Lisa had disappointed almost everybody I had ever talked to about it. They invariably said it was much smaller than they had expected. Based on this, I had pictured a painting the size of a laptop or paperback book.

Yet, as I pushed through the crowd to get a better look, I was stunned and amazed by its beauty. I was pleasantly surprised to find it much larger than I had been led to believe. Despite the dense crowd, I was very pleased with the experience. The artwork was a masterpiece.

Because of the massive crowd, we were unable to spend too much time basking in the glory of *The Mona Lisa*. We soon had to step out of the room. We were both growing incredibly tired. The Louvre was far too large to see and because we didn't pay anything we didn't feel bad about leaving. We agreed to go back to the hostel room for a nice nap.

On our way out, we popped into another random hallway so at least we would see more than one single painting. In this hallway, picked for no reason, we were stunned at the walls and ceilings. They were covered in glorious paintings and amazing woodwork.

The Louvre was the seat of the monarchy until Versailles was built. In these older wings, it was apparent that the monarchy used to reside in this palace. The ceiling was covered in spectacular paintings, reminiscent of the Sistine Chapel. In the center of the room was a glass case holding the royal jewels of the restored Bourbon dynasty. The Bourbons used these jewels after they reclaimed the throne from Napoleon.

Satisfied, we headed for the exit. On our way out, I glanced around at the artwork. I stopped in my tracks when I saw a painting hanging a few feet in front of me. It was one of my favorite paintings, *The Coronation of Napoleon.*

The painting was massive. I paused in front of it, swallowed up by its majesty and awe. Napoleon stands bedecked in glorious robes, wearing a Romanesque oak leaf band around his head. He holds in his uplifted hands the crown of the Emperor of France, soon to place it on his own head. His wife, the nobility, the army, the Pope and foreign dignitaries look on in reverence. The painting was so much more impressive in real life than in a textbook. I had seen and studied this painting for years and I was now right in front of it. Nothing can compare to knowing a piece of art and then at last seeing it with your own eyes. It's a wonderful feeling to enter each new major museum and know I would see at least one work of art I'd had studied in school.

We left the museum. The largest museum in the world, filled with priceless works of art, and we left after forty minutes, having seen two paintings and some jewels. We were utterly exhausted and shelled out some precious euros for the metro to ease our aching feet. We got back the hostel in no time.

Samie and I napped in the warm Parisian air that rolled into our room. The sounds of muffled voices and the far-off whine of cars lulled us to sleep. Drifting off, I wished that the moment would never end.

Later, we awoke from our nap. We had made plans to again meet with Oksana and Max at the Notre Dame. It was such a convenient spot in the center of the city. We opted to ride the metro instead of another two-hour journey on foot. Although I didn't mind the metro it was truly one of the dirtiest and sketchiest I had seen. Standing on the platforms I would set my face in stone and hope the local drunk would pass by me without stopping. Every single time, without fail, some poor bum would start yelling or pissing himself. Everybody would look straight ahead, pretending it wasn't happening. Later on, my other friends will tell me they encountered jazz bands playing impromptu sets, or strippers putting on a free show to boom box music, but me, I just saw beggars.

Soon we got to our destination, mercifully unmolested, and climbed the stairs to the Notre Dame plaza. There, in the same spot as yesterday, we saw Oksana and Maxime chatting in front of the church. The cathedral was no less impressive in the evening. We sat in front of it for an hour, watching its spires reach high into the Parisian night. We told them about our adventurous day and then heard about Max's walking tour of Montmartre. Oksana surprised me with her tale.

"I was leered and catcalled constantly," she told us with a resigned sigh. "Men would not leave me alone, and I didn't feel comfortable. I liked Paris, but I don't know anymore, I really didn't like it."

Then, without a pause, she described how a huge group of shirtless Frenchmen had been screaming and yelling in a threatening manner while a wall of riot police advanced slowly on them.

"I think they were an anti-EU protest or something," she said. She had tried to relax in a park, but the harassment had only gotten worse. Her experience had been the opposite of Samie and I's.

We decided to get some food and walk off the day's experiences. We were pretty hungry, so we walked into the first place that we passed. This time it was an Italian restaurant.

As we sat down at the table, waiters would carry plates of food over to us, showing us each plate, before placing them in front of the actual paying customer. Max asked them in French why they are doing this.

"In order for everybody to see of course," they responded.

Enjoying the vibe, we each ordered individual pizzas. As we sipped wine, the waiter sang to us in Italian.

We had an enjoyable meal. Another hour soon melted away. I really enjoyed my time with these guys. After a glass or two of wine, I had Max ask where the bathroom was.

The waiter pointed down a corridor. He told me through Max that it was down the stairs down the corridor. I walked down it and saw it took a sharp U-turn to where a descending staircase was.

I turned the corner and was confronted by dozens of stuffed animal heads staring at me. Lions, zebras and tigers stared at me from their perch over the stairs. The Italian décor had not led to me believe they would have twenty taxidermy animal busts hidden in the back.

When I got back to the table, I told the others about the heads. They each soon went to the bathrooms to see the unexpected trophy wall. Later, after we paid our bill, we stood up to leave. The waiters jumped up to help the girls put their jackets back on. It was very classy.

The four of us decided to take the long walk back to the Eiffel Tower to see what it looked like at night. Along the way Max pointed out things he had learned on his French walking tour, such as the French language institute. Apparently, the French refuse to use loanwords, so instead of using words like 'computer', they come up with uniquely French equivalents like *'ordinateur'*.

We got to the Eiffel Tower just after eleven. The Tower sparkled like a Roman candle at the top of each hour. We were still a bit away when the Tower lit up and the lights danced on the waters of the Seine.

Once we reached the Mars Garden, we were surprised to find the place almost completely empty. A few scattered couples sat in the grass along with one man walking around selling champagne bottles.

The dazzling view was intoxicating enough without champagne. We had the best view of the Eiffel Tour as gentle yellow lights inside its frame lit it up. I couldn't believe how I was sitting with my friends in front of the Eiffel Tower at night. It felt like a surreal dream.

We sat there for a long time. In due course, our throats grew hoarse from talking, and we sat in a comfortable silence. The night was getting colder, but nobody wanted to leave because we know it is the last time for us to be together.

Max was going back to Quebec very soon and Oksana would be leaving the day after that. We had been the basis of a small, tight-knit friend group for months and now it was starting to come to an end.

The moment was too perfect to leave but we knew it could not last forever. Reluctantly we walked to the nearest metro. Again, it was too surreal to be walking through the darkened empty Mars Garden, with the electric lights of the Eiffel Tower behind us, half past midnight.

We boarded the metro in silence. As we passed stop after stop a feeling of sadness welled up inside of me. The four of us stood in a semicircle and looked out of the windows at the passing platforms. Nobody said a word until we were one stop away. We couldn't put it off any longer.

Sam and Oksana went in to hug Max. He gave each of them a warm embrace. Sam's eyes were watery as she told him he was welcome to visit us anytime.

He asked, in his earnest style, "Even if it has been two or three years?"

Laughing at his question we told him, of course he could. The metro slowed down for our stop.

"Goodbye Nate," he said and he held his hand out for a shake. I pulled him in for a hug instead, and then next thing I knew we were on the platform and the metro was pulling away from the station. It was midnight in Paris as we watched Max speed off into the darkness back towards home.

Max was the second person I had to say goodbye to since arriving in Europe in January. Our time was brief but so intense and joyful that these people became some of my best friends. The goodbyes got easier, but never any less sad.

Paris, Day Seven: 3rd of April.

I woke up with a heavy heart. Having just bid farewell to Max, I knew I had to do it again with Oksana later this evening. It was our last day together for the rest of the trip. She had to leave early the next morning to catch a train back to England.

We went downstairs for one last breakfast. As we descended the winding wooden stairs, Chloe told us about her time at Disneyland the previous day. They had had a great day taking pictures with Mickey Mouse and such. I still didn't understand it but was glad she had a good time. If there was any ill-will from the other day, she didn't show it.

After a breakfast where I successfully evaded the madam and ate *two* croissants, we went into the city on the metro. As I leaned against the subway window watching the subterranean lights whiz by, I thought about how desperately my feet still ached from the yesterday.

I hopped off the subway a few stops before the girls. They were heading on to see the inside of Notre Dame, but I wanted to see the Tomb of Napoleon.

I climbed out of the metro and walked up the imposing tree-lined boulevard to the tomb and attached museums, Le Invalides. The building complex used to be a military hospital, hence its name, built during the reign of King Louis XIV, but it had been converted to museums and a mausoleum not long after Napoleon died. I only had two hours to see it, before I meet the girls at the cathedral.

I walked inside the 19th century building and bought a ticket. The former hospital hosted several museums in its many wings, in addition to the tomb. I had forgotten to grab extra cash, and I was grateful that my only bill, a ten-euro note, covered the student entry fee of nine euros fifty cents.

Mindful of the limited time, I went first to a Charles de Gaulle exhibit, which was located in the basement of the building. I planned to rush through the special touring exhibit, and then head to the main military museum on the ground floor, but the detour ended up taking over an hour. I became engrossed by the overview of this controversial and pivotal figure.

After quickly skimming the parts about de Gaulle's World War One experience, I got to the part of his life where he became president of France in the fifties. I knew nothing of this time period. In America, de Gaulle is remembered for withdrawing from NATO. I remembered hearing patriotic stories where, upon hearing this news, the American NATO commander simply asked whether he was supposed to remove the American war dead as well.

The story illustrated the common American perception that the weak-willed French were only saved by the grace and grit of hardworking Americans. To Americans, postwar France would act in bullheaded and strange ways, seemingly with no patience for the rest of the Western nations. To many Americans, France should have acted with more deference and gratitude.

So, quite unexpectedly, I was confronted with a totally different point of view. I learned how France was an ancient and proud nation that spent millions of lives fighting Germany in the first war. Then, only two short decades later, France was quickly and brutally laid low by Nazi Germany. Frances' self-image was destroyed during the occupation, as the nation was ripped apart, by both foreign and domestic forces.

After their surrender, France was mostly ruled by the Vichy government, which was largely seen in the West as a Nazi puppet. However, domestically, the Vichy government had a fair amount of support. Once the war turned in favor of the Allies, most French turned against the Axis government, but the fact that millions of French people had supported the fascists would not be easily forgotten. The fact that France, the birthplace of modern democracy, had seen a semi-popular fascist government caused a massive identity crisis.

De Gaulle ended up helping win the war and liberate France. But France had been deeply shaken by the fascist experience and desperately wanted to reclaim its lost pride. By standing up to stronger nations, like the US, de Gaulle was trying to make the French feel like the powerful people they once were.

Contemplating this different perspective suddenly made de Gaulle's actions much more reasonable. Although it was definitely biased towards de Gaulle, my eyes were opened in ways I had not expected.

It was profound to see recent history from a foreign perspective. It dawned on me how much I considered America to be the center of the world in more ways than I'd ever thought. Of all the places I had half expected to realize this, I certainly did not think it would be in the basement of a museum about Charles de Gaulle. I was thankful the exhibit was fully translated into English. If travelling is about opening one's eyes to new points of views, this certainly did it for me.

Completing that moving exhibit, I went up to the next level where I entered a conventional military museum. In this portion of the museum, I walked through the armies of France and watched them evolve from 1640 to 1871. It was a good look at the wars that France fought in that time period, of which there were many. There were many artifacts and fully preserved uniforms to admire.

The parts about the Napoleonic Wars were exceptionally well done. There were many well-kept uniforms, sabers, guns and cannons. There was also brief section on the American Revolution I found interesting. It was readily apparent that France was very proud of the fact that it helped birth the United States.

In fact, this was a recurring theme throughout Paris. It seemed like I couldn't turn a street corner without finding a massive street named Franklin Roosevelt Avenue or a tasteful Thomas Jefferson statue. In the De Gaulle exhibit, they stressed that when France left NATO it was not because they disliked America. Although both museums did not shy away from examining our complex and sometimes strained relationship, both stressed the deep and important bond between our two countries.

In some ways I found France to be more familiar than England. Despite the language barrier, I could see at times how influential the French culture has been in my country. After all, France was our principal ally and partner for a hundred years before Britain. The French have a more relaxed attitude in day-to-day life than the English. Their daily interactions were much closer to mine than the stuffy and reserved English manner. Their attitude, bordering closely on arrogance, was a trait deeply ingrained in both France and the US.

Beginning to run out of time, I hastily texted Samie from my cheap flip phone, asking her to push back our meeting time. I had to pay for each text, so I tried to never use it except for emergencies.

I ran through the World Wars museum. I didn't have time to look too closely but they seem well done. Unlike the other parts of the museum, the displays were exclusively in French. It was still interesting but I wanted to get the French perspective instead of just seeing artifacts. It would have been interesting to see a French take on the wars, but unfortunately my French was limited to vegetable names.

Leaving the museum, I made my way over to the Dôme des Invalides itself. It was a giant, multi-story marble building topped by a golden dome, built directly behind the military museum. The mausoleum housed the heroes of France.

The great dome rose over me as I entered the building. Directly inside the rotunda I saw a few smaller tombs, although they were still quite ornate. Most were of Napoleon's family, but also people like General Ferdinand Foch, the French commander during World War One.

I was later surprised to learn that the little-remembered Napoleon II, son of Napoleon, had actually died in Vienna and been buried there for a hundred years. Adolf Hitler was responsible for moving his remains from Vienna to Paris in 1940, as gesture of good will towards the occupied French.

I was witnessing history by seeing the tombs. They were on the ground level and were laid out in different places along the circular interior. In the center of the building, the floor dropped away. I stepped up to the railing around it and looked down.

There, I finally saw the sarcophagus of Napoleon. It was easily fifteen feet high and another twenty across and made of gleaming red marble. I was in awe.

I descended to the lower level. The subterranean chamber was quite chilly due to all the marble. The casket was no less impressive from below. From the lower level, it towered above me and I could barely even see around it.

On the walls around the tomb were marble inlays which featured Napoleon with the body of a Greek god. In one, his impressively muscled body proudly gave his set of laws inscribed on tablets to a grateful mankind. In others he was seen, half-naked, fighting the allegorical figures of oppression. The epic reliefs alone were worth the admission price.

The Tomb of Napoleon was everything I had expected and wanted. Unfortunately, I was definitely late to meet the girls.

Leaving the museum, I found myself again running down the banks of the Seine on my way to the Notre Dame. I wondered if this was as common of an experience for other visitors as it was for me.

I met up with the girls in front of the Notre Dame again. They hadn't had to wait too long for me, as their tour had taken longer than expected. They told me the inside was spectacular and had they spent a long time admiring it. On the steps of the cathedral, we ate a standard lunch of Nutella sandwiches. After eating, we went to explore the city on the north side of the Seine.

I looked up at the towering stone buildings, with their shallow balconies and tall narrow windows. During the 1830 Revolution, Parisians had barricaded the streets we now walked, and fired on the French Army from these very balconies. These random citizens won their battle and toppled the Bourbon dynasty that had ruled France for a thousand years.

We walked deeper into the city, having a good time talking and stopping in shops. We ran across a photoshoot where the models wore the kinds of artistic and colorful clothes you only see on the cover of magazines. The tall skinny models leaned against the walls of the building looking bored while a swarm of men snapped their pictures.

Before long, we were back at the glass pyramid of the Louvre. We snapping some more pictures in front of it, but decided not to go in. We had all been in the museum at different points over the years, and we were pretty burnt out on museums. Instead, we went west, away from the entrance of the Louvre toward the Arc de Triomphe.

Or at least what we thought was the Arc. The monument was located just across a small roundabout near the pyramid. We strolled over to it, passing the Africans selling their tiny Eiffel Towers, bottles of water, and other cheap goods.

Reaching the Arc, we stood under its pinkish stone and craned our necks. I would guess it was about fifty feet high. I was underwhelmed. It was far smaller than expected and frankly looked unimpressive.

"Uh, guys," Oksana said. "I don't think this is the actual Arc de Triomphe."

"Oh," the rest of us said in unison. I wonder how many other tourists make the same mistake.

Double checking the map, we saw that the actual Arc lay a good deal further west, through the Jardin de Tuileries and up past the Champs-Elysees. The Tuileries garden was located adjacent to the smaller Arc, so we walked right in.

The Tuileries Garden was magnificent. Open to the public since 1667, the gravel paths were wide and shaded by dozens of trees, small ponds, reflecting pools and statues of Greek gods. Walking around, one would never guess one of the bloodiest battles of the French Revolution had happened here, when the people of Paris fought and massacred the personal guards of the king. This event kickstarted the bloody phase of the French Revolution.

I stopped to get some ice cream from a small food cart.

"Strawberry?" I asked, stressing the questioning sound. The lady nodded back at me.

"*Fraise,*" she said smiling.

"Ah *fraise*," I repeated, also smiling. She obliged my follow-up questions and taught me a few other fruit names in French.

Ice cream in hand, we sat in front of a huge fountain on some green metal chairs. We sat in the stunning garden, the former Royal Palaces surrounding us, our feet propped on the side of a fountain eating ice cream. It was one of my many moments when I wondered if this was all really happening. Paris was unreal.

Throughout the garden, Chloe would identify the various gods depicted in statues. She was something of an expert.

"Oh, and that's Hestia," she said excitedly, running up to a statue of a cloaked woman. "You can tell by her veil!"

Her excitement was contagious.

We exited the gardens and crossed over a vast intersection of several huge streets. In the center of the roundabout sat a giant obelisk, looted during the days of colonialism. It was here, that King Louis XVI, Marie Antoinette, and many others were executed. Even Maximilien Robespierre, with a gunshot wound in the jaw and broken legs from his fall at the Hotel de Ville met his end at the guillotine here. Endless waves of cars drove by as we crossed over it.

Soon we were on the famous Champs-Elysees. The sidewalks were massive and broken up by grass and trees with benches and food vendors. We saw a crepe shack and bought some of the delicious cheap treats.

We happily staked out an unoccupied bench to eat our hot crepes. Before long, our peaceful snack was broken by a man staggering towards us. He looked to be in his fifties, with red eyes and a can of beer in his hand. He staggered around in front us, making eye contact the whole time. He came to a stop, faced us fully and slowly lifted his finger to point at us, never saving a word.

The four of us fell silent and tried to ignore the man. He kept pointing at us, swaying slightly in the breeze like a big ungainly drunken tree, not saying a word.

Oksana sighed wearily. We took that as our cue and stood up. Before the man could react, we quickly strode away. After a few meters, I looked back and saw the man still swaying, facing us and looking confused.

A little further up the street, the green spaces ended, and we were once more at a giant roundabout. I felt like I was at the mouth of a roaring river, except instead of water and rocks it was concrete and cars. Straight ahead, we saw the distant outline of the Arc de Triomphe.

We crossed the roundabout and continued up the Champs-Elysees. The further up the street we went the better people were dressed and the more expensive the stores were. We were in the epicenter of a rich, world city.

A few more blocks up we saw doormen standing in front of stores gilded in gold. The crowds grew thicker as we passed these guards. I didn't think they let people like us in stores like those.

The sidewalks were twenty feet wide on each side of the street. Despite the large number of people, I didn't feel terribly congested. I had enough personal space to feel at ease.

The Arc de Triomphe by now had grown from a speck on the horizon to a huge building right in front of us. As we at last approached it, I was a little dismayed to see it was in the center of a busy roundabout and that about a quarter of the building was covered in scaffolding.

We stood for a moment at end of the Champs-Elysees as cars and tourists rushed by. The roundabout that surrounded the Arc was three lanes deep and swarming with traffic. How to get closer? Was it even passable?

We pondered for a moment, but then Oksana spied people disappearing into what looks like a metro entrance.

"Let's check it out," she said.

It soon became apparent that it was an underground tunnel that took us underneath the road. We came up out from underground right beneath the Arc. It was a daunting and imposing piece of architecture and art. Each enormous pillar was covered in beautiful reliefs depicting victorious battles.

Suddenly, the traffic died. This was unusual because the drone of traffic was so common, that the sudden silence felt alien. We watched in amazement as the busy intersection in the heart of this metropolis turned completely quiet and empty.

Then, from one of the many streets emptying into the roundabout, we saw a procession of older men in civilian clothes, a few people playing military tunes on drums and horns, and a small contingent of uniformed young men. They marched across the now empty roundabout and crossed over to the Arc.

I had no idea what the ceremony was, but I watched it from no more than a few feet away. The large, international crowd was respectfully silent as the French laid down a wreath and somebody gave a short speech.

Travelling, I thought, *is all about the unexpected moments like this.*

By the time the ceremony ended it was getting late and we were tired from hours of walking. We took the metro back home and grabbed dinner from that same Subway we'd been eating at. Subway, at the time, was definitely my comfort food.

We popped into a supermarket to buy a few bottles of wine to enjoy with dinner. The labels were in French and I was uncultured in wine drinking. I grabbed a bottle at random.

As I came up to the counter, I said *"Bonjour"* to the woman behind it.

The cashier seemed nice until she said something to me in French and looked at me expectantly.

I said *"no Anglais"* and shook my head. I felt my cheeks blush with embarrassment. I instantly realized that I had just said 'No English' and that just made no sense.

The woman rolled her eyes, as if she couldn't be more exasperated by my inability to speak French. She pointed at the screen, where my total was clearly displayed. I paid and slouched away in defeat.

When Chloe exited the store, I told her my experience.

"Oh," she said shrugging. "When she said that to me I just handed her a large bill. The cashier said a few more things and handed me my change. I told her *merci* and walked off."

Chloe paused, and then added, "I think she was complaining about you."

As a tall skinny white girl with dramatic features, Chloe was often mistaken as European. At several times, strangers would come up to her and speak the local language. They were always surprised to find out she was American, not a local.

Back at the hostel, we sat at the tables in the common room. The room was comfortable for a cheap hostel. It was all wooden benches, high ceilings, and tasteful lighting. While Samie went upstairs for an early bedtime, Oksana, Chloe and I drank the bottles of red wine.

We chatted and enjoyed our last few hours together. Just as I drained our last glass, a guy at the table across from us waved us over.

"Do you guys want to drink some champagne?" he asked us in an unmistakable American accent. We squeezed in next to him. He was a tall blond American from Reno who was studying in Madrid. Next to him, we met his friends, Jose from Bakersfield, and Juan from Brazil. They insisted we drink champagne with them.

The three gentlemen had bought too much of it and were desperately trying to finish it in before heading to the club.

They graciously invited us along, although we didn't take the offer.

As I talked to the American from Reno, I mentioned I studied at Kent State. As soon as I said the name of my school, two blonde girls, perched on the table across from us giggled loudly, and yelled out to me.

"Hey we are from Hudson!"

I turned to face them. "Hudson, Ohio?" I asked incredulously. "Near Twinsburg and Streetsboro and Kent? With an old town square?"

"Yes," the girls exclaimed happily "that's it!"

I couldn't believe it. These people were from a place fifteen minutes away from my parent's house. I had spent countless hours in quaint little Hudson, Ohio.

Running into a random American from California in front of the Notre Dame is no special coincidence. Meeting somebody who lived fifteen minutes from you in a hostel common room late in the evening? That's a damn coincidence.

I was ecstatic to be finally hanging out with fellow travelers in a hostel. When I had gone to Chicago the previous year my friends and I spent a bunch of time with our hostel-mates. We had met cool people and hanging out with them had really made the trip worth it. I fondly remember just sitting on the steps of the hostel with these other travelers, watching the busy Chicago street bustle with life.

Since January we had been staying in hostels all over the UK and hadn't once met somebody interesting. In fact, the only people we'd seen in hostel common rooms had been creepy older drunk men. All spring I had been consistently disappointed at the lack of social interaction in hostels, so this hour or two had been great.

My new acquaintances from Hudson soon left to go to bed. The three champagne drinkers then left to go clubbing, leaving just Chloe, Oksana and I.

It was getting late and Oksana had to sleep, to get rest before getting on the Eurostar train to London early tomorrow. She announced to us that she was going to bed. I hugged her goodbye and although I knew would see her again, I was sad to see her go.

"It's been a great trip, Oksana, and I really wish you could stay for the rest of it," I said to her.

Oksana hugged me back. "You guys are going to have an awesome time."

All of our trips this whole year had been the four of us travelling together. Oksana was an integral member of our little tribe. I knew the rest of the journey wouldn't be the same without her pushing us to eat at nice restaurants or go out for drinks and dancing. She injected a certain rebellious and carefree attitude in our group that Sam, Chloe and myself lacked.

Chloe joined Oksana as she went back upstairs. They were going to bed but I decided to take a little walk first. I always loved night walks and I wanted to enjoy my Paris adventure just a tiny bit longer. Outside, I drunkenly looked up at the stars hanging above the city. I still couldn't believe that I would ever end up in a place like this. The pleasure of travel washed over me.

Later, I happily crawled into my bed, just as the girls were turning in.

"Goodnight all," Chloe said softly as the light was turned off.

I was groggily aware of Oksana leaving around six the next morning. Although I was only half awake, I saw her slip out of the door in the gray light of dawn, shutting it quietly behind her. I drifted back to sleep as her footsteps faded away. I never could have predicted how the next forty-eight hours would unfold. We didn't realize what a wild ride we were in for, as the hostel door in Room 108 closed shut that morning.

The girls in front of the real Arc

Chapter 3: Spain

Madrid, Day Eight: 4th of April

Leaving Paris was the easy part. We slept in late and ate breakfast leisurely. We were mostly quiet as we climbed back up the stairs and packed our things. We were feeling Oksana's missing presence acutely.

We were in no hurry to leave because our flight wasn't until five. I took one last shower in our private bathroom. I left the tall and narrow window next to the shower open, allowing beautiful morning sunlight illuminate the bathroom.

This is like a resort, I thought to myself. After a wonderful shower, we lounged about in the spacious room for a while longer before leaving around noon. We took the metro one last time. It took us to a bus depot downtown where there was a shuttle to the Charles De Gaulle Airport.

With Oksana being gone the old tensions were beginning to simmer again. Perhaps it was nerves or just plain exhaustion. As we ate a meager dinner at a small table, I had to excuse myself as we began to bicker. Better to walk away then get sucked into a downward spiral.

It had been a tough decision when we picked to fly on this leg on the trip. Having paid considerable money for the rail passes, we had been very reluctant to pay additional cash for a flight.

We had ultimately decided on a cheap Ryanair flight because our rail passes would not cover the full cost of a night train. Additionally, the ride from Paris to Madrid would have taken at least twenty-four hours and would have included a layover in Marseilles at midnight.

Marseilles, despite being on the coast of Mediterranean, was known for being quite the shithole. I had heard, not least of all from Chloe, that it was not a safe or nice town. I had read guidebooks before I left which euphemistically referred to Marseilles as 'developing' and having certain 'areas not advisable to be in after dark without a local guide.'

When Chloe had been in high school they had taken a school trip from Rome to Madrid via the midnight train. They had arrived in Marseilles late at night and needed to switch trains.

"The ticket man threw me against a wall and screamed at me in French," Chloe would recount the story with wide eyes. "People were sneaking onto the train and getting thrown out and it was horrible!"

Between the guidebooks and Chloe's story, we were in no mood to check out that particular destination.

So, we had decided to fly from Paris to Madrid. The flight was dirt cheap as intra-European flights often are, and only a few hours instead of a full day. I was excited to travel so far, so fast. Coming from America, I had wrongly assumed everything in Europe was close to everything else.

After walking around and writing in my travel journal, things had cooled down a little and we got on the plane at peace.

The flight itself was short and unremarkable. During the flight, I looked out of the window to see Spain below me, with its dry grassy hills and hardy-looking shrubs. Spain physically looked very different from the other countries we'd seen. We were only a few hundred miles south but the climate looked totally different. I was excited as we touched down in Madrid just before sunset.

The Madrid-Barajas airport, like most major cities, was located a fair bit outside of Madrid proper. We quickly found ourselves a metro station inside the airport. Sam connected to the wifi and pulled up directions to our hostel, Sleep Madrid.

Train Seats and Hostel Beds

We had booked the majority of our rooms before leaving Leicester. We attempted to balance between budget and comfort. We were not fussy travelers, so long as the room was quiet and clean we really did not ask for much more. Figuring we would not be spending much time in the room, we usually ended up picking lower priced options over more comfortable ones.

We had also decided to balance the number of cities and length of our stays. The last few cities had been an exhausting whirlwind of constant travel. Amsterdam was supposed to be four nights, but we had cut it in half to visit Bruges. So, before we left Leicester, we decided to stay in Madrid for a good number of nights. Sam spoke fluent Spanish and Chloe was proficient so we figured there wouldn't be much of a language barrier. We knew Spain was cheaper too, so we knew we could stretch our money there.

Typically, we found that renting three beds in a four-person dorm to be the best mix of price and privacy. With Oksana, it was even better because the four of us would essentially get a private room for the price of a dorm bed. On average we would pay about twenty to thirty US dollars a night per person.

Sleep Madrid, we were excited to find out, would only cost us fourteen, yes fourteen, US dollars a night per person. For this price, we had decided, from our comfortable rainy English town, that we could afford to spend a week in sunny Spain.

So, there we stood in the metro station of the airport. Both were sleek and new. The metro and airport of Madrid looked much nicer than the Parisian ones. Before we bought our tickets, I wrote down the key code to enter the hostel. The reception would be closed, but they had emailed me a code to punch into the keypad outside the door. The code would let us in, and we would find the key to our room in an envelope at the front desk.

The code was a simple series of numbers, five-two-two-five. We punched in the address thirty-two Lavapiés and a route came up on Samie's phone. The route looked simple and we were not worried in the slightest. We had been doing this for months now and the routine was second nature.

Our plane had touched down as the sun was setting, so by the time we got to our metro stop it was around nine thirty. The metro ride had been quite long.

We exited at the Tirso de Molina metro stop. It was a less than ten-minute walk from the metro stop to the hostel. Climbing out of the crumbling stone metro we saw a crammed square with towering buildings multiple stories high covered in neon signs and iron-wrought balconies. The square was bustling with life and there was hardly room to stand without running into somebody. When I went to Asia later in life, the cities there would remind me of this.

People were sitting and eating food, while kids kicked soccer balls and throngs of people were moving around. All around us cars honked and drove by on narrow streets. I looked up to see a balcony high above me jammed packed with shirtless men drinking beer.

What the hell had I got myself into, I thought to myself. Overwhelmed with the amount of people, and disoriented from our long day we wanted nothing more than to reach our beds. We shouted over the crowd, trying to find which street was Lavapiés, the street the hostel was on. We cut through the crowd and walked into a darkened street between two buildings. As we entered it we saw the street name, Calle Jesus y Maria. Perfect.

Yellow, old-fashioned streetlights stood every ten or fifteen meters, leaving bits of darkness between them. Walking down it, we saw it was strangely deserted. We were only a few meters away from that square which was so crowded. Becoming aware of my surroundings, I noted that the buildings were all padlocked, with gates pulled over the doors and bars on the windows. There was graffiti everywhere. The graffiti was not the nice artistic kind but the dirty scrawls of gangs and violence.

I stiffened at this. It was not what I'd come to expect in Europe. It reminded me of the rougher areas of Cleveland, not the Europe I'd seen so far. I unconsciously started to go into defensive mode, setting my face into a scowl and walking faster, as if with a purpose.

We turned right onto Calle de Cabeza and saw a few dark figures hurry past us. We heard noise everywhere but nobody else was around. We turned left onto to our destination street, Calle de Lavapiés. We were finally on the correct street.

Now Calle de Lavapiés was a long street that intersected with Calle Jesus y Maria like a Y shape. These two streets came together and then continued as one single street stretching south. At the intersection of the streets, at the center of the 'Y', there was a smallish plaza. Further down the shaft of the 'Y', there were stores and restaurants but not nice tourist ones. These were more like rough local joints you can find in places like East Cleveland or Youngstown. We were not in a touristy part of town.

We were on the right branch of the 'Y', on Lavapiés. Not seeing a building numbered thirty-two we walked into the plaza at the intersection. These streets were very narrow, only able to fit the tiniest of cars and motorbikes. Spilling out of one of these narrow streets between huge decrepit buildings we walked past a man with dark skin and dreadlocks.

He was leaning on his motorbike, yelling out "Rasta! Rasta!"

He stood with his back to the buildings that faced the intersection, so he could overlook the entire plaza as if he ran it.

Next to him were two other people yelling "Hey *guapa!*" as we walked by. Unnerved but ignoring the comments we saw the number thirty-two. It was on the side of the street, just past the plaza, and looked like it was still on the right side of the street.

Unfortunately, underneath the address was an empty storefront, dark and gated. It was obviously not a hostel nor anything else.

We didn't say a word and instead immediately turned back up the street into the plaza. We were accosted every few feet by men stepping directly in front of us, saying things in Spanish, or beckoning us to go down even tinier dark alleys. In Spain, as I was finding out, when people want to pester you they would get right up in your face. They would put their faces inches away from yours and speak to you while staring into your eyes.

We were three white people in a part of town that was obviously not white. We had huge backpacks on and I was intensely aware how we looked increasingly lost and vulnerable. I hated being in public with my pack because it so clearly marked us as outsiders. We had a fair bit of cash on us, not to mention two laptops, three passports, and other valuables. We fell into single file, just trying to curb the verbal assaults.

"*Hablas Español?*" some guys yelled at us. A man tugged at my arm, beckoning us to go with him.

The rasta-man cackled menacingly and screamed in accented English, "you can ask ME for directions, white people. There is no shame in asking for help!"

He let out a piercing wordless scream.

"They are white and they look rich," we heard somebody else say in English. Although we kept looking at the address numbers the yelling was completely unnerving and we quickly exited the neighborhood, finding ourselves back at the metro we came from earlier, chased out by the shrill cries of the fine people of Lavapiés.

We gathered underneath a streetlight. The square was bisected by a one-lane road, with occasional cars driving by. There were still some people milling around eating food and talking, although it was much calmer than last time we were here.

We felt safe here because it felt like a normal city and not that hellhole we had just walked into. We had a quick and forced conversation and decided to ask for directions, thinking a local would point us in the right way. We saw a hostel sign across the road so we crossed and walked into its tiny reception hall.

There was a woman who must have been in her sixties sitting there looking at us expectantly. She shook her head when we asked if she spoke English. Sam then spoke to her in Spanish and they have a brief conversation.

"*Gracias,*" Sam thanked her and we walked outside.

"She said that she didn't know where Sleep Madrid is, so I asked her if she had rooms, but she said that since we already paid for the first hostel that we should go there. She gave us directions to a different hostel that might know where the Sleep Madrid is though."

Sam sounded frustrated. The three of us were frustrated. Luckily the next hostel was only a few blocks up the road away from Lavapiés. We walked, ten thirty at night, lost in a bad part of Madrid with no room yet for the night ahead.

We got to the other hostel. This one was bright and well lit, inviting and familiar. The Russian woman at check-in spoke good English. They didn't know where the hostel was but the Russian woman and her boss looked up directions on Google. We made the mistake of telling them we had already paid for our night there, so when we asked if they had beds for us they told us we needed to go to Sleep Madrid.

"You already paid, you can't lose that money," they insisted. They turned the computer towards us and showed us that the hostel was located just before the plaza on Lavapiés.

The number thirty-two we had walked to was on the left side of the street past the plaza, while this new one was on the right side, before the plaza. We had been close, but none of us wanted to return there.

"You must go back," the hostel workers insisted again.

We walked back out into the dark night, exchanging no words, all of us steeling ourselves for another trip. We walked slowly down Lavapiés like condemned men to the gallows. We stopped just one or two buildings away from the square where we heard our friend the rasta-man screaming. I shuddered as he unleashed another banshee-like scream.

At the correct door this time, we saw a tiny piece of paper with a figure dancing over the words 'Sleep in Madrid'. We were overjoyed. This was the place!

There was keypad by the door. Nearly collapsing with relief, I punched in the code..

The keypad flashed red. I put it in again. It flashed red. My heart sank as I put it in, again and again, it still flashed red each time. I tugged at the door and it wouldn't budge.

"Oh no no no," I heard one of the girls say.

I couldn't think straight for a moment, and my vision swam. We turned and walked again to the metro stop, packs heavy, adrenaline rushing through us. The vulnerability of our situation was driving me crazy.

We gathered at a streetlight. Chloe looked very white, like she was going to faint. I was sure I did too.

"What do we do?" Chloe asked, her voice quiet.

"Let's go back to the second hostel and look up the email," Sam suggested, thinking on her feet. "Maybe the code is just wrong".

I nodded in agreement, my throat too dry to speak.

In silence, we went back to the second hostel. We stood outside and tried to reconnect to the wifi. Luckily, I somehow remembered what the password was, for I had seen it written down inside. Sam connected to the wifi and I checked my email.

"They sent me two codes," I said softly and I wrote down the second code. It was five-two-two-seven, very similar to the first. We walked back, again single file, again silently, again hearing the screams, the cackles and the sounds of this strange city.

As we walked down the dark narrow streets, I looked around at the buildings. Most of them were dark and shuttered with iron bars over the windows. However, we pass one store lit by fluorescent lights shining through the barred windows. I saw rows of books alongside red and black anarchist flags. The logo of the store was a skull with a punk rock Mohawk.

Being familiar with anarchist bookstores from Cleveland, I wondered aloud if we should get help from these friendly neighborhood anarchists. Chloe and Sam immediately shot down the idea.

"We are not bringing anarchists into this," one of them said curtly and we continued to trudge on.

Arriving once again at the hostel, I punched the new code in. I was afraid to even look at the light.

After a long moment it flashed....red.

I slumped onto the door. We were so close. Chloe moaned softly behind me. I tried the code a few more times, not expecting anything. I tried the first code again. Nothing. We turned and left the hostel. The door was firmly locked.

We walked, defeated and tired back to the second hostel. Inside, we flatly told them we needed beds, the door doesn't work and we just need a damn place to stay.

The woman looked surprised. "It will be thirty-eight euros for the beds," she said.

I was relieved it was relatively cheap. Just as we were about to hand over the money, the receptionist asked us which one was not staying.

"What?" Chloe asked incredulously.

"Yes, we only have two beds open."

"An hour ago you had three."

"Another person came in," the woman responded. Unreasonable anger flashed through me as I thought about her forcing us out earlier.

I mentally prepared myself to find another place. In the worst case, I reasoned that I could stay in the metro station so that the girls would be safe, at least.

"Well we are not splitting up," Chloe said, putting a quick end to my idea.

The woman shrugged, uncaring. We asked her if there were other hostels around. She told us of another a few blocks over, called Cat's Hostel. We walked towards it, as if in a daze. It was well past midnight and we were numbed from the night's events.

We saw lots of young people milling around outside the hostel. Normally we wouldn't think twice, but now I scanned the crowd wearily, hands on my wallet, ready for a fight, amped on adrenaline. But, the crowd was just drinking, smoking and having fun. They were no threat. We entered the place and passed a bar bumping loud music. We found reception and this time, just flat-out lied.

"Our plane just got in," Sam said in Spanish. "We are really tired, do you have three beds?"

The man nodded and we paid an outrageous price of forty euros each. At this point in the night, I would have paid any price. I would have gladly traded my passport and British visa if he had asked.

He took our money, and gave us a keyfob. The doors were electronic and we were on the second floor. Past the bar, in the middle of the room, there was a stunning Moorish fountain in the shape of a star. The room was shaped like an octagon and stretched up at least six or seven stories, up to a beautiful glass roof. The floor was made of marble and the walls of mahogany. I later found out this was a palace from the 17th century. Even in my exhausted state, I could admire the beauty of this building.

We staggered up to our room and I held the keyfob up to the door. It glowed red. I couldn't handle this. I drew my hand up to beat wildly on the door in terrible anger.

Just before I started to beat down the door, a young man came up to us.

"Oh I'll get it," he said in accented English "It is really weird and at first it wouldn't let me in." He chuckled happily and swiped in the key in a rectangular pattern.

"You'd think they'd explain this at check-in," he said, chuckling again. We entered the room and saw twelve bunks.

We stared stupidly for moment, before claiming different bunks. The young man studied us for a moment.

"Jesus, you guys look wasted," he said

Yeah, buddy, I thought to myself. *We are fucking wasted.*

He introduced himself as Juan from Chile. He was quite chatty and I forced myself to make small talk as the girls went to shower. Juan obviously meant well but he was one of those people who can't help but be offensive by accident.

I told Juan about our misadventures and he just grinned at me.

"Don't you know to never arrive at a new city in the dark?"

Yeah, thanks Juan, I thought. I was in no mood to deal with his chipper as fuck attitude.

The girls came back and I went off to shower myself. There was a huge bank of showers with little privacy. Two young men yelled happily at each other in Spanish and all I heard was "yar yar yar yar TripAdvisor yar yar yar." I chuckled in spite of myself.

The shower was terrible. It was freezing cold, moldy and smelled strongly of semen. Gagging, I dressed quickly, still wet, desperate to escape.

I stumbled back down the stairs to buy a sandwich from a vending machine. It tasted like cardboard and was probably old but I hadn't eaten in twelve hours. My last meal at Charles de Gaulle felt like a million years ago.

After 'dinner', I saw a beer vending machine and put in my very last euro coin. The vending machine ate my coin and dispensed no beer. I stared at it for a while then sat down near the fountain. My mind was broken. I don't know how long I sat there before eventually go back up to bed.

I fell fitfully asleep in my top bunk. I did not sleep very well because a loud group of French people would come and go, every so often, talking loudly and turning all the lights on.

It was the exact kind of hostel I have always sought to avoid. Later I heard people puking in the bathrooms, which were directly next to our room. The walls were paper-thin. I dreamt of dark alleys, rasta-men, and the sound of party people puking.

Bienvenido a Espana!

Madrid, Day Nine: 5th of April

I woke up exhausted after a few hours of pathetic half-sleep. It was seven o'clock. Juan, unsurprisingly, was wide-awake.

"Good morning!" he said and immediately launched into conversation. I forced myself to be friendly.

"Good morning, Juan."

The girls ignored him.

"Hey guys," he said to us, "I have no plans, can I hang out with you guys today?"

We exchanged glances as we dressed. I could tell none of us wanted Juan to come. But, too polite to say no, I hesitatingly responded, "Yeah...sure."

"Great!" Juan beamed at us and walked out of the room, no doubt excited for the day ahead.

We went down to breakfast. Breakfast was disappointing, as it was just some cereal and coffee. I was still quite hungry after my meager meal. We were still a little edgy and were seriously considering cutting our losses and spending the rest of the week in Toledo. Juan overheard us talking and was shocked.

"Leave Madrid? For Toledo? Toledo is a day trip!" he said. "It's so tiny and old and boring!"

"That sounds wonderful," Sam said dreamily, closing her eyes and picturing herself far away.

Instead, after more discussion, we decided to try Sleep Madrid one last time before ditching the city. The reception should have been open by now, and we figured we might as well try before we got the hell out of Madrid.

As we headed out of the Cat's Hostel, Juan ran up to us and apologized. He was so sorry to break plans but something else had come up and he would be meeting with friends who just arrived in Madrid. It was hard to keep my grin down.

It was still early when we went back to where our nightmare had happened last night. I peered into the square and it was completely empty. *Madrileños* don't wake up early. Unlike the crazed and unnerving scene the night prior, the square now looked innocuous. It even seemed like a pleasant place to relax or eat lunch.

Chloe tugged on the door. It swung open immediately and we at long last entered. The white stucco ceiling was low slung, almost touching my head. Right inside the door were three couches draped in white sheets and a small bookshelf. Besides a few generic paintings on the walls, the room was empty.

Immediately to the left of the entryway, was a small nook containing a desk and a nice looking young lady who couldn't be more than sixteen years old sitting behind it. She welcomed us and then Sam proceeded to have a long conversation with her in Spanish. It was apparent English was not as common in Spain as it had been in the last few places.

They both walked outside and I saw the girl punch in the codes I had tried to use to no avail. They came back inside and spoke more. At last, Samie thanked her and turned to us. She told us they apologized the code didn't work and as compensation, they wanted to offer us a stupidly low rate for the rest of our stay. We huddled up and made a quick decision to stay. At this point it was basically free, costing only a couple bucks a night.

The young lady, whom Samie informed us was the daughter of the owner, showed us around. The doorway near the couches led to our dorm room, where there were two bunk beds. To the left was a hallway that led to a full kitchen and a dining room with two round tables, each with four seats. Directly adjoining the dining room were the female and male bathrooms. There were two more dorm rooms across the street, apparently connected via an underground tunnel, which was awesome, but sadly I never got to experience.

I set down my pack in our empty dorm room and sank into the bottom bunk, facing the wall. All at once I was flooded with all the feelings I couldn't feel last night. All the fear, stress and frustration my body had pushed aside as it had entered emergency mode hit me at once. I had been numb for a good number of hours and they crashed over me, materializing in big wet tears as I hid my head beneath a blanket. I was so exhausted.

I cried for a minute or two when Samie came into the room and sat with me, cheering me up. I felt a little better having let my feelings out. Chloe came in a little later, having used the shower. *She is,* I thought, *absurdly cheerful and ready to go sightseeing.*

"C'mon Nate it'll make you feel better," Chloe urged, drying her long hair with a towel. "I booked us spots on a free walking tour." Sightseeing was the last thing I wanted to do. I'd much rather lay in bed all day and recoup.

Chloe had been to Madrid before and had very positive memories of it but I had already decided that I hated this shit city. Nonetheless, I knew I couldn't lay in my bunk all day. I begrudgingly got up.

Forced to leave my bunk bed safety zone, we took the ten-minute stroll to the Plaza Mayor. I was leery of everyone. It was still pretty early in the day but the huge plaza was already full of people. The plaza was made of cobblestone and probably the size of a football field. It was literally a square, with different historic buildings surrounding it. A large equestrian statue dominated the center of it. There were two or three small entrances into the square with no access for any vehicles.

People were walking around, taking pictures and talking while the street performers did all sorts of crazy antics. Some dressed in outlandish costumes and made loud noises. One, in particular, was dressed up as a baby and screaming gibberish, while others dressed normally but had some kind of device in their mouth that allowed them to make loud duck noises. Surprisingly, the man-baby was a hit with the tourists and he was raking in tip money.

We walked around the length of the square and stopped into tourist shops selling swords and soccer balls and such. Inside, we found a poster advertising a free walking tour that met in this spot in an hour. Free sounded good to us and we hadn't done a walking tour in Europe yet. We had just enough time for a quick lunch.

Hungry, we looked around for some food. We looked at restaurants in the plaza but they were far too expensive. Stepping just outside the plaza, we found a sleek glass and metal building called the Mercado de San Miguel.

Inside there were vendor stalls everywhere selling relatively cheap food, drinks and produce. I took a picture of a large fish that was four and a half feet long. On Facebook, I would see this same fish multiple times over the next few weeks because all of my friends who passed through the same market also took pictures of it. We bought some Spanish rice, *paella,* from a tapas vendor. The paella was cheap, filling and tasty. I felt marginally better.

Soon it was time for our free walking tour. Although this was our first tour in Europe, we had grown to absolutely love them in the U.K. Walking tours were always cheap, after the tip, and they usually pointed out good places to eat or drink. The guides were typically young people and they told us the places they like to go. Normally their schedules were loose and they took groups wherever the specific guides wanted. Walking tours were the best way to find historical sites and buildings and the guides were almost always aware of the deeper history of their cities.

Walking back to the Plaza we saw a group of people gathering under a big red umbrella. That certainly looked like the start of a free walking tour. We joined the small crowd just as it was starting. They broke the tour into two groups because there were so many folks wanting the tour. Our assigned guide was a feisty young Madrid native. This was her first tour conducted entirely in English.

We started the tour in the Plaza Mayor itself and learned that they used to hold public executions in it. The preferred method was the garrote.

A garrote is a weapon used by somebody who takes a corded rope or piece of silk and wraps it around your neck. Then, they insert a little piece of wood between the rope and your neck. The executioner turns the wood, tightening the rope until you are strangled to death. It is an incredibly violent way to die.

The guide pointed out that the benches we had been sitting on were engraved with worn images of the executions. I was shocked to find out that the last public execution had taken place in 1973. My parents had been in high school.

These actions occurred under the dictatorship of Francisco Franco. The *Caudillo* or Leader as he was known, ruled Spain with an iron fist for fifty years. It's easy to forget that even liberal Western Europe had been home to dictatorship within living memory.

The guide talked more about the Franco legacy and the effect it had on Spain. She was not afraid to discuss this dark chapter of Spanish history. In general Spain is a country not eager to discuss this period, so I was happy the guide was willing to dive into it.

Leaving the plaza, the guide then showed us the allegedly oldest continually operating restaurant in the world. She let us know never to trust any signs that the bars hung up, claiming Hemingway drank there.

"He drank a lot and he drank in every single bar in Madrid."

Further along, she pointed out another unassuming side street. There, in the early days of the 20th century, an anarchist tossed a bomb at the royal family as they passed below his window. It was part of a worldwide trend of anarchist assassinations, including a Russian Czar and an American President.

At one point she told us the story of the Spanish Robin Hood. Unlike the English one, this guy stole from the rich and gave to…himself. Along the way, he seduced many women and was eventually killed by a jealous husband.

I was at all not surprised this asshole was a national hero because he just about sums up the 'Spanish Dream.' Rob the rich, sleep with the ladies and die young. Sounds about right.

We walked to the Cathedral of Spain, which was ugly, and to some old Moorish architecture, which was beautiful. The guide told us *Madrileños* are known as *gatos* or cats, because they stay up all night. That explained why there were always vibrant crowds in the evening. I was finding the tour very illuminating.

The tour ended in front of the royal palace. The tour guide claimed it was the largest royal palace in the world. Funny, because a different guide told me that Buckingham Palace in London was the largest. In France, I read that Versailles was the biggest royal palace. Later I will read that the Schönbrunn Palace in Vienna was the biggest. Hmm….

Regardless of that questionable bit of trivia, I tipped her well. I felt that her commentary really explained Spanish culture. Perhaps my initial discomfort was just plain culture shock as I adjusted to place with different values and ethos than where I am from.

During a short break on the tour, the guide told us about a tapas tour taking place later that evening. Normally we avoided paid tours, but we signed up on the spot, figuring it would provide dinner. Spain was definitely culturally different than the rest of Western Europe and the UK.

We left the royal palace after the tour. The palace was too expensive for us to go in. However, once a week, on Thursday afternoons after two, they let South Americans in for free. These limited free hours serve as an apology for the centuries of slave labor the Spanish had forced onto South America. Back in Ohio, we told our Columbian friend about this and she nodded happily. Her and her husband had taken full advantage of that policy when they had visited Madrid. While to me the policy sounded almost condescending due to the very limited hours of it, my South American friend was genuinely touched by it.

Just past the royal palace, we stopped at a shop to buy and eat some *tirujunas*, a Spanish Easter delicacy. It was like French toast but better and made with wine, a lot of wine. It was literally soaked in wine. We munched happily as we leisurely strolled through the congested streets and tiny alleyways of Madrid.

Madrid is an interesting city. The architecture consisted of towering, unique buildings. Each one was different than the next, as if they were built with no unified plan in mind. The streets ran in crazy zigzags, with no obvious layout.

Colorful paints lit up each building, each a different tone than its neighbor. Madrid struck me as a very old city that had had a layer of modernity forced over it. I'd pass a tiny medieval stone street with a mess of wires and satellite dishes propped up over my head. I'd see a weird mix of what I'd call Hispanic architecture mixed freely with Gothic and Germanic-style buildings. In Madrid I could see the fusion of several cultures that melted into one, making this puzzling Spanish nation.

We went back to the Plaza Mayor to wait an hour before the tapas tour started. As we sat there, it was jam-packed and the so-called entertainers were constantly making obnoxious noises. They all were using the duck call whistle. It was apparently some kind of tiny kazoo they hid in their mouths. I was going crazy because their constant squawking.

I really dislike Madrid I let myself think. I pictured my bed back home and missed it. *I could be there, safe and comfortable in Ohio.*

Getting to the tapas tour proved to be more difficult than we expected. The city was vaster than we initially thought. We almost got lost two times. Sam and I were still shaken by the idea of being lost in this city. In the back of mind, I dreaded having to go back to Lavapiés at night.

Eventually, however, with Chloe leading the way, we found the small nondescript plaza where our tour started.

We meet with a few other people and the tour guide, and then headed to our first restaurant. Our tour guide was a jovial young man, tall and skinny with a blond afro and a big smile.

There were about fifteen people in our group, and the tiny restaurant probably only had about twenty-odd seats. We crammed around one long table, taking up the whole room. The restaurant was a hole in the wall, never something we would have found on our own. I was already loving the tour.

Once we were seated, the cooks brought out several little traditional Spanish dishes, called tapas. Traditionally the cooks would serve these small plates and the guests shared them as they drank.

We ate paella, calamari and deep fried potatoes amongst other dishes. The seafood was particularly good. We passed around a big jug of sangria and poured liberally from it. Each bite and sip was wonderful. Each dish was a new experience. Having so many little dishes allowed me to taste a wide variety of exotic food. While always an adventurous eater, I had never been exposed to much world cuisine. I wholly attribute my gastronomical evolution to all the beautiful new food I tried in Europe.

We were seated next to two American students, an American girl travelling around Europe, and an Austrian woman who was hanging out with two bogan friends she met while studying in Australia eight or nine years ago. There was also a nice young Indian man who was studying in Germany.

The Australian bogans were straight trailer trash, both looking frumpy and wearing dirty wife beaters. It was jarring to see them amongst the well-dressed *gatos*, but also somehow comforting. Bogans are the exact same as our rednecks, except with Australian accents. They were not going to dress up for anybody or anything and I could respect that.

I overheard the one girl sitting next to Chloe speak English. I leaned over and ask if she was American. She said yes and told me she was from Colorado, but living in Prague. She was meeting up with her friend who happened to be in Barcelona and they took this tour to check out the city.

They were nice. We chatted for a while and eventually the third American, Melissa joined in. We bonded over our study-abroad experience and how enjoyable it had been so far.

Next, we went to the second stop, chatting with Melissa on the way over. She was from Hong Kong but had spent the last ten years in Boston. She was American in both accent and action. It was nice to be with someone who was such an unabashedly East Coaster.

I love how friendly Americans are. I never noticed it until I was abroad. Like many Americans of my age, I came of age during the Bush years and the Iraq invasion. Some of my earliest political memories are of tortured prisoners and protests against the war. Although Obama had softened the image some, I never really considered myself particularly American.

But, then I lived in England. I was surprised to realize how much I liked my country after living abroad. Sure, the British healthcare system was far superior, but damn I found out how much I enjoy casually talking to Americans. As a people, we are incredibly friendly and welcoming, something Europeans just aren't. I was still aware of my country's flaws, of course, but traveling across Europe genuinely made me appreciate my home culture. Hanging out with these Americans brought that into focus.

The second stop was a bar with large amounts of ham hanging on the walls and ceiling. This practice had started back in the Middle Ages when the Spanish needed to hang ham to prove that they weren't Muslim or Jewish. As terrible as this was, it turned Spain into the land of the most wonderful pork products I have ever had. Every piece of *jambon* I ate in Spain was magnificent.

At this bar, it was tradition to throw one's trash onto the floor. The guide told us that in Madrid you could tell which bars are the best by how much trash is on the floor. The more trash, the better the bar. Apparently throwing your shit on the floor was how you showed that you loved the food at this place.

We drank light beer and ate some meat filled finger sandwiches. The Indian guy, Praveen, joined our little circle. He was Tamil and lived in Germany. We spoke a little in German and he told me about the casual discrimination he faced there.

"They never speak to me in German, assuming I don't speak it" he said.

I drank my beer, polished off Sam's and then Chloe's. I even got to eat two little sandwiches before we headed off. This bar was very busy and the older people in our group decided to stay behind. As the night went on the streets got increasingly busy around us.

As we walked to the third and final location, the guide made little effort to keep track of us. The throngs of people were crushing around us. The guide sometimes held up a folded red umbrella, but we ended up losing at least a few more people before he paused in front of the last building. I had been to some busy cities but none as busy as Madrid. I later find out there were well over three million people in this city, a huge metropolis by any standard. Even Hanoi wouldn't feel quite as hectic.

We gathered around the tour guide.

"I am very happy my boss has picked this one," he yelled at us. We were barely able to hear over the crowds and traffic.

"This is a Northern Spanish place, the place I am from!" he said excitedly, and let us in.

We entered the narrow building and climbed the wooden stairs to a private lounge on the second floor. We sat on a leather couch around a coffee table laden with cured meat. The sausages on the table were cured to the point of blackness. They were quite spicy and very delicious. As we snacked, the guide set out three or four bottles of alcohol.

"In Northern Spain, this drink is our tradition," he said happily. "It is cider but it needs more oxygen to make it perfect" he continued in his accented English. He looked super happy to be doing this.

He uncorked the bottle and held it high over his head. At the same time, he positioned a glass in his other hand as low as he could reach, effectively separating the bottle and glass by four feet or so. He began to pour.

"You must be able to do this without looking," he said confidently, looking straight at us. We, the audience, were in rapt attention.

He did not spill a single drop. He poured a few more glasses and passed them out to us. It was very sour and was much stronger than the English cider we were used to. It was superb. We ate more meat and drank more glasses of the Spanish cider.

"You may now try to pour yourself," the guide said. "You have already paid for the bottles, so have fun."

Not needing more encouragement than that, the girl studying in Barcelona gave it a try. She was much less graceful, and cider spilled to the floor.

She sat down laughing as I jumped up to try. It was very hard to do and I got as much cider on the floor as I got in my glass. Yet, there I was holding a bottle of cider over my head, pouring it into a glass held below my waist in a dimly lit bar in Madrid while my friends, new and old, watched from a couch.

They cheered me on. The night was fast becoming one of my favorite memories from the entire trip.

The tour guide got up to leave, telling us we should finish the cider and meats and that the tour was over. We had paid only fourteen euros per person and had gotten more than our money's worth. Stuffed full of great food, we were more than a little drunk.

"Hey so do you guys want to get some churros with us?" the girl studying in Prague asked.

"Yeah of course," Chloe enthusiastically responded. Samie and I nodded while Praveen agreed to come as well. Kat, the Austrian, joined us too. Her bogan friends had inexplicably ditched her on the way to this last bar.

"They don't like the big city I guess," she said in her Austrian accent. Melissa had signed up for a pub-crawl and so couldn't come, but we made plans to meet up tomorrow to visit a flea market. She gave her number to Chloe and went off into the warm Spanish night. The remaining six of us headed to a churro place in the heart of Madrid.

Along the way, we passed a big plaque in the ground, which marked the geographical center of Spain. Excitedly we all put our feet on it and took some pictures. The night was entertaining and I begrudgingly began to like Madrid a little bit more.

We arrived at the churro place, which was apparently famous in the world of churros enthusiasts. It was packed full, so we descended some white marble stairs and nabbed a booth in the basement.

I sat with my back to the wall. Next to me sat Kat, and the group ordered churros and melted chocolate. As we ate them, I listened happily to Kat tell me about all things Austrian and Australian.

"I saw a very funny shirt once, 'No kangaroos in Austria' as we say, it is very funny."

"Oh, the fast food in 'Straya is so good and cheap, I gained three kilos there"

'The town was full of bogans; there was only one street which is where I lived".

She spoke with low deep voice typical of German-speakers. I got to talk to her in German, which was great. She was hilarious and a pleasure to hang out with.

Praveen joined us in speaking German. He said he doesn't get to speak it much, as in Germany the Germans speak English to him, assuming he can't speak their language.

The American students gave us nifty tips about places to go in Barcelona and Prague. We hastily wrote down their advice on napkins. After finishing our delicious churros and chatting for what seemed like hours it had grown late and was time to head home.

We hugged goodbye outside the door. The night had been very enjoyable. Travelling is strange because you spend fantastic nights like this with people you bond with, but know you will never see again. You promise to keep in touch, but everybody knows that nobody actually will. Saying so, and trading Facebook invites is just one of those things you do, a common courtesy among travelers. The three of us meshed well with these people and the goodbye was heartfelt. I wished them the best of luck, and we all went our separate ways.

Getting back to Lavapiés was surprisingly not a problem. This time the crowd in the little plaza seemed normal, with people eating at tables and drinking sangria.

There was no sight of screaming drug dealers or scammers. This, I suspected, was probably Lavapiés in its best light, a troubled neighborhood that occasionally glows with light and happiness. I was familiar with these kinds of communities from America, having grown up in one. The day had been rough but the walking tour and tapas night had lifted my spirits.

Inside our room, we climbed into our bunks and turned a dehumidifier on. The room was almost entirely underground except for one tiny window near the ceiling, a window that looked out onto the street. The room would grow sticky in the humidity, but the dehumidifier would make the room comfortable, if a little warm.

In my bed, I turned on my laptop. I dimmed the lighting on it, plugged in headphones and played some Otis Redding. I fell asleep happy and content, the bad memories forgotten. *I wouldn't trade this for the world,* I thought happily to myself, my bed in Ohio far from my thoughts.

Madrid, Day Ten: 6th of April

I opened my eyes to scan our dungeon-like room. It was uncomfortably warm and dry, thanks to the dehumidifier. I went down the hall to the kitchen for breakfast. I met our other roommates there, a young Japanese couple with spikey hair and leather jackets, and a bearded guy from Eastern Europe.

I sat with them because there it was the only seat left. Of the two four-tops, the other table was full. I set down my cup of coffee I had grabbed from the coffee pot on the counter next to the sink and looked around for the promised breakfast. My new friends pointed to the middle of the table where I saw that 'breakfast' consists of a single piece of white bread and some packets of jam.

I imagine that the maximum occupancy of our hostel must have been only about twelve people. I was pretty sure it had three rooms with four bunks each. The hostel was a good size but had only two bathrooms for all of us. The bathrooms were located right next to the tables, so I waited patiently for my turn while eating 'breakfast.'

I finally got my chance after twenty minutes or so when a man with a heavy-metal chin beard exited one of the bathrooms. I brushed my teeth, and got ready for a shower.

I opened the curtain to find the showerhead on the floor of the shower. When I tried to put it back up, I saw it was broken and that I had to hold the showerhead the whole time. *No big deal* I thought, as I washed myself. The water wasn't very hot, but at least wasn't freezing cold.

As I washed myself with the lukewarm water, the bathroom lights suddenly went out. They must have been motion activated. I waved my arms wildly over the sides of the shower door to no avail.

The sensor must have been located right by the door. The rest of my shower was in the pitch black because there were no windows. *Ah, home sweet home* I thought. At least we were paying less per night than the cost of a Subway sandwich. I used this justification often here.

The night prior we had made plans to meet with Melissa at the Tirso de Molina metro stop and go to the giant local flea market. It was still early in the morning as we went to the metro stop to wait for her. We had no way of contacting her once she left her room and was no longer on Facebook.

We hung out on the concrete wall, dangling our legs over the metro stairs. The air had a chill to it, before the sun started to beat down and would spike the temperatures into the high nineties.

The sky was bright baby blue, and the few trees swayed gently in the breeze. The city was waking up around us. A few children ran around laughing, and couples were starting to stroll around. People were setting up booths and tents to sell handicrafts and anarchist literature.

We had started our journey in Madrid at this stop just two days prior, but it felt like a lifetime ago. We were talking about the quirkiness of travel when Melissa ascended from the bowels of the metro. We greeted each other and walked up the street to the flea market, called El Rastro.

Melissa was in a chatty mood. Personally, I had always found Clevelanders to be more similar to East Coast types rather than other Midwesterners. I felt very comfortable with Melissa. The four of us wandered to the flea market

El Rastro was insanely big. It consisted of people setting up stands and booths and selling anything from underwear to adapters, to one-eyed broken dolls. The flea market stretched for blocks and blocks. It billed itself as the largest open-air flea market in the world, and it can't be far off. It was a spectacular sight.

We wandered street after street of people selling stuff. The crowd was thick and lively as we browsed the various stalls. People weren't as pushy as I would have expected, perhaps because the volume of buyers was so high. If I lived in Madrid, I would undoubtedly be shopping at this market frequently. I passed a big old globe the size of a big exercise ball. This was precisely the kind of thing I'd love to own if I wasn't backpacking the next three weeks.

While I was enjoying myself, I was careful to keep my hand my wallet the whole time. Pickpockets are known to strike commonly here.

Pickpocketing is a common crime in Europe, but a little precaution goes a long way. Keep your hand in your pocket and don't keep your wallet in your back pocket. For women, always keep your purse on your shoulder and an arm over the zipper. Both make a thief want to target somebody else who is more careless, and in Europe, there is always somebody more careless. It's not about being adequately protected, just being a little more protected than the guy next to you.

We finished up the flea market near El Museo Nacional del Prado, or El Prado for short. We hadn't been to a museum in a while, so we were excited to visit this one, the national art museum of Spain.

My stomach growled as we walked on the broad road to the museum. In Madrid, one can be walking along a narrow stone street and be suddenly dumped out on a broad eight-lane road unexpectedly.

Having had only one piece of bread for breakfast, Chloe, Samie and I were starving. As we turned onto Paseo del Prado, we spotted a little McCafé built into a corner building. The three of us unanimously decided to eat there before the museum. These small McCafé's were pretty ubiquitous in European cities. They were usually pleasant and clean, and a solid notch better than its American counterparts.

After the long line, long wait and high prices (*six euro for a combo??*) we grabbed our food trays and sat down.

"Are you sure you don't want any?" Chloe asked Melissa thoughtfully, offering her some of the fries.

"No, I'm good," Melissa responded, giving our food the side eye. I sensed that Melissa was judging us hardcore for eating McDonald's. I could tell because I did the same thing at home. I NEVER ate McDonald's but hey it was relatively cheap, I knew what I was getting, I was hungry, and I didn't need to goddamn explain myself.

Bellies full of Spanish McDonalds, we finished the rest of the walk to the Prado. The museum was free for students, which was a happy surprise. I don't know how I'd have traveled across Europe without a student ID. We blew a few hours there hanging out with Melissa.

The museum, in addition to typical paintings, had a large exhibit on Goya's Black Paintings. These were dark and ominous paintings. The brutal *Saturno Devorando A Un Hijo*, Saturn Devouring his Son, totally captivated me. It was a dark painting of the Greek demigod bloodily ripping apart his son with his teeth. Chloe gleefully pointed it out to us, as it is one of her favorite pieces of art.

Melissa had to leave before too long, and we had an awkward, if heartfelt, goodbye. We hugged, and I think all of us were a little sad to part. Later she messaged us each on Facebook saying that we were really cool and she had a good time with us. She implored us to let her know if we ever made it to Boston.

"I know travel buddies aren't real friends," she told us before she left the museum. "But I think we would make really good actual friends."

The Travel Friend is a curious thing. It's often people you meet that speak your language and share a love of travel. Although you might have nothing else in common, you find yourself doing crazy awesome things with these strangers and a remarkably intense bond can form. You might hate these same people in your day-to-day life at home, but when you find yourself partying in Berlin or Budapest with them, then go out for dinner at three in the morning, well, they don't seem so bad then.

It is always understood that these are friendships of convenience and are temporary, i.e., the people you meet on your walking tour and join for coffee. The next day they might be heading to Seville while you are boating to Rome. You compare itineraries and trade tips: "I'm going to Barcelona next," "oh I was just there! "Oh man, we missed Avignon this time, but maybe next."

Now travelers can get extremely pretentious, so I always tried to feel people out before I told them where I had been and where I was going next. A good traveler will always build you up ("that's so cool, you'll have an awesome time there") and never shit on you for doing touristy things.

I found that the people most likely to look down upon 'touristy' things are people who are seeking a more 'authentic' experience, which ironically only seems to mean getting drunk. Now I have been to a few bars and I know that every local bar is filled with the same drunk a-holes from Prague to London, to Pittsburgh. I'm not so sure what's so 'authentic' about this, but hey whatever floats your boat I guess.

After Melissa left, we went to the Museum café to buy some cappuccino. The food was costly, but the coffee was affordable and delicious. We poked our heads in one more wing, and I was shocked to see *El 3 de mayo en Madrid*, *The Third of May* right in front of my eyes. It is a beautiful and moving painting by Goya that commentated the shooting of Spanish guerillas by the French under Napoleon. Goya himself had lived through the rebellion and suppression and was deeply affected by it.

I was surprised at how big the painting was, as it was the size of a wall. I distinctly remember looking at pictures of this painting in my seventh-grade history textbook. Like most paintings, it is so much more moving and glorious in real life.

We went back to our hostel to do some laundry. We were walking down one of the more prominent streets when a trolley passed us by. It looked like a little bus except it was powered by ten or twelve people facing each other, peddling furiously, drinking beer and shouting "I don't care...I love it!" There was no music playing along.

As we entered the hostel around three in the afternoon, I immediately saw there were two bearded men were sitting on the couches, facing each other, in the living room area near our room.

They didn't say anything to either each other or me. The men looked shady and given the neighborhood, I was sure they were up to something. As we popped in and out the rest of the night, they were there for at least five hours, never talking or making any sound or acknowledging anybody else. Eventually,

I came back to the room, and they had left without a trace. It was another little mystery and charm of Lavapiés.

Laundry, not bearded mystery men, however, was our primary concern. We had been washing our clothes in sinks by hand and hanging them out to dry. It was a hassle because none of us had many clothes. If I was air-drying one pair of socks, I was wearing the other pair. In Bruges and Paris, we had private rooms and big windows where we could wash our clothes and leave them to dry.

In Madrid, our room was windowless and humid so drying our clothes would have been impossible. As such, we needed to find a laundromat. Finding one proved to be somewhat challenging, as we couldn't locate the first few we tried to. We walked to each address only to see it converted into a market or apartment complex. Given we had the same issue our first night in Spain, perhaps the Spanish just use an address system I can't comprehend.

After a couple of false starts, we finally found one. We didn't trust the locals enough to leave our clothes and come back later, so we just stayed. We had ended up having an enjoyable time in the laundromat, the three of us, laughing and fooling around. At one point, Chloe was animatedly telling some crazy story, standing on a chair and waving her arms wildly. Sam, sitting down, had a wide grin on her round face and was laughing along enthusiastically. *Man, I love both of these guys so much*, I thought to myself, smiling along. Sometimes you have perfect moments in front of the Eiffel Tower at night, and sometimes you have them in laundromats in the heart of Madrid.

As we walked back a few hours later, with our clean clothes in our packs, we saw kids playing in the park next to our hostel. It was a makeshift, graffiti-covered jungle gym, and I'm pretty sure I saw prostitutes hanging out there after dark. The children were laughing and having a blast, while the parents sat nearby and chatted with each other. Other kids ran by kicking a soccer ball.

That evening I would read an online review about Lavapiés that read 'this neighborhood has life if you're tolerant and patient. You can find the best kind of life in a place like Lavapiés.' As the sun went down that late Sunday afternoon, I saw that 'best kind of life.'

That evening we left the hostel, past the silent, bearded men, to look for a grocery store. We had as much trouble finding one as we did finding a laundromat. But of course, we did locate one and had dinner back in our little kitchen.

We ate tasty *jambon* sandwiches. The ham was very thinly sliced, and each bite was full of flavor. It only cost us five euros each. We also replenished our Nutella stock, because we ate so much of it. Almost every single lunch was a Nutella sandwich and some fruit.

Later I sat on the couches that the mysterious men had finally vacated. I flipped through a few books that were lying around and wrote in my journal by the light of a single lamp. I looked around the quiet and calm apartment and felt quite content. *Maybe, it wasn't so bad here after all*, I thought.

Toledo, Day Eleven: 7th of April

I was excited to get out of bed. Today we were going to Toledo. We wanted a change of scenary after so much time in Madrid. After a cold, dark shower and our morning toast, we packed our daypacks and walked to the main train station downtown.

At the station, we headed over to the Eurail Office to see how to use our passes on the high-speed rail to Toledo. When we got to the service counter Samie asked if they speak English. The young man behind the counter shook his head. *'Hablo Ingles'* was often met with this response.

As Samie and Chloe switched into Spanish, I was left wondering what they were talking about. There was a lot of questioning sounds on their part, and a lot of head shaking by the young man. A few minutes later the girls informed me that our Eurail passes were generally not accepted in Spain, except for a handful of commuter routes. We were going to have to buy the tickets to Toledo.

Toledo, incidentally pronounced Toe-LED-o, not like the Ohioan To-LEED-o, was not far from Madrid. We bought our tickets at a terminal, and then boarded the next train out of town. We had been delayed a little bit at the counter, and the ride was about an hour. It cost about fifteen euros each way, and the ride was very comfortable.

Arriving half past eleven, the weather was beautiful as we got off the train. The station itself was stunning. It was about a hundred years old and rivaled the splendor of cathedrals. The station was built at a time when rails were a luxurious way to travel. The tiled ceilings were high, with huge glass windows letting the sun reflect onto metal chandeliers. The floor was beautifully tiled. The exterior was a great example of Moorish Revival and looked like a grandly decorated Spanish mosque. I couldn't help but be excited to notice that there were far fewer people than in Madrid.

The city was a short distance away, perched on a big hill. We gasped as we turned the corner and saw the medieval walled city rising out over the river ahead of us. The city was remarkably persevered. Tan brick buildings rose over the high stone walls. Each building looked like it had been there for a thousand years. Stone bridges spanned the river at three or four points.

At the highest point of the city a massive stone fortress, the Alcázar de Toledo dominated the skyline. It was a big rectangular building with four great towers rising out of each corner. Toledo probably looked much the same two hundred years ago, or even five hundred years ago, as it did now. The city was in a naturally defendable location, and I could easily see why the Romans, Vandals, Arabs, and Spanish had fought over this spot.

We crossed one of the bridges, Puente de Alcántara. I later learned the stone bridge had built by the Romans and was still standing. At the time I just knew how neat it felt to walk across such an obviously old bridge. It was only open to foot traffic, and we were the only people on it, giving it the feeling of traveling in time.

Just across the bridge, we found stairs cut into the steep walls. We climbed them to enter the city. The stairs were much more numerous than they initially appeared and we ascended them under the burning sun with no hints of shade. We were alone as we climbed the ancient walls.

The view from the top was terrific. I looked out over the brown hilly countryside to see green shrubs and a few beautiful buildings in the distance. It was surreal to stand on these medieval walls and see that view.

From the walls, we entered the heart of the city. The buildings were all old, and the streets were cobblestone. We saw almost no cars and the roads were medieval and narrow. We soaked up the hot sun. Chilly Amsterdam and damp England felt a million miles away as I took off my flannel, sweat dripping from my forehead.

We walked through the winding streets with no real plan. Before too long we ended up in front of a magnificent gothic cathedral. Seeing people step in, we also entered. The doormen were wearing suits, and I felt terribly underdressed in sweaty t-shirt. Sam and Chloe asked if we are allowed to go in, and the man nodded. He told us we have about five minutes before the Mass started.

The inside of the stone cathedral was calm and cool, a welcome break from the hot sun. The interior of the cathedral was awe-inspiring. There were towering stained glass windows, beautiful arches, a marble sanctuary the size of a hotel room and beautifully carved Catholic statues. We didn't have much time to admire before the ushers gently shooed us tourists back out to the hot sun.

From there we unhurriedly wandered around looking for lunch. We continually stumbled from narrow stone streets to small open plazas that offered impressive views of the desert landscape around us. The city sat on a series of hills, so these little walled plazas usually either offered views of the countryside or of the town, depending on the angle.

The streets were decidedly uncrowded as we wandered joyfully. It was not unusual for us to be the only people on the street. Even though the sun was still high above us, the stone buildings casted cool shade over most of the roads. Although there was still a lot of ambient noise, like the sounds of voices carrying over buildings or the low hum of cars, Toledo was startlingly silent compared to Paris or Madrid.

We came across a little shop that sold sandwiches. We ordered in Spanish, even me. The man spoke with dramatic flair. His shop was compact, but he proudly showed it off to us. We were his only customers, so the man was quite amiable, letting us sample different dried meats to pick our favorites for the sandwiches.

I pointed at the cured chorizo, and he beamed at me, happy I enjoyed his work. He added some oregano and olive oil "at no extra cost" because he liked our company. We paid him and walked out, happy after our interaction.

We ate the delicious, unelaborate and cheap *boccadios* outside, perched on another stone wall, overlooking the starkly beautiful semi-desert landscape. The sandwich was only bread, chorizo, olive oil, cheese, and oregano but couldn't have been better, especially because we had watched the man proudly make them. We washed them down with Orange Fanta.

Toledo was a magical city. It was wonderfully persevered, like Bruges, but Toledo was a grander and more important city in its heyday than Bruges. As such the scale of everything was bigger. Each corner we turned onto sat in front of some spectacular historic site. Each street name was wonderfully named after a historic, if usually blood-soaked, person or event.

On the Calle de Los Reyes Católicos, Street of the Catholic Monarchs, we marched past the Monastery of San Juan de Los Reyes. High above the street, we saw metal chains hanging from the walls. The map I had somehow acquired told me these chains were hung up in 1494 during the final push of the Reconquista. Christian prisoners had once been shackled with them, and they were hung up to remind people of their liberation.

Toledo was home to many museums, and there was no way we had time or money to see them all. One of the museums we ended up going into was the home of the famous painter El Greco. By complete coincidence, the museum was free because it was the anniversary of his birthday.

The museum was a beautiful reconstruction of his home, but I did not spend much time in it. I breezed through it and then sat in the garden. Directly influenced by the Islamic Moorish gardens, this area was peaceful and relaxing. The trees provided gentle shade as I admired the elaborately trimmed hedges and bountiful flowers. A reflecting pool sat in the center of the garden. There were comfortable lounge chairs, and I happily dozed off in one. The luxury that wealthy people in that time enjoyed must have been truly unimaginable. The girls woke me up when they were done with the museum.

Another highlight was the Mosque of Cristo de la Luz. Built at the end of the 10th century, the mosque was in nearly the same shape as it was built. The three of us fit in comfortably. Although cozy by modern standards I read that it was considered to be quite roomy in those times. Toledo had been the capital of Al-Andalus, Islamic Spain, for a time. The arches recalled the beautiful vaulted arches of Cordoba.

When the Christians captured the city, they converted the mosque into a chapel, then used it for the next thousand years. By the time we got there, specialists were in the process of restoring the mosque to how it was originally built. It was interesting to see a building that looked so obviously like a mosque but had fading medieval portraits of Jesus and Mary on the walls. It made me think, how on a much larger scale, the Hagia Sophia in Constantinople been converted into a mosque under the Ottoman Turks. In America there are not too many examples of a new religion just claiming the building of an old one and grafting their stuff on top.

On a different note, I was again stunned, as usual, at how cool the inside of the building was. It's hard to picture the world before our technological age, but the people gathering for afternoon prayers a thousand years ago were just as cool as we are in air-conditioned buildings.

Later, we sat in a park with afternoon sun high overhead, the trees providing cool shade from the dry heat. We sat just looking at the countryside for a long time. I had not expected Spain to look so much like New Mexico or Baja California. I pictured it as more temperate, but everything in Spain looked hot and dry. I don't know if there is a connection there, but it seemed to me that the Spaniards colonized a lot of warm places.

We continued to wander up and down the staircases cut into the hills of the city, down random alleys and across cobblestone streets. We went into a shop run by a kindly old man who made his own jewelry. When he held up his work to hang on the necks of the girls, it didn't seem like a scam as it would in Madrid. Instead, it just looked like a man who took pride in his work and wanted to show it off.

Near this shop, Sam found a leather goods store. Leather, along with swords, was a speciality of Toledo. She had been looking for a leather backpack since January and was finally able to buy a beautiful homemade bag for a reasonable price. All the people we talked with were warm and friendly, with none of the hustling we'd seen in the bigger cities.

Also placed around the city were green markers, at about eye level, which commemorated the fictional path that Don Quixote had taken through the city. Don Quixote was a huge deal in Toledo, and I saw numerous memorials to this hero of Spanish literature. Chloe and Sam were able to appreciate it a lot more than I, both of them having read the book.

The day was growing longer as Samie suddenly spotted an interestingly named street.

"Look at that!" she said pointing to where the street name was posted in tiles on the side of a building. It read Calle de Toledo de Ohio, the Street of Toledo of Ohio. We gushed in excitement over this small reminder of home.

We slowly made our way back to the main square. It was getting late in the day and we had a narrow timeframe to catch our train back to Madrid. The main square was much busier now with school buses dropping kids off, adults greeting each other and the tourists getting ready to go home. We hung out there for a little bit, enjoying the amiable scene.

Next, we made our way to the bridge out of town. Just outside the main bulk of the city, located halfway down a sloping hill, we came across a candy shop. Naturally, we had to step in.

The owner greeted us in Spanish. We said hello and started to look over his barrels of candy.

"Where are you from?" he asked, switching to English after hearing our accents.

"America," we told him.

"Yes, but where in America?" he asked politely.

"From Ohio," we chorused.

"Ohio? Have you seen the street here named for Ohio?"

We laughed and told him we had just come from it. It turned out the man had travelled very extensively in his youth and had been to Ohio himself. He had good things to say about our beautiful state, which is always a pleasure to hear.

With some hard candies in hand, we said goodbye and left. On our way down the hill, we came across a quiet Moorish gate made of stone. The gate, tucked away seemingly randomly, was cut in that flowing bulbous pattern typical of medieval Islamic architecture. We posed for a few pictures. The gate, which was about thirty feet tall, connected two alleyways. There was absolutely nobody else down there, so we goofed around in this quiet old entryway for a while by ourselves.

The gate was adjacent to a hill, as most of Toledo was, so it was just a few jumps to get to the top of that gate. I had to give it a go. Up top the walls were only the width of one of my feet. I walked across the gate putting one foot in front of the other. I was balancing on a medieval Moorish stone wall in a beautiful old city in sunny Spain. It was a great feeling, although Samie did not appreciate my balancing act.

Reaching the train station that late afternoon, tired and sunburned, I was sad to leave the city. I had enjoyed Toledo. The town was romantic and charming, filled with picturesque alleys and buildings. The desert landscape was visually pleasing and the people were warm and inviting. Toledo was the Spain I had heard so much about, and it stood in contrast to dirty sprawling Madrid. Despite what Juan from Chile had said, I could have easily spent a week walking around Toledo, and I doubt I would have gotten bored.

I stole one more look back at Toledo before we got to the train station. I saw the city perched on its many hills, protected by its river and high stone walls, with gothic cathedral spires and palace minarets reaching toward the setting sun. One day I hope to make it back there.

The rest of the night was uneventful. In our dingy dining room, we ate a dinner we had scrapped together from leftovers. As the girls got ready for bed, I stayed behind to work on my school papers for a few hours, and to catch up in my travel journal. As I typed away on my tiny laptop, it occurred to me that the hostel was starting to feel almost like home.

Madrid, Day Twelve: 8th of April

After our daily breakfast of bread and jam, we took the metro to the central train station. We needed to book our train tickets to Barcelona. Not having the Eurail pass be accepted in Spain was seriously biting into my carefully planned budget.

Getting to the train station, we went up to the counter. They told us to take a number. We naively thought this would be a quick and fast transaction. Instead, we ran headlong into the infamous Spanish bureaucracy, as we watched the line to move extremely slowly.

We waited an hour and a half before at last hearing our number called. We were able to purchase our tickets, but left the station in a crabby mood. We had planned to sightsee more, but the diversion had taken much longer than we had expected. No wonder the Spanish Empire had told fallen apart a few centuries ago. Spain was one of the more inefficient countries I had been to. I was very grateful Sam and Chloe spoke Spanish, otherwise, I don't know what I would have done.

Next, we needed to book our journey from Barcelona to Italy. By doing it right now, we would be able to enjoy Barcelona without worrying about our next step. We hopped on the metro to ride back home.

When we first arrived from France, I had been pleasantly surprised by the size of the metro cars in Madrid. They were huge. They were also very clean and modern, unlike the grimy Parisian cars.

How pleasant, I had thought to myself, *they made these cars so big and comfortable.* As I stepped into the car, an old man gently pulled me further in, tugging on my shoulder. *How odd,* I thought.

At the next stop, a huge crowd of people entered the car. There was no room to breathe. People were packed in like sardines. My body smashed into those around me. I had not realized Madrid would be like this. I clearly realized in this moment why the cars were so large. It was physically challenging to exit the car at our desired stop.

We got out at the Puerto Del Sol. It was the Times Square of Madrid. As we ascended the stairs to the plaza, we passed a full band set up in the corner of a metro tunnel playing 'Keep on Rockin' in the Free World.' I tossed them a euro coin for the unexpected awesomeness.

Although we had passed through Puerto Del Sol previously, we hadn't spent any time there. During our tapas tour, it had been so crowded I had had to shove my way through the crowd just to move a few feet forward.

This time, around noon instead of midnight, it was much less crowded. In Madrid, this meant it was still packed to the gills, naturally, but just not as much. We checked out the main attraction, a seven-story department store called Corte Ingles.

It was nothing but a big department store. I wasn't impressed and found it as dull as any other department store. We wandered through the floors slowly, checking out the different things, but primarily enjoying the air conditioning. At the very top level, there were books and Legos, so the store wasn't a total bust.

Making our way out of the store, we found an all-you-can-eat buffet. It cost eight euros. We grabbed trays and piled them high with food. The food was greasy and low quality. Each bite hurt my stomach. However, I was determined to get my eight euros worth and kept returning for more food.

It had been a weird day. Our nasty lunch over with, Chloe split off from Samie and me. She was going to the central park in Madrid where there were trees, ponds and a statue of Lucifer. It sounded pretty cool, but Samie and I needed to figure out how we were to get from Barcelona to Florence in just a few days.

Back in our underground hostel room, Samie and I looked over our options. The train from Barcelona to Florence was an absurd twenty-five hours and included long layovers in the middle of the night in Marseilles. To avoid these middle of the night drop-offs, we would be forced to buy sleeper car tickets, the cost of which was nearly twice as much as a hostel bed. Even with the sleeper car, the journey would still have been over twenty-four hours. The train option did not look appealing.

We then looked into taking a boat over, which would have been fuckin' awesome. Sadly, for me, I was not able to garner enough support from Samie for this option. The cost was just too high and the times didn't line up as nicely as we have liked them to be. The Eurail pass gave us a small discount on the boat, but not enough to justify the price.

After some discussion and a much needed nap, Samie and I finally figured out the most efficient route was to fly from Barcelona to Bologna, then ride the train the rest of the way to Florence. Our flight was due to leave super early at five in the morning, so I figured we would deal with sleeping arrangements for that night later.

Chloe came back to the hostel around seven. She had seen a bunch of cool stuff in the park, and her pictures were fascinating.

"Oh, and I perfected my resting bitch face to stop the people from talking to me," she told us proudly as she set her face into a fierce scowl. It was always necessary to scowl because of the aggressive panhandlers. According to our tour guide the other day, Spain had a very high unemployment rate, and a lot of these guys were desperately trying to survive. The poverty was why these guys would get in our faces so aggressively.

It being our last night in Madrid, we wanted to go out for dinner. We might be on a budget, but it was still vacation. We had no destination in mind, so we walked around until we saw a middle-aged man wearing a sandwich board. The pictures on his board had some tasty looking food on it. With the disappointing lunch, we were ready for something better.

"*Tiene calamares?*" Sam asked, looking to see if they had calamari.

"*Claro!*" The man shouted and happily led us to the restaurant he represented.

We followed him down a few twisting alleys before we reached the restaurant. It was a compact sit down place stuck in a quiet little corner away from the constant hustle and bustle. We would not have found the restaurant without a guy in sandwich board leading us there. We took a table right outside and sat down, the setting sun casting a warm golden glow over us.

For drinks, we ordered a big pitcher of red sangria. I came to love the simple drink. It's tangy and sweet flavor nicely complemented the heat and the spiced food. Samie ordered her calamari while Chloe and I tried some beef fillet dishes.

A bum came up and asked us for money as we ate. We waved him away dismissively, not even breaking our conversation. The bum then moved on to the next table, where four businessmen sat. One of them made the mistake of handing the man a few euros.

For the next twenty minutes, the bum incessantly badgered those poor guys. He waved his arms wildly and would squat down next to each one individually. They tried to call the waiter over, but the waiter just shrugged, clearly putting the blame on the men for encouraging the bum.

The meal was great. *Sipping sangria in Spain at sunset ain't too bad* I decided, my belly satisfied. We paid the waiter and wandered around for a while, eventually drifting back to that sleek glass and steel tourist trap, the San Miguel market. Our tour guide detested this market where we had eaten paella a few days ago.

"No true Spaniard would go in there," she had hissed, jabbing her finger in its direction. The place was so slick and new, like an upscale grocery store that puts farmers markets out of business.

But, you can't live like a local all the time. Through the glass walls, we saw it was full of people eating and drinking and having a good time. It looked pretty fun, so we went in.

It was a great experience. People were crowded in front of the food stalls, buying little plates of rice or desserts. We drank a few more glasses of sangria and wandered around, taking in all the artisanal foods. The marketplace was quite the scene and best experienced a bit boozy. With glasses of sangria in hand, we hopped from stall to stall, looking at the big fresh fish on ice and buying little deserts.

Hey, sometimes you just want to visit the inauthentic tourist traps where you can drink in public and eat flavored rice. Not everything needs to be authentic all the time.

We drank and ate to our heart's content. Then, we made our way back again to the Plaza Mayor, a place where we had spent so much time already. We sat until half past ten on the benches enjoying the unusually calm and pleasant plaza.

We had come full circle from our first morning in the same plaza when we were tired, exhausted and fighting with each other. That felt like years ago as we sat and enjoyed each other's company.

Lavapiés and Madrid had both grown on me in unexpected ways. They reminded me a lot of places where I had grown up. They were hard places, but places with soul. They were places that challenge its inhabitants every day, places that not everybody can live in. I'm glad I had the experience, although I wouldn't stay there again. A little adversity can go a long way. I felt that I had earned my right to visit Lavapiés and walked away the better for it.

Later, as I showered in ice-cold water and the lights went off again, I knew I was ready to leave Madrid.

Barcelona, Day Thirteen: 9th of April

I met the girls for breakfast in the dining room early in the morning. Walking in, I started a fresh pot of coffee, nodded hello to the guy with the heavy-metal chin beard, and sat down. It was our last breakfast at these cramped plastic tables. As a parting memory, the bread tasted strongly of cleaning fluids.

We packed our things quickly and efficiently, strapped our backpacks on and hit the street. The air was crisp, the sun was weak, and the neighborhood had yet to awaken. I turned around to take a picture of Sleep Madrid. I got a good photo of the graffiti-stained door with bars on the windows. In later years I'll periodically resend this picture to Chloe and Sam. 'Remember this??' I'll write, and, boy do they.

Soon, we were stowing our bags over our heads and relaxing on the luxurious and expensive Spanish high-speed train. I popped in some headphones and wrote in my journal as the desert landscape rolled past.

I think about how crazy my teenage years were, and how they were followed by such seriousness. Trying to atone for my youthful mistakes I became a studious young man, religious, focused, and a total killjoy. I took everything so seriously. I was shopping for a wedding ring when I was twenty-one, and less than a year after that it all came crashing down. Three of my friends died.

My friend Jessica died alone in her car, overdosing in the wee hours of dawn, the morning she was supposed to enter rehab. I had been her friend for two years, had laughed and cried with her many times. Her adopted son was only ten.

Heroin then took Doug shortly after. He had always struggled to stay clean, and this slip would be his last. Only a week prior had we been smoking cigarettes in the park, bullshitting for a while.

They say tragedy comes in threes. A few weeks later Donny got drunk, fired a gun in a bar and then led the cops on a high-speed chase. It ended in a fiery wreck when he smashed his car into a wall.

I'll never forget my last conversation with Donny. It was at a friend's wedding. It was an outdoors wedding and it had rained all day. Donny and I stood there in the pouring rain, getting our suits soaking wet, our shoes sinking into the soft muddy grass.

"I feel good," he said. "I always want to be there for my little niece. I want to be a good uncle for her".

He died one week later.

I was sick of living in suburban Cleveland, doing nothing except watching my friends die in the hurricane of an opiate epidemic and under waves of senseless violence.

After the deaths, other shocks followed. My would-be fiancé left me. People who I thought I knew turned out to be criminals of the worst kind. I left religion, bitter and disillusioned. I would walk around the quiet suburban streets at night, and wonder if this was all there was to life.

Then, like new flowers sprouting after a harsh winter, I found balance. I quit smoking cigarettes and made new friends. I didn't think I could date again, but I soon was. I loosened up and now here I am backpacking through Europe.

I can't believe my reality right now as the Spanish landscape slides by, barren and beautiful, the dry plains broken here and there by dry shrubs and low hills. I feel like I am being reborn out here.

On the road like this, we rarely make plans. We just relax and think on our feet. Travelling has made me realize that everything is going to be ok. Travelling has given me confidence that I can do anything if I try, and if it doesn't work out the way I planned, well, then something even better is coming.

I felt a great release as I processed my emotions by writing them down. I smiled to myself as I listened to Samie's iPod. She slept peacefully as I wrote.

We arrived in Barcelona and got on the metro. In Madrid, I only ever heard Spanish, but now I listened to a symphony of different tongues. A group of foppy-haired and tanned German youth stood in front of us. I was happy that I could eavesdrop and understand their banal conversation about soccer.

We got off at our stop and climbed the stairs out of the metro. I looked up as the concrete ceiling gave way to bright blue skies. There were palm trees on either side of the street, and I felt a fresh breeze. I inhaled deeply, savoring the salty smell of the nearby sea.

The journey to the hostel would prove to be much easier than our last one. The hostel was close to the metro stop. We found the right street quickly, walking between tall tan colored buildings. The street was narrow and endless clotheslines hung with laundry flapped in the wind above our ends. In three different directions we could see sand and blue water beyond it. The hostel was located in the middle of a little urban peninsula. The peninsula was small, only a few blocks across.

Despite the finding right street, we struggled to find the entrance of the hostel. We scanned the buildings for the name of the hostel, Barceloneta Beach Club, but saw only nondescript apartment blocks. After fifteen minutes of crossing the same streets over and over again, we were getting frustrated. We were about to backtrack once more when all of a sudden, an older man came walking out of a building and started loudly spouting off Italian

We stared at him blankly, and then he slapped his forehead lightly.

"I am so sorry" he said kindly. "I was just speaking with an Italian man. Are you looking for the hostel?"

I nodded. "Barceloneta Beach Club?"

"Yes! Follow me!"

The man turned and gestured us to follow him. We trailed him as he walked into an unmarked door. There was a tiny sign above the entryway that displayed the name of the hostel. I got the sense that we are not the first people unable locate the hostel.

The man said he was the owner and led us to the reception desk. He explained the rules as we checked in.

"You come home a little drunk, this is ok, but always be considerate of other guests. Party at disco and beach, enjoy yourself, but do not party in hostel please."

The hostel sounded like our kind of place. We climbed a flight of stairs to our room. It was six beds, but two would be empty.

"You will be staying with a South African man who is working in Barcelona," the owner told us as he headed back down to reception. I pictured a dark-skinned man selling plastic Eiffel Tours from a ring.

As we walked around the hostel, we were surprised to learn it included a large fully equipped kitchen, and that all the rooms had huge windows with beautiful views of the streets and beaches. The bathroom was huge, modern and clean. Compared to Madrid it was a veritable palace.

I felt almost out of place, having got used to the broken bathrooms, dirty kitchen, shady characters, and sticky humid underground rooms. I was finding myself scowling at strangers and found it almost too easy to turn bums and beggars away. In Barcelona, they would leave me along I would say no and walk away, whereas in Madrid they took 'no' as an invitation to stand in your face and ask louder. The bums in Barcelona have nothing on the bums of Madrid.

We claimed bunks and putt our backpacks in the lockers, changed into swimsuits and hit the beach. It was only a minute's walk away.

As we laid out our towels, the wind coming off the Mediterranean was downright cold. The chilly air didn't stop us from lying out in the sun. It didn't stop a couple of nude sunbathers around us either, although most people keep their bathing suits on.

The sand was soft and cool beneath me, and the sea was a beautiful dark blue. The sky was clear. Sitting on the beach, looking over the Mediterranean, I felt the tension in my shoulders relax. I'd never travelled this long in my life and I couldn't believe how it just kept getting better.

Despite the chilly breeze, every few minutes a man walked by calling out "Mojito!" while others would carry buckets and say "auga, cervesa, cold beer" over and over like a mantra.

Women walked by selling their wares.

"Henna tattoo" they called out walking in long lines up and down the beach, "mas-sage, ten euro."

The massage ladies would squat down next to me and give me a preview by gently squeezing my leg or foot. It didn't feel too bad, and we were very tempted by the mojitos. The sellers were annoying at first, but hey that's Europe for you. At least these people were making an honest living instead just asking for free money.

We briefly stepped into the sea, but it was much too cold to swim. We saw only one or two brave souls swimming despite the throngs of beach goers. It felt so good to relax and do nothing.

Refreshed, we went to purchase some groceries. Every other storefront was home to mini-markets, called *Mercats* or *Supermercats*. Chloe and I laughed like dumb kids each time we passed one. Mercat just sounded silly.

We stopped in one near our hostel. The stores were pretty little by American standards, but I managed to stock a wide array of cheap food. We picked up some pasta and vegetables for dinner and muffins for breakfast.

Arms full of groceries, we made our way back the hostel. It was time for an actual cooked meal instead of our Nutella sandwich diet. I took a long warm shower as Sam cooked up some pasta in the kitchen. I felt renewed as I toweled off.

Walking back to our room, I saw a shirtless man with a chisled physique laying in one of the bunks. He greeted me.

"Hi I'm Greg," he said in a vaguely British accent. It soon hit me, that this was our South African roommate. I was way off the mark earlier. He was a tall blonde haired man, with a body fit from manual labor.

Greg and I spoke for a bit and then went to the kitchen. Greg wanted to say hi to Chloe and Sam before he went out for the evening.

The girls immediately fawned over Greg. He had rugged good looks, perfect teeth, and tan skin. He oozed an easy confidence. He told us about his job in his impeccably proper accent. He worked on yachts for rich people and traveled around the globe. They had been at port in Barcelona for a few weeks, and his leave was just coming to an end. We told him about our plans too.

"Oh, is it spring holiday already?" Greg bemusedly asked when we told him we are still in school. We must have seemed like children to him. Greg had to leave shortly after, so we sat down for our little family meal just thee three of us.

We ate the pasta, cooked with fresh tomatoes and some summer sausage from Madrid. We ate around a little three-seater table in the kitchen with the windows open.

Sam was rightly proud of her whipped together meal, so we made sure to get a group photo in before we ate. For college kids, this was damn fancy. For dessert, we had fresh green apples. I hadn't seen these since I left Ohio in December.

Wrapping up dinner, we went to check out the town for a bit. None of us wanted to do anything too crazy, but our time in Barcelona was quite short, and we needed to make the most of it.

Back in Madrid, our friend from the tapas tour told us to check out La Rambla, the main street of Barcelona. She had told us it was full of shops, restaurants, and bars. It was only twenty minutes away on foot.

The way to La Rambla took us along an enjoyable boardwalk along the water. Barcelona was full of wide-open streets, palm trees, and impressive sculptures. I walked under a giant eighty-foot metal lobster with a smiley face on it. The city was bustling with the people, but nobody seemed to be in a hurry.

We turned onto La Rambla. It was a broad shaded street, full of business and bars. We passed by a few places selling sangria and thought about stopping in for a drink. Just then we came across a generic pub. Feeling suddenly homesick for Britain, we went right in.

Immediately we felt like we were back in the U.K. There were dark paneled wooden walls, English accents and a football game playing on the Sky TV. As we slid up to the bar, we saw they were selling mojitos for a reasonable five euros.

We ordered some and watched the bartender muddle the fresh mint.

We had never had mojitos before and were blown away by the meld of sweet and minty flavors. Wow! We promptly indulged in several more. The bartender told us the mojito originated in Barcelona, so we drank up, happy to be enjoying the local drink.

I later found out mojitos are a Cuban, not Spanish, drink. Like the palaces, everybody claims to be the first or the best. Regardless, these were finely crafted cocktails, and they soon hit me harder than I expected. We left the bar more than a little tipsy.

We made it a few more blocks into the city but soon turned around. Tired of seeing cityscapes at night, we went back to the beach near our hostel.

The darkened beach was now empty. We sat on the cold sand and talked for a while. Beaches are always magical at night. I was kind of hoping to come across some kind of raging beach party around a bonfire, but it was not to be. Instead, we enjoyed the solitude of the waves lapping the shore.

Going back home to the hostel, we ran into Greg again. He was having a quiet night in, as he needed to report back to duty tomorrow. Today was the last day of his month-long break. Greg loved his job, but I don't know if I could put up with such a lifestyle for a long time.

All of us decided to head to bed around the same time. We turned the lights off and climbed into our bunks.

From my view on a top bunk, I could just see the soft yellow streetlights behind the window curtain, and I could hear the waves in the background. I was delighted with Barcelona. Picking a beach town like this was a great decision. It had been a late addition to our plans, but as I fell asleep that night, I was sure as hell glad we had picked it.

Barcelona, Day Fourteen: 10th of April

We woke up excited to start our short stay in Barcelona. We only had two days here and didn't want to waste any time. Our hostel did not provide breakfast, so we slathered some muffins in Nutella and ate them while we walked.

We were heading to the Castel del Monttjuïc, a big castle perched on a mountain on the edge of town. We had googling around yesterday, and this looked like a cool place to visit. We never had many plans when we got to these new cities. We just looked up directions to the hostel. Once we arrived and settled in, we would make a short list of stuff to do and would go into town based on that. This approach left us with a lot of freedom to improvise. Traveling with a strict itinerary was too limiting.

The beginning of our trek took us along the boardwalk. Between the early morning sun and the agreeable sea breeze, it was quite lovely. On the boardwalk, we passed by old men playing tennis in courts shaded by the palm trees. Barcelona was a charming city.

Reaching the park, we found ourselves at the base of the mountain. The path up the steep side was long and scenic. The entire route had gardens all the way up it. Unlike the exotic French gardens in Paris, these were full of local plant life, so there were a lot of long grasses, cacti, palm trees and other dry climate plants. The cacti were in bloom with lovely pink flowers. There was also a bunch of graceful green statues that blended in seamlessly with the natural plants.

Unfortunately, a lot of inconsiderate people had been up this lovely route. People had carved their names into the plants and rocks along the path. I saw some cacti that were big as exercise balls with names cut into them. The marked ones were cracked and dying or already dead. These plants couldn't survive with twenty nicknames and hearts carved into their flesh.

Near the top of the mountain, there was a restaurant and flat vista where we could view the city. The views were fantastic. From this point in the southwest of the city, I could see all of Barcelona, the harbor, and the Mediterranean stretching out beyond that. The city sprawled out deep off into the distance, while a light gray mist shrouded the small mountains that surrounded the city on three sides.

The harbors were strange to see. They were big blue squares cut into the natural coastline. Even from this view, the harbors looked massive. I don't know why I was surprised at this, but these harbors were very busy with gigantic ships coming in and out of them. Although I had been to port towns, I guess I had never actually saw the ports themselves. I reflected that the ports were the very reason the city existed at all and the continued engine and lifeblood of Barcelona today.

Looking extra tiny next to the enormous freighters I even saw the cruise ship that we had almost booked. I pointed it out to the girls who politely nodded. Damn, it would have been neat to go on that ship.

Continuing, we climbed the last little bit of the mountain and came to the entrance of the fort. The sun had gotten pretty hot and the three of us had slipped back into bickering. We were with each other all day every day. This much contact was bound to create friction at times.

However, our desire to explore and see new things tempered our spats. The three of us were happy to see that the entry fee was only five euros. The price was gentle on our daily budgets, and we entered the castle.

Unlike the cramped medieval castles we had seen in England, this was from the early modern period. It was surprisingly open and airy. It had been built with guns and cannons in mind. It was originally constructed in the 1640's, then captured and recaptured several times for a hundred years. The limited English language exhibitions told us that in

1750 the Madrid government turned the cannons from the sea to the town and let loose a devastating bombardment.

For the next two hundred years, the fort was not for defense but was mostly used to bombard the Catalans into submission. The fort became a hated symbol of Spanish oppression over Catalonia. During the civil war, Franco had executed numerous political opponents in this fort. There was an interesting memorial in one corner of the fort to a prominent Catalan leader killed at this spot, Lluis Companys.

Lluis had declared an independent Catalan state during the war. This act made him a hero to Catalans but sealed his death warrant after the Nazi's captured him and sent him back to Spain.

We climbed up onto the highest walls, then to a twenty-foot tower on top of that. We ate our packed lunches, overlooking the vast harbor and the beautiful seaside city. The sky was bright blue above us. We ate sandwiches and oranges on this fort, which had caused so much misery for so long.

Finishing our lunch, we looked at a few more of the exhibits. The main museum commemorated the long years of Franco's dictatorship. The photographs were moving, but the language barrier limited my understanding. The explanations were written in Catalan and Spanish, but barely any English. There would be five paragraphs in those languages, but only one or two sentences in English. It was a shame because most European museums shy away from their darker bits of recent history.

Linguistically, I was surprised to see that Catalan is very different than Spanish. Catalonians have long chaffed under Spanish subjection. Every few years Catalonia tries to break away from Spain, but is blocked at every turn by the government in Madrid. I heard much less Spanish spoken in Barcelona than in other parts of Spain. These folks are fiercely proud of their identity.

We walked around the fortress a little bit more before heading out. The military historian in me was impressed by the classic 'star' layout. The stone walls of the fort were built in jagged, angular patterns. The design was to deflect and minimize the effect of incoming cannon balls. This style replaced the big tall walls of the medieval era, as those would easily collapse under a gunpowder siege.

We also posed on the big World War Two era artillery gun. It was in good fun, despite the fact that this gun was actually designed to shell the unruly inhabitants of the city, rather than incoming Allied ships. I felt a tiny bit guilty about having fun on it.

On the way down the mountain, after leaving the fort, we almost took a cable car down. It looked entertaining, but none of us could spare the ten euros it cost. Oh, the life of a student traveler!

We walked back to the hostel. We had a homemade lunch and washed our laundry by hand in the kitchen sink. When we opened the window next to the sink, we found a clothesline and clothespins attached to it. Delighted, we hung our shirts and socks out to dry, joining our laundry with the hundreds of other clothes lines. We were several stories up, so if our clothes got blown down, we would never see them again. It was only slightly nerve-wracking to leave our laundry there.

Afterwards, we hit the beach again. It was notably warmer than yesterday, making for a more enjoyable beach experience. This time Chloe and Samie jumped into the Mediterranean and swam around.

"Come in!" they yelled to me, splashing around. I waddled in up to my thighs.

"It's too cold," I said to them quietly.

The water was freezing. I stood there, halfway way in the Mediterranean, in awe at the beauty of the beach. The sea was a deep blue color while the sand was white and soft. The sky was cloudless and palm trees swayed gently back and forth. The beach was full of people yet was not overcrowded.

It was strange to see eight-story buildings a hundred feet from the shore, but they were aesthetically pleasing with their warm brown hues. We could not have asked for a better day in a more beautiful place.

Getting out of the water, we laid out to warm up in the sun.

"You two are literally the whitest people here," Samie said to Chloe and I as we sprawled out on our towels. Chloe and I looked at each other and shrugged. It wasn't the first time either of us had heard this.

We stopped talking and enjoyed the sounds around us. We listened to the waves hitting the beach, the seagulls crying out, and the gentle sounds of the city behind us. We also heard the other natural sounds of Barcelona.

"Auga, cerveza cold beer."

"Auga, cerveza, cold beer."

"Mass-age."

"Auga, cerveza, cold beer."

And so on. The same monotonous voices kept repeating these phrases, and they became almost hypnotic. They were not unpleasant. We spent the rest of the early afternoon there.

Back at the hostel kitchen we yet another bowl of pasta. We had plans to eat later, but this way we would save more money. As we eat our pasta, Greg poked his head in to say goodbye.

"Bye Greg," the girls called lustily to him as he left. They were visably disappointed to see him go.

During this meal, I was messaging our friend Abby on Facebook. Abby was just arriving in Barcelona as we messaged. She went to Kent State with us back in Ohio, and we had all became friends in Leicester. Abby was one of those people with a bright and warm happy-go-lucky personality. She charged headfirst into life and did so with humor and humility. We were looking forward to hanging out with her again.

We agreed to meet beneath a statue of Christopher Columbus near our hostel. We had seen it from afar and figured it was a good prominent landmark that was nearby.

The statue sat on top of a grand stone pillar, flanked by statues of lions and trumpeting angels. It was a massive monument, with plenty of room to sit beneath it. It was in the center of a roundabout. Unlike at the Ac De'Triomphe, there were traffic lights and walkways to the monument on the street itself.

We sat on the stone base of the monument and waited for Abby and her friend Emily. Behind and above us was this magnificent monument. Around us were grand buildings built in Gothic and Neoclassical style, while the sea and mountains stood in the background. Crowds of people swarmed to and from La Rambla. A mass of cars roared around the monument. Occasionally they would all halt when the traffic lights let people cross the street. A brilliant orange and dusky red sky framed the whole scene.

High above us a larger than life Columbus had his hand outstretched. We made idle conversation about how we assume his hand was pointing west.

"Wait a second," Samie said to us. "He is pointing to the sea, and away from the sun."

"He's pointing east," Chloe finished for her. "He's pointing to India."

We laughed. That was pretty funny. Was that a slight to Columbus? Taunting him with where he tried to reach?

As far as random monuments go, this one was pretty odd. It was well made but super weird. Why Columbus in Barcelona? He wasn't from Barcelona, never lived in Barcelona, and didn't make his name anywhere near Barcelona. One does not associate Columbus and Barcelona at all.

As we pondered the Columbus statue, we saw Abby and Emily across the street, waiting at the crosswalk. Emily was from Arizona, and she had become great friends with Abby over the past few months in Leicester.

They practically had a skip in their step as they crossed the street. Both had irrepressible energy in their gait, amplified by their short statures.

"Hi guys!" Abby shouted when she saw us. "It's so good to see you again!"

We greeted each other and exchanged hugs. Abby and Emily had just arrived in Barcelona an hour ago and were starving, so we walked back down the boardwalk near our hostel to find some food.

At the end of the boardwalk stood a touristy restaurant called Makamaka. We had heard about it in Madrid. It was a burger and beer place that looked like a bamboo shack.

Inside, the food was not remarkable. The burgers were ok but hideously expensive. We bought a pitcher of sangria for a costly nineteen euro and only got one glass each. I thought the sangria tasted like fruit juice and was not amused by it.

Although the food was disappointing the conversation was great. We caught them up on our travels, and in turn, they regaled us with stories from Morocco. They had just arrived from there that afternoon, and it was still fresh in their minds.

"We had to wear veils," Emily told us.

"Yeah and we had to be accompanied by a male at all times," Abby added. "The food was so good though!"

It was fascinating to hear about their experience. Both girls were very religious and had somehow connected with underground Christian missionaries. Prostelizing was illegal in that Muslim country, and they could have faced pretty severe penalties for doing this.

"The missionaries can't even tell people what they do until they totally trust them," Abby told us.

"Well does that work?" I asked, incredulously.

Abby and Emily nodded, eyes bright and full. "They are building a Christian community there."

Neither Chloe, Sam nor I were particularly religious. We especially just couldn't imagine making this your life's work. I'd personally be more inclined to let the Moroccans continue to practice their ancestral religion. If Crusaders and then centuries of French rule hadn't successfully converted the Moroccans I wasn't too sure silent underground missionaries would either, but hey that was just my take on it.

Abby and Emily told us about their other adventures in Morocco, things like riding camels, eating fantastic food, and soaking in a culture that is very different than ours.

"I don't want to seem like I'm bragging," Abby said earnestly, "but it was an eye-opening experience."

Their stories enthralled me. It is an ironic part of traveling. Meeting with other travelers, you tend to talk about your past experiences and future travels. It's funny how, when hearing about Morocco, I got transported to another place. At the same time, we can forget that we were in a crazy new location right then. We had literally climbed up to a five hundred-year-old castle that morning, after all.

The sun had set by the time we left Makamaka. Abby and Emily were exhausted, so we walked them back to the nearest metro stations, and made plans to meet the following day. The route to the metro again took us underneath that big smiling lobster statue.

"Hey, so you do guys want to grab a drink?" I suggested as we walked back from the metro.

"Yeah, let's buy some and go to the beach," Chloe said excitedly. Drinking in public still felt new and wild after all these months in Europe.

We stopped into a mercat and grabbed some cans of Rekorderlig, a Swedish hard cider drink. We took a few different fruity flavors and went to the beach. We sat in a row in the sand and drank our ciders as we looked up at the starry night and listened to the crashing waves.

I took my shoes off and buried my feet in the cold sand. It felt surreal to sit on the Mediterranean beach drinking cider. A million and a half people in Barcelona, and we were entirely alone. We stayed out there for a long time.

After a while, it got late, and we were tired from a long day. We grabbed our empty cider cans and walked back to the hostel. Having our hostel so close to the beach was unreal. We lucked out with our location.

As we entered our room a glazed-eyed white dude with dredlocks came stumbling out. He was wearing a dirty but colorful poncho and khaki shorts. He muttered what might have been a greeting and headed straight for the door. He stank heavily of weed. I had no trouble figuring out which locker was his because it also reeked heavily of marijuana.

The three of us exchanged a knowing look. It was just our luck we'd have our suave South African friend replaced with this guy. Fortunately, he was apparently heading out for the night, and we did not see him again. I fell asleep quickly.

Barcelona, Day Fifteen: 11th of April

I woke up to the sunlight streaming through the windows onto the hardwood floor. From my top bunk in the corner of the room, I could see Chloe was already packing up. She was always such an early riser. On the bed above her, I saw Samie sleeping with a t-shirt draped over her face, trying desperately to keep out the morning light. I have never met a person who enjoyed sleeping as much as Samie does. The dichotomy was striking.

I climbed out of my bunk. I couldn't believe it was already our last day in Barcelona. As I went to brush my teeth, I felt a little sad to be leaving. I had really liked the city and our hostel.

We packed our bags within a few minutes. We were old pros at this. We did our automatic scan of the room for cell phones, laptop cords, and souvenirs. With everything looking good we stepped out of the room and closed the door, letting our dredlocked friend sleep off whatever kind of night he had had.

In our little kitchen, we ate another quick breakfast of muffins. Our bags were piled in the hallway outside while the three of us sat at the wooden table. I took one more look out of the window. Fresh sheets of laundry were strung up again and fluttering in the gentle wind. Far below us, the streets of our neighborhood were quiet.

I stepped away from the window as I heard Chloe and Sam stand up.

"Time to go?" I asked wryly.

"You know it is," Chloe responded with a slight smile.

We were comfortably slipping back into travel mode. I was feeling confident about traveling again. Although nothing terrible had happened in Madrid last week, it was hard to overstate how much it shook my confidence. Our experience there had shown me that this was real life, not a game or a movie. I had to be always aware of what was going on around me.

At the same time, I was starting to relax again. I think a good traveler is somebody who possesses a mix of foresight and spontaneity, somebody who goes with the flow but with a grain of caution. For a little while after our arrival in Madrid, I had thought perhaps I was in over my head. But, as we climbed down the tiny stairwell and walked to the reception, I felt great.

"Can we leave our bags here and pick them up in the afternoon?" I asked the owner as he sat behind the desk.

"Of course, follow me!" The man responded, just as energetic as the first time we met him. He led us around a corner to a big wire cage sealed with a padlock. Removing a key from his necklace he deftly unlocked the latch and swung the door open. Inside the cage sat five or six large backpacks already.

"You may store them here and retrieve them when you are done sightseeing."

We thanked the man and set our stuff down. As we hit the streets of Barcelona, I felt like my old confident self again.

It was going to be a weird day. Because our flight left absurdly early the next morning, we had decided it would not be worth it to rent a hostel room. Instead, we planned to sightsee all day and then head to the airport in the evening. From there, we would get past security, sleep in the airport and go straight onto our plane the next morning. We had found a website that rated the sleep-ability of each major airport and were happy to see that Barcelona had a decent rating. What did people do before the internet?

Feeling upbeat about our upcoming day, we walked to the metro station and headed deep into the heart of the city. Our first stop was to the renowned Sagarada Familia.

The Sagarada Familia was a vast, unfinished Catholic cathedral. Construction had started in 1882 and was still ongoing. While this was the norm in the Middle Ages, you would be hard-pressed to find many buildings that take this long to build these days.

The architecture of the building was utterly unique. Called 'Catalan Modernism,' no label describes it adequately. The church towers were not stiff and straight but were organic and almost alien in appearance. The six massive towers rose up from the building, resembling abstract tree trunks. The flying buttresses mimicked tree branches and circular stone halos capped each tower. We did not see the interior, but pictures of it are incredible.

We got as close as we could to the outside of the church. High above our heads, men worked on the towers. Their cranes were so high above us that they looked tiny from our vantage point on the ground. I had read that the church was still under construction, but in spite of that, I was surprised that it was a real, literal construction zone.

We could only gape at the outside of the building for so long. One day I would like to return there after the construction is over and see how it looks. But for now, we had seen the church and were growing hungry for lunch.

We walked away from the church and stopped for a coffee at McDonalds. We ordered our drinks and looked for a place to sit down. Chloe and I discovered these strange booths that hosted two barstool type seats facing each other. Between them was a small table and a thin wall separating the table from the area around it. The wall didn't hide one's body, only the table, and possibly head if the person leaned in towards the divider.

What were these tiny strange booths for? Dates? Interviews? I was not sure, but Chloe and I had a fun time playing around in them, poking our heads out the other side and acting like children.

"You guys always embarrass me," Samie scolded us as we played. She was looking up our next stop on her phone. Sam made an executive decision to take us to Parc Güell, a prominent public park designed by Antoni Gaudi, the same man who created the cathedral. We finished our coffees and headed out.

So far, the day had been overcast and nice. It had not been too hot out. As we started to walk to the park, however, the clouds suddenly broke, and the sun began to beat down on us. The hot sun and lack of substantial food was taking its toll on us. We kept an eye out for a cheap kebab stand but only walked past high-end restaurants. Our walk was entirely uphill.

Barcelona was a beautiful city to walk around. Trees lined the streets, and the whole place had a pleasing aesthetic to it. It seemed much more cohesive than Madrid, which had felt like it had been slapped together randomly. Like most cities, once we left the Sagarda Familia, and before we got to the park, there were next to no people on the streets.

After a long forty-five minute walk, it appeared Samie's phone was taking us to a dead end. The street ended in a brick wall within our eyesight. We dubiously continued forward, passing a schoolyard behind a metal chain-link fence. Young grade-schoolers stopped playing their games to stare at us.

Just when we almost turned around, Chloe spied something.

"Oh, I see!" She said. "There are stairs in the wall!"

And indeed there were. Although the street was a dead end for cars, there was a nifty stone staircase sent into the brick wall. The stairs weren't apparent until you were on top of them. It was like Ali Baba's cave. Was this to throw off tourists? At the top of the stairs, we were rewarded with a beautiful view of the city.

During our whole trip, I was vaguely aware that I walked a lot. Long afterwards, I went back and tried to calculate how many miles we walked each day. It turns out that on an average day, we might have walked between ten and fifteen miles. On a particularly busy day, we would walk upwards of twenty miles. We walked everywhere in Europe. I couldn't believe those numbers. By the end of this day, we were definitely on the high end of the scale. My legs ached.

At the top of the hill, we joined a growing stream of people heading into the park proper. Immediately upon entering the park I was blown away by its beauty. Gaudi had created a grand vision of art and nature. He built archways and benches that blended organically into the trees and shrubs. Their brown and olive colors mirrored the natural hues of the earth.

We walked inside a pavilion built into the side of a hill. The stone pillars looked like they had sprouted up organically. Different size stones, all tan colored made up the pillars. Plants spouted out of niches built just for them. The style in the park was so futuristic and unique that is hard to describe. Like the unfinished cathedral, the park looked more like an alien landscape than a park designed and built a century ago.

We climbed to the top of the pavilion and looked out over the magnificent city. We could see the Sagrada Familia and the Castel Monttjuïc beyond it. The sky was bright blue and cloudless, and it blended seamlessly into the sea beyond the city. I looked around at the palm trees growing next to the beautiful sandstone benches we sat on. It was so progressive and perfectly designed.

I laid down on the bench and put my head in Samie's lap. I saw Chloe's flaming red hair blowing in the wind as she gazed out over Barcelona. I suddenly had the feeling that traveling was the most wonderful thing in the world. I looked back over at the surreal and beautiful artwork in the park. Moments like this more than made up for any shitty moments. *This is the best feeling in the world* I thought to myself.

We walked around the rest of the park slowly, taking it in. The amount of greenery visible in the city around us was stunning. We went to the central area of the park, where there was a famous salamander sculpture by Gaudi. A while into our slow wanderings, we came to a little clearing.

In front of us was a big cylindrical stone mound with a narrow set of stairs wrapping around it. On top of it sat three human-sized stone crosses. The mound was maybe twenty-five feet tall, and fifteen feet across at the top. Plenty of tourists were standing at the top.

Because this wasn't America, there were no fences or wires around this summit. If you fell off the top, you'd probably break a leg. Something like this would never be allowed in a prominent touristy place in the States. I guess people worry less in Spain.

Samie stayed back as Chloe and I climbed the stairs. At the base of the monument stood a man with long brown curly hair, done in a perm. He wore pink sunglasses and tight leopard print pants. He was playing guitar and singing at the top of his voice.

"In the jungle, the binga bonga, the lion sleeps tonight!" I don't think he knew the other words because all the lyrics were variations of this line. Sometimes he would playfully roar at ladies who passed by too close. He wasn't very talented as a musician but sure as hell knew how to work a crowd.

Like I usually do with musicians, I tipped him some coins. Right after me, somebody else tipped him a sandwich, placing it in his money jar. He laughed at me and winked at the sandwich giver. He looked very pleased.

As we left the park, two buildings that resembled giant gingerbread houses flanked the exit. They were weird and playful. The entire park was a surreal and neat experience. I would definitely recommend it to anyone.

Leaving the heart of the city, we took the metro back to Barceloneta, our little beachfront neighborhood where the hostel was. It was late afternoon, and we still needed to print our boarding passes for our flight tomorrow. I had seen a library as we explored a few days ago, so we went towards it.

We got out of the metro and took the short walk to the library. The neighborhood was great because so it was very compact, and had everything from libraries to mercats to restaurants, to a sunny, sandy beach. The library was built into one of the narrow buildings and looked exactly like the other apartments.

Stepping inside, I was immediately comforted by the familiar look and smell of books. The library felt much like any other library I have ever been in, despite being on a Mediterranean beach.

The three of us walked up to the front desk where the only person in the library was sitting. She was a lovely young woman in her late twenties.

"Do you speak English?" we asked her politely.

The woman's eyes grew big, and she looked terrified. I would hate to have to speak English as my non-native tongue too. We mimed printing out papers. The woman nodded and then pointed her finger straight up. Then, she pointed over to a nearby set of stairs.

We thanked her and walked to the staircase. On the way up, Samie tugged at my arm insistently.

"I really need to pee."

"Ok, I'm sure there is a bathroom in here."

"No, I really, really need to pee right now." Sam looked like she was in pain.

If you have ever been to Europe, one of the first things you notice is the lack of public bathrooms. For whatever reason, Europeans seem much less inclined to have these readily available. Europeans are much stricter about only letting paying customers use their bathrooms. Often the bathrooms will be locked, and you will need a specific key to access them.

With Samie hunched over in pain, we climbed up to the next floor. The stairs took us to what was apparently a children's section. There were kids books and colorful children's posters on the wall.

In front of us was a table of little girls wearing cute dresses and coloring happily. We stood there dumbly, unsure of what to do. After a minute or so, the girls noticed us, stopped coloring and started to chant "Up! Up! Up!" in unison and pointed their fingers at the ceiling.

We turned around and saw another set of stairs that kept going up. We took it to the next floor and found, to our delight, a room with a row of computers and a librarian behind a desk. To the other direction was a locked door that had a bathroom symbol on it.

Samie ran over and grabbed the handle. It did not turn.

"Fuck!" she exclaimed.

We went over to the librarian. When we asked if she spoke English, she shook her head. Bladder nearly exploding, Samie pointed to the locked door.

The librarian smiled and produced a key from under her desk. Samie grabbed it, ran over and opened the door. Did this have to be so hard?

Crisis solved, Chloe and I asked via miming how to print our boarding passes. After much back and forth the librarian understood our questions and after even more gesturing we understood her answers. With Samie rejoining us, we printed our boarding passes, thanked the librarian and left, mission accomplished.

We went back to the beach to relax just a big longer. We took off our stinky shoes and dug our bare feet into the sand. We sat near the boardwalk and watched people create massive and elaborate sand sculptures.

Samie rested her head on my shoulder and told me how homesick she felt. I think every traveler gets this at some point. The three of us kids sat on the boardwalk, legs dangling over, and watched the beach people go about their business for a long while.

As the afternoon began to give way to evening, we went back to the hostel, grabbed our bags and thanked the owner one last time. He had run an excellent hostel.

As per our plans made the night before, we got on the metro and rode northeast across the city. We were going to meet with Abbey and Emily at their hostel.

We got off the metro and walked up the street to their place. We could see a bunch of scruffy looking young people hanging out in the little alleyway where the entrance of the hostel was. Since we couldn't get in without a keycard, we waited outside the door until they came down to us. Soon, Abbey and Emily came bounding out of the door, happy as always.

"Come on in guys," they yelled at us cheerfully as they held the door open. They led us in past the common room, greeting a few people as they led us to the stairs.

"People are so friendly here," they gushed. Their room was down a long hallway with dozens of doors. The hostel was far bigger than the small quiet hostels we usually stayed in.

"You could put your stuff on our beds," Emily told us as they swung open their door. Their room held eight or ten bunks.

"Our dormmates are super cool," Abbey told us. "They are really nice."

We unstrapped our heavy packs and placed them on the two bunk beds nearest the door. We were grateful we did not have to carry the bags for the evening.

"There is a cool rooftop bar we went to check out last night. There are a lot of people partying up there".

The hostel did not sound like my type of place. The girls took turns quickly showering to refresh for the evening. I chatted with Abbey and Emily as we waited for them.

It was a welcome change to talk with people who weren't with us constantly. It was like a breath of fresh air for us to have new conversations. At times it felt like all we did was rehash the same stories and memories, and talk about the same things all the time.

For dinner, Abbey suggested a nearby place she had heard about from a hostel friend. The place, named The Surf Bar, was a hole in the wall joint in a quiet square, tucked away only a few streets from the beach. Walking in we saw white tile floors and plain white walls adorned with a few surfboards and a Tex-Mex menu. A TV was playing an old Chuck Norris movie on mute.

The only other people in the place sat at one of the four long metal tables. They were a group of fifteen large men. We sat at the table next to them, and before too long a woman came out wearing a cook's apron.

"Do you speak English?" was our first question. A shake of the head was her reply.

"*Español*," she said. Spanish was no problem for Chloe and Sam, and it turned out Emily spoke some too. We ordered a ton of different cheap seafood dishes and nachos.

Once we ordered, we started to listen to the men next to us. They were a rowdy but jovial group of Englishmen on holiday. They were drunkenly watching the Chuck Norris movie, spouting their own commentary and ribald comments to the TV and each other.

Abbey leaned over her seat to shout over the din of voices.

"We're from Leicester!"

One or two of the men looked at us with glassy, bemused eyes.

"In Leicestershire?" he asked as if there were multiple cities in the UK named Leicester. Their accents made us feel at home. It turned out the men were from Birmingham. Birmingham (pronounced 'burming-IM not 'burming-HAM') was very close to Leicester, and we had each passed through the city at one point or another. Like true Brits, they were spending their whole holiday completely drunk.

The language barrier had proven to be a significant obstacle for them.

"Tell her to give us that," one of the men slurred, pointing at our plates of nacho. "Those look good."

Abbey ordered some in Spanish for our new friends. As we ate, I quickly deduced that while the food was not very good, the company was unparalleled. Between the Englishmen's banter and our conversation, it was a good time.

An older American couple came in about halfway through our meal and sat near us. They heard our American accents and quickly started up a conversation. They were from California and on a cruise around the Mediterranean. At first, I didn't mind talking to them, but they soon grew condescending.

"Do your parents know you are spending their money here?" they asked me in an accusatory voice after learning I was on spring break.

"Well. I'm paying for this myself," I said coolly and turned my back to them. For better or for worse my college debt would be entirely my own. I was acutely aware that I would be paying for all of this for many more years to me.

We finished our meal and went to walk around the city one last time. Abbey and Emily were also leaving tomorrow, going onward to Paris. It was dark by the time we left the Surf Bar to wander around. We found ourselves on the boardwalk again, between the Olympic Village and the beach.

The Olympic Village had built back in 1992 for the Games. The Village had been used to house the athletes, but now were expensive apartments and tourist shops. The Olympic pools had long been connected to the sea and packed with docked yachts. We walked through the darkened sea of masts and sails towards to beach beyond it.

We were going to the beach one more time. As we walked to it, a voice called out from the darkness.

"Cocaine?" The disembodied voice was soft, and the word whispered. "Cocaine?"

Ignoring the kind offer we sat on the cold sand again and watched the waves roll in. We didn't speak much this time.

Instead, we sat in silence. The lights of the city behind us gave way to the blackness of the sea in front of us.

"I can't believe we're here," I said softly. The girls nodded in agreement.

"It's like a dream," Abbey said. "A really awesome dream."

In time, we walked back to their hostel. We walked past a sorbet shop on the way. Who could turn down sorbet?

The shop was on a pedestrian-only road. We ate the sorbet while sitting on an iron-wrought table underneath strings of lights hung up between the buildings. I felt alive, eating my mango ice cream alongside my friends underneath sparkling lights. Our voices carried down the empty street.

All good things must end. Too soon, we had to go. We went back to Emily and Abbey's hostel to grab our bags. We put them on and then hugged them goodbye. It was time for our next journey.

We boarded the metro and shot off into the heart of the city center. Despite the late hour, we had found a cheap shuttle that would take us to the airport. As we left the metro and climbed up the stairs to the street, we were a little nervous that we would not be able to find the bus time. It was the last outgoing shuttle of the evening.

We got to our stop and looked around the street. Right across the street from where we stood was a bus with the word 'Aerobús' emblazoned in big letters across its side.

"Well that was easy," Samie said dryly. Chloe and I had been much more worried than she had been. Grateful for the ease of this transition, we boarded the bus and rode to the airport. We were the only passengers.

We arrived at the airport a half hour before it closed at midnight. Boarding passes in hand, we leisurely joined the line of a handful of other travelers going through security. All the flights had already left for the evening, so security was slow and relaxed. Everybody was peaceful and calm. It was the best security experience I've ever had in an airport.

It's funny how so many airports are so similar. The Barcelona aiport was no different than most airports I'd seen. It had a typical layout of one central hub and several wings shooting off from it. These wings were open and spacious, with big metal blocks every two hundred feet or so. These blocks had TV's and flight information on them, along with outlets. Next to them were metal benches. The floor was cold hard marble.

Finding our terminal, we settled down next to one of the big metal blocks. We sat between the block and the glass wall facing the runway, giving ourselves a tiny bit of privacy.

Samie immediately built a cozy nest out of clothes and her backpack. She draped a black t-shirt over her eyes and promptly fell asleep on the cold hard floor. She slept peacefully through the whole night.

With Sam out, this left Chloe and I up. We plugged in our laptops. Connected to the wifi, Chloe watched a movie while I worked on my school papers. At midnight all the TV's and information screens shut off, leaving the place in silence and semi-darkness. Only a few dim lights remained on.

After a while, Chloe shut off her laptop and curled up on the metal bench. The benches had unmovable armrests every three feet, so I am not sure how she managed to sleep on it. I tried to lean back and rest but could not do so. My eyes would flutter open as soon I shut them. I was far too uncomfortable to sleep.

I sighed in exasperation and pulled my laptop back out. I knew myself well enough to know I would never fall asleep like this. I can be very particular when it comes to sleeping. In this way, I am the inverse of Samie. While she can sleep anywhere at any time, I can only fall asleep in a comfortable setting.

I turned my laptop on and settled into a semi-comfortable position. While I didn't have Netflix at the time, I had downloaded a few things in preparation for times like this. I started by watching *Memento*, a critically acclaimed film about a man who can't remember stuff.

I had heard about *Memento* for years, and my film buff friends had highly recommended it. As a cinephile myself I was excited to watch a good meaty film. Unfortunately, I could not get into the movie. I watched it for about half hour before closing it down. I have still never seen it.

I was too tired to follow such a brainy movie. I needed something a little more straightforward, so I started up my other pirated files, the first season of *Game of Thrones*.

I watched several episodes. I had only seen three or four, so I soon worked my way to the end of the season. In between episodes I would take short walks around, try to fall asleep, and inevitably end watching another episode.

It was strange being inside an airport so late. It was nearly empty, save for a few small clusters of people. Like us they were hidden in quiet corners and curled up on the cold floor, trying to catch a few fitful hours of sleep.

I wandered, half delirious from lack of sleep, at the end of each episode. I would linger long in the bathroom, check out the closed food court, and hang out in front of shops with metal grates over their entrances. Being in an empty airport felt a lot like being in an abandoned mall. There was a sense of awe in the vast depopulated place.

At about four in the morning, I was halfway through one more episode. I had been awake for nearly twenty-two hours. The world of Westeros enthralled me. My fatigue and dreamlike state made me feel like I was actually there.

Suddenly and unexpectedly the unthinkable happened before my eyes.

"Ser Ilyn Payne, bring me his head!" King Joffrey said with bloodlust in his eyes.

"No this isn't happening," I muttered to myself. I still didn't think it was going to happen. Then the executioner swung his great broadsword and cut Ned Stark's head clean off. I was in shock.

"What the shit," I spoke aloud as I shut my laptop off without finishing the episode. I had to stand up. The room was spinning around me. I tried to walk off the shock. My body twitched from exhaustion and surprise as I took one more walk around the dark and empty airport. How could they kill the hero of the story? I could not handle this right now.

Our home sweet home in Madrid

Chapter 4: Italy

Florence, Day Sixteen: 12th of April

I was still awake when the sun rose and people began to file into the airport. I saw the other sleeping people wake up and grab coffee. Sam woke up refreshed. I did not talk, for I was too tired to speak.

We gathered our things and lined up for the plane. We were the first ones there. Within a half hour of Sam and Chloe waking up, we were sitting on in our seats. As soon as I sat down, I immediately passed out. I slept through the preflight speeches, the takeoff and the flight over the Mediterranean.

I woke up to Sam shaking me awake.

"We're in Bologna," she told me.

I stumbled out of the plane and grabbed my bag from the storage above me. The inside of the Bologna airport was as nondescript as the one we just left. We needed to get to the train station to get a train to Florence.

We usually weren't ones to ask for help, but we were worn out and unwilling to spend much time looking for the right bus. Instead, we walked up to the first guy behind a counter who looked like he knew something.

Luckily, he spoke English. We told him where we were trying to go, and he deftly explained which bus to take. There was a shuttle from the airport straight to the train station, and it was leaving soon.

We thanked him and went off to catch our bus. It was boarding right outside the exit of the airport. We were some of the first ones on the bus, so we claimed a few seats in the back.

Before we had much time to relax, a bunch of people entered the bus. Then, a bunch more came on. Soon there were no more seats left. Then, even more people came on. I was grateful we had arrived early because there was standing room only on the shuttle.

When the bus was finally packed full, it pulled away, into the city. I was smashed in the back seat but had a window view. I watched the gritty, dirty industrial town of Bologna slide by. I saw a lot of graffiti and barred windows. Bologna did not look nice. Perhaps there was a better part of town, but if there was, I didn't see it.

The bus pulled up to the train station around ten in the morning. We disembarked only to find the train station even more crowded than the bus. I couldn't believe how many people were trying to leave Bologna. Well, maybe after seeing the city, I could actually believe it.

We pushed our way through the crowd and got in line for the ticket kiosk. Or rather, I thought there was a line. Several people cut in front of me before I figured out the system. There wasn't so much a queue, as there was a mad dash for the booth as soon as somebody else left one. When the kiosk nearest me opened, I quickly cut off some Italians to claim it.

At the kiosk, I found some good news and some bad news. The good news was that our Eurail passes were accepted again. It was a relief after Spain, after all, we had paid a lot of money for these passes. Unfortunately, I also found out that the next train to Florence was four hours away.

We settled down on the platform to wait for the train. We sat and sat for hours. I borrowed a paperback copy of *The Time Travelers Wife* from Chloe and read a big chunk of it. We read and sat in silence as a few Roma beggars came by us. They left empty-handed. In Europe, I was never too worried by the beggars.

At last, our train arrived, and I looked for my seat. In Italy, and a few other countries, we needed to reserve a specific seat with our rail passes. I walked down the aisle looking for mine.

My eyes settled on my seat number, then drifted down to the occupant of the seat.

I looked down to see a middle-aged black haired Italian woman and her two bratty teenage sons. They looked and acted like shitheads. They stared at me staring at them until I mimed that I was trying to sit in that seat. I had to climb over one of the kids. As I climbed into my seat, the kids went back to being dumb sullen teenagers to each other and their mother. Great. I tried to make myself comfortable.

Suddenly, Sam, who was standing next to me, was shaking me awake. The family was nowhere in sight.

"We need to get off right now!" she said urgently.

Adrenaline shot through me as I jumped up. I couldn't believe I had fallen asleep like that. I hadn't even known it had happened. My seatmates were long gone, and it had been two hours since I sat down.

I grabbed my bag from the overhead bin and followed Samie to where Chloe was standing by the doors. Not a moment after I got there did they slide open. Most trains are only at their stops for a few minutes if they aren't terminating. I was fortunate Samie had been able to find and grab me. Otherwise, I probably would have woken up hours later in Rome or Naples.

It was late in the afternoon when we got off the train. We paused for a moment in the train station to pull up a map to our hotel. As soon as the maps loaded on Sam's phone, we were off.

We exited the Santa Marie Novella train station and walked across the city center. I wasn't yet familiar with the compact nature of Florence, but the train station and our hotel straddled the two ends of the historic city center. We walked through the narrow cobblestone streets.

Typically I'd be captivated by the yellow apartments, the stone streets, and beautiful plazas. Usually, I'd bask in the fact that the city still looked much like it did five hundred years ago. But, for now, I was too tired to care.

It was only a half hour walk to our hotel. The hostels in Florence had been unimpressive. Most were too far away from downtown or too expensive. Instead, we had decided to splurge on an actual hotel room. It was much more expensive than our typical lodging, but the location was great. Additionally, we had booked it thinking we would need a break from the world of hostels. We were damn right about that, we joked, as we thanked our past selves.

Finding our hotel was unproblematic for once. Unlike some of our other stays, our hotel was clearly marked, with a big neon 'Hotel' sign near the door.

One of the owners, a lovely Asian immigrant to Florence, greeted us. As she checked us in she gave us a list of places to check out. She even the took the time to mark them on a paper map of the city.

"These are good cheap places, local prices not tourist prices," she informed us as she marked different eateries. This information served to soften the blow when she told us of the 'tourist tax' on hotel rooms.

"That will be forty euro," she said politely. I was astounded. Forty extra euros? That was significantly more than what I had budgeted to pay. In a bind, we had no choice but to pay the tax.

Once we paid, the lady walked us up to the second floor to our room.

"This was a palace built in the early 19ᵗʰ century," she told us as we walked. There was a finely crafted stone staircase up to our room. We walked down a hall of terracotta tiles to the heavy wooden door.

"Here you are," the owner said, inserting a metal key into the lock. It was beautiful. The floor was marble, complemented by handcrafted wooden dressers and chairs. There was a small

TV in one corner, a big queen-size bed, and second smaller twin size one next to it. The ceiling was vaulted high above our heads. There was a large double window facing the street outside, with wooden shutters you could swing open or shut. It was magnificent.

We dropped our bags and began to relax. When I went to the bathroom, I was surprised to see two toilets, one being much smaller than the other.

"Hey check this out guys," I called to the girls, showing it to them. Chloe just laughed at me, while Samie looked away grinning.

"What's so funny?" I asked indignantly.

"Just google it," was all Chloe and Sam would say to me, despite my questions.

We took turnings taking quick showers, and then tried to nap. I closed the wooden shutters, but some golden Tuscan sun rays still entered and cast shadows on the white walls around me. Half asleep, I watched the shadows play on the high stucco ceiling above us.

I was in a weird state where I was too tired to sleep. Instead, I just lay there under the covers and admired the rays of this setting sun illuminating this room that was hundreds of years old.

Perhaps I drifted to sleep after a while, for I opened my eyes to see the girls getting dressed. We had stopped worrying about such privacy a long while back. There was none to be had when we lived this close with each other.

We were very hungry. It had been nearly twenty-four hours since we had last had a proper meal. Since none of us wanted to do anything too crazy, we decided on takeaway pizza and some wine.

We gathered up our things and walked out into the dusky evening. We hit the grocery store on the way to the pizza place. The hotel owner had recommended both spots.

The grocery store was similar to most other ones I'd seen in European cities, a tight space with just a few aisles of items. We grabbed some wine and Nutella and prepared to get out of there. Near the checkout, I impulsively picked up some antipasto. When I saw the jar of marinated olives and red peppers, I felt a sudden spell of homesickness. It hit me like a punch to the gut.

"I gotta buy this," I said to the girls as they looked on in surprise. I was not one to break my budget on weird little things like this. But to me, everything in the store reminded me of my childhood. The rows of pasta, the roasted red peppers, the fresh tomatoes and onions, all of it brought me back to the big Sunday parties of my young life.

Back when we still lived in Cleveland, it seemed like every Sunday we would host a big gathering with our older relatives. We would feast on Italian sausage, stuffed shells and pickled antipasto. Some of my happiest moments of childhood are from these parties.

The parties had all but ended years ago. Most of the older relatives died off, and the rest of the family scattered to different states and countries. Our old familial Italian feasts were rarer these days, although just as beautiful when they did occur.

So, when I saw those jars of antipasto, I knew I needed them. I had never been away from my family for so long, and I missed the sense of belonging.

Wine and other items in hand, we walked up a block or two to the takeaway pizza joint. We bought some freshly made pizzas and went back to our hotel for dinner.

The pizza was surprisingly disappointing. I had expected Italian pizza to blow my mind, but my expectations had greatly exceeded reality. The Florentine pizza was much less greasy and more savory than American pizza. It was probably objectively better, but it wasn't anything like I thought it would be like. The antipasto was good enough to enjoy at least.

We finished our less-than-stellar meal and sat back in our beds. We had had no table to eat at.

"So, how about we go for a walk around town?" I suggested. Both the girls nodded wearily. We were still tired from the night before, but also profoundly aware we had such limited time. Samie later told me that she expected a nice quiet, leisurely walk through an empty part of town. She was quite mistaken.

Although I didn't know it at the time, we took the route straight into the city center, near to where the Duomo stood. It was dark enough that we had no sense of the spectacular scenery as we walked through the darkened streets of *Firenze*.

We didn't talk much as we took smaller back roads heading west across the city. We passed a few little restaurants and a darkened market, past vague statues in the night and up narrow streets. We walked by cigarette vending machines where very young teenagers hung out. I took a closer look at these cigarette machines a few days later. They said you had to be eighteen to use them, but there was no way to check ID's on such a simple machine. It certainly seemed like we would see more people smoking in Italy than elsewhere, and perhaps this ease of purchase was part of the reason.

Before too long we were in the heart of the city center, narrowly missing the famous and spectacular works of architecture so close by. All we knew is that we were weary, sore and sick of each other. As we got deeper into the city center, the crowds grew larger. There were a lot of well-dressed people walking through the streets, eating gelato and talking with each other. I had expected a sleepy town like Bruges, but this night was pretty lively.

The further we walked, the tenser it became in our group. We needed to go to sleep, but none of wanted to admit it.

Finally, Chloe suggested that we get some gelato. She often retold this story of eating it in Rome when she was in high school.

"We just kept saying to each other 'we're eating gelato in Rome on the curb,'" she would say with a big smile each time.

We had heard so much about Italian gelato, so we stopped into one of the shops the owner had recommended. The inside looked a lot like the interior of any other ice cream store in America. Behind the glass counter, we looked at the rows of flavors.

We picked the kinds we wanted and paid the low price for them. They handed us the scoops of gelato in little paper bowls, with tiny white plastic spoons to eat it with. We ate the gelato as we turned around to walk back in the general direction of the hotel. The gelato was phenomenal. It tasted much like ice cream but sweeter, richer and denser. The flavors were intense and delicious. Our gelato did not last long.

Unfortunately, neither did the peace between us.

"I want to go to a wine bar," I said as we walked past a marketplace with Neoclassical pillars. "You guys can go back to the room if you want, but I might never be here again, and I want to see what it's like," I announced my plan with no room for questions. I had been doing this for months. This trip was my trip, and I was going to do it my way, with or without anybody else.

For Samie, this was the straw that broke the camel's back.

"This trip isn't all about you!" she exclaimed angrily. "You can't just go off and only do what you want to do all the time."

I was genuinely taken back, unclear why she was suddenly mad at me.

"You've been doing this all trip!" she continued. Before she could say more, Chloe interrupted with some comment about something insignificant.

Her comment had the unintended effect of redirecting Sam's anger and frustration at Chloe. The two of them had been at loggerheads all evening. Mainly due to fatigue and overexposure, the girls were at wit's end. As we continued to walk, they erupted at each other.

Happy I was no longer in the crossfire I stayed quiet for a while before I tried to break it up. My attemped backfired right away.

"This trip was supposed to be just Sam and me!" Chloe told me, before taking several big strides away. "I need to be alone now," she said, walking far in front of us.

Chloe and Sam had initially talked about this trip long before Sam and I had even known each other, a fact that occasionally caused tension.

With Chloe a block ahead of us, this meant I was back with Samie. We quietly bickered until we got back to the hotel. We spoke briefly with Chloe on how to split up the two keys between the three of us. Even though we were fighting, we weren't stupid. Safety was always our first priority, even in times like this.

Making sure Chloe got in ok, Sam and I headed around the corner to a nearby urban park, Piazza D'zeglio. It was a pleasant little park with some trees to sit under and wooden benches to sit on. Surrounded by beds of flowers, we proceeded to have a big fight.

We exchanged some heated words, before Samie collapsed in my arms and sobbed wholeheartedly. She cried in this park built when Italy was just becoming a united country. I held her in my arms this park where Nazis had executed resistance fighters.

We held each other for a long time, letting the stress and exhaustion escape. Samie was on sensory overload from these big cities and huge crowds, and I was tired of not having any alone time. We talked through our issues and went back to the hotel after a long time.

We went back to our room, and found Chloe asleep. Maybe we just needed some time apart. Samie and I got ready for bed together. When we climbed into the big queen size bed, we started laughing. Only now did we realize that this 'queen' bed was just two twin mattresses pushed together. This was classic Europe, and not something we'd see in America.

Feeling a lot better, we fired up my laptop and watched the final episode of the first season of *Game of Thrones*. I had no time to contemplate it, as I feel immediately into a deep and dreamless, my body grateful for the rest.

Florence, Day Seventeen: 13th of April

I woke up feeling refreshed for the first time in thirty-six hours. It was wonderful to get the much-needed rest. Before our breakdown yesterday, Chloe and I had planned to join a walking tour across the medieval and Renaissance parts of the city. Since Sam disliked walking tours, she was going to sleep in, and then meet up with an old friend. In a stroke of luck, one of her best friends from high school was studying abroad in Florence at the moment.

Letting Sam sleep for now, Chloe and I headed out back near the train station, to Santa Maria Novella, a magnificent white and blue building with a distinctive curved roof. On the way, we ate little snacks, as this hotel did not include breakfast. The walk was brisk but enjoyable. The city was much better to look at during the day than at night.

We quickly found our tour guide near the entrance of the church. He was holding the ubiquitous red umbrella that our preferred tour company used to mark their tours. He was an older, refined gentleman with neatly combed silver hair and a red sweater vest. He was a knowledgeable guide, but we soon found out that he spoke exceptionally softly and was often hard to hear.

When our little groups grew to about fifteen people or so, we started the tour. The guide pointed to the nearest church, the Santa Maria Novella and started talking. We got a brief history of the building and the artwork inside. A lot of people would probably find this dull, but it is the exact kind of nerdy thing Chloe and I like.

In front of the church was a big ovular courtyard surrounding a couple of green grass gardens. Two twenty-foot tall obelisks anchored each end of the oval courtyard.

"During the Renaissance, Florentines would race horses around this courtyard," the guide told us.

Years later I will be in the Cleveland Museum of Art, looking at Italian works from the 16th century. I will look a bit closer at a painting of a horse race, with familiar looking buildings in the background. All of sudden, I will recognize those very buildings and the museum will fall away from me. I will be transported back to this morning in Florence. I can't believe my eyes when I read the description of the painting. Florence was indeed the setting. It was incredible that I can recognize a scene painted five hundred years ago.

In fact, as our guide pointed out, most of Florence looked more or less the same as it always had, just minus the cars, streetlights, and odd neon advertisement. I love cities like this.

From Santa Maria Novella we headed west as a group through the fashion district. The streets were narrow and mostly one-way. People thronged around us as we moved through the neighborhood. There were high-end stores all around, some with only a few pieces of clothes inside. I couldn't even imagine the price of these pieces. We were in one of the great fashion capitals of the world after all.

From there we made it to the Basilica di San Lorenzo, one of the oldest and largest churches in Florence. The inside was undoubtedly splendid, but we did not go in. The exterior brick dome and long halls look great in pictures, but scaffolding and canvas completely covered it. At the time, unaware of the history of the building and its famous patrons, I did not much care for it.

Down another one of the charming alleyways of Florence, we saw the site of the house of Leonardo da Vinci. It had been torn down long ago, "before people cared about preserving the past," as our tour guide stated.

As we walked up and down these streets, from quiet alleys to crowded main roads, I would sometimes catch sight of a giant red dome. This great dome would be briefly visible from one place on the street, only to disappear behind some three-story yellow Florentine buildings. As we made our way through the streets, the dome got bigger and bigger.

Walking down the Via de' Cerretani, we pushed out of the tight streets and into a smallish crowded square. In front of us was the famous Baptistery of St John. Although I will later marvel at its beauty in pictures, for now, it was completely covered in a cloth façade. It was utterly unremarkable in this state of repair. For us, the real sight lay just beyond.

We walked, as if in a trance, towards the indescribable cathedral. I was too captivated to notice that people were packed as tightly as sardines. I was in awe. We paused, just a few steps past the Baptistery, now forgotten completely. In front of us stood the Santa Maria del Fiore, also known as the *Duomo* or Dome.

The Duomo was a massive grand cathedral. It dominated the skyline of Florence. It was far more massive than any other building in the city. The Duomo was mind-bogglingly large, even by modern standards. Considering it had been built in the 15th century, it was even more impressive. The eponymous dome itself was made entirely from brick. How it still stands today, I do not know.

At that moment we were standing in front of the front facade of the Duomo. It was nearly as impressive as the dome itself. Statues, friezes and gleaming white, green and red marble decorated the front of the church. It was incredibly intricate, even gaudy. It resembled a magnificent wedding cake.

Our tour guide was dismissive of the façade.

"It was built in the 1800's for tourists," he said, waving his hand in contempt. He was still in awe of the rest of the building however, even after living his whole life in Florence. The guide also told us about how spectacular the interior is, but sadly I never made it inside. The damn budget constraints were such a drag.

Next, we re-entered the maze of narrow pedestrian streets of the historic city. We stopped in front of a rounded conical tower, three or four stories tall, with odd stone bricks poking out of it. Here we got a history lesson about these towers.

The Duomo completely dominated the modern skyline of Florence, but this was not always so. Back in the medieval era, there were at least one hundred and fifty big stone towers, hundreds of feet tall all over the city. The affluent families of Florence had owned these little mini-castles, and they would be used to launch violent attacks on one another. The higher they were, the more prosperous the family was. Dante came of age in this iteration of the city.

The stone bricks, which were poking out at seemingly random intervals, were put there to support wooden planks. Allies and families with multiple towers would connect their towers with wooden catwalks. Some of them would be hundreds of feet off the ground. The ground level would have been dark, dirty and nasty, and these catwalks allowed the wealthy to avoid such filth. Every once in a while, one wealthy family would succeed in demolishing a rivals' tower.

In the end, most of these towers were destroyed over the years by various causes. After the Medici took control of the city, they sought to limit the powers of other families. The surviving towers had to be knocked down to an appropriate height, lower than the Medici towers.

Of the few towers that survived the long Medici reign, a number were taken down in the 19th century, as the city modernized. More were destroyed during World War II. Now, only a tiny number of towers existed in recognizable form, although many buildings have parts of them in their foundations. It was captivating to stand there, in the shade of one of these towers and hear this story.

On our way past this lone remaining tower, we passed a food cart.

"Here you can buy a Tuscan specialty, a hamburger in a cow stomach," the guide said, gesturing to the dingy looking truck. I looked at it excitedly. Cow stomach? Now that's something I could get behind. We didn't have time to stop there now, so I marked it in my head for future use.

Unfortunately, I never did make it back to eat some cow stomach. Oftentimes, when traveling, if you don't seize the moment right away, you miss your chance forever. This cart was a good lesson for my future travels.

The cow stomach food truck was in a quiet little stone courtyard. There were lots of tiny plazas, narrow alleys, and odd little museums all over this town. Almost everywhere we had gone on this tour was eerily deserted. From the food truck, we walked one block over and were suddenly in a massive crowd of people. Rarely do cities offer such an extreme contrast. It seemed that all of Florence's tourists crammed into three or four places.

In the immense square ahead of us, I first spot a big bronze equestrian statue, turned green with age. Nothing too unusual there, so my eyes wandered ahead. There was a big ornate fountain beyond that. A towering naked figure made of white marble rose out of the middle of the fountain, flanked by smaller bronze satyrs at the base of it. The guide would explain this was a statue of Neptune, built in the late 16th century to show off the Florentine domination of the sea.

Beyond the fountain stood the famous square castle of Palazzo Vecchio, also known as the Signoria. The palace was impressively severe. It was not ornately gothic like other palaces but instead seemed to be more functional. The tan stone walls were perfectly smooth, with windows at even intervals. Above three perfectly symmetrical stories, stood the battlements. These jutted out a bit over the lower levels, but they were still crafted with perfect symmetry and proportion. There were arches where the battlements met the rest of the building, and under each one was painted the crest of some family. Above the classic medieval battlements stood a clock and watchtower, similarly designed and executed.

The Signoria was where the semi-democratic government once ruled from. Once the Medici's took over, it became their seat of power, although they cleverly kept up the façade of democracy for centuries. The guide pointed out they used to keep the torture chambers underneath it. Machiavelli was tortured there, leading him to write his famous book.

We worked our way through the crowds to the front of the Signoria. There was a copy of the Statue of David there, but we did not have to time to examine it. Our tour guide was behind schedule, so we quickly made our way out of the Piazza della Signoria and over a few more streets.

The tour ended in front of the Church of Santa Croce, another beautiful massive church from the height of Florentine power. White marble made up the façade and it was topped by statues of various saints. It overlooked a large stone square filled with vendor stalls. It was less gaudy than the Duomo but no less impressive. Near the top of the façade was a massive blue Star of David. It was jarring to see such an obviously Jewish symbol so prominently displayed on a Catholic church.

The tour guide explained that a Jewish architect designed the façade in the 19th century. As a Jewish person, burial within the church was forbidden. He would not rest alongside other famous Florentines like Michelangelo, Galileo, and Machiavelli. Instead, he was to be buried at the entrance of the church, underneath the stone steps we were now standing on, forever on the outside looking in.

To the left of the church, stood a larger than life statue of Dante. He wore a Roman crown of leaves, was propped up by fasces, the bundle of sticks used to show political power, and was flanked by a large eagle. Dante scowled out over the plaza, looking surprisingly angry.

The square itself was handsome, as it was large and inviting. Here, our last stop, the tour guide told us this was where soccer was invented.

"You will find that the size of this plaza is the same as a modern football field," he said, wrapping up his tour. I was highly skeptical of this claim. The English had told me that they invented soccer. This claim reminded me of the largest palace claim.

All in all, it had been a wonderful tour. The man was very knowledgeable. He had been quiet at times but had given us some of the most concise and illuminating histories I'd had heard. I tipped him well, and the group broke up. Chloe and I stayed behind, sitting on the stone steps of the church.

We had made vague and fuzzy plans to meet our other friends from England, Patrick, and Parker, at this spot. We had been in sporadic contact via Facebook for the last two days. We had made tentative plans to meet at this church around noon. They were working their way around Europe in a similar direction as us, although we had not been in the same cities at the same time yet.

We people watched as we sat beneath the statue of Dante. It was always interesting to see the flow of life in a place like this. Dirty kids begged for money, tourists bought postcards, and locals sold food and trinkets from their stalls. Watching the busy plaza hum with life was better than any TV show.

As we waited, we popped into a few stalls and stores around the perimeter of the piazza. I was surprised to find that you could buy an image of the pope stamped onto literally anything. Pictures of *Papa Francesco* emblazoned everything, from cups to lighters, phone cases, makeup cases, and even napkins. Italians love the Pope!

We poked around for an hour or so before leaving. Our plans with the boys were vague anyways, so we didn't feel bad about going.

Just when we ultimately decided to leave, we spotted a familiar figure walking across the square. She was wearing a long black skirt and a blue blouse. The dark sunglasses on her face were framed by her long brown hair. She looked like she was gliding gracefully across the stone plaza.

"How did you find us?" I ask Samie incredulously, as she came up to us.

Samie shrugged. "I knew where your tour started so I was just going to start furthest away from there and stop at all the landmarks. This was my first stop."

Sam looked up at the church. "Huh, a Star of David. That's weird. How was the tour?"

I was surprised Samantha had been able to find us in a city this big. I did not quite realize yet how compact the historic city center was.

"Did you meet up with your friend Rachel?" I asked. They had once been best friends back in their high school days.

Sam frowned. "It fell through. Rachel said she had a bad headache and we couldn't make it work. I might see her later." She sounded disappointed.

Samie, like myself, tends to take plans pretty seriously. I could tell she was upset she couldn't see her old friend.

"Oh hey, I brought lunch," Samie said, slinging her leather backpack off her shoulders. She was already putting her purchase from Toledo to good use. She set it down and pulled out three sandwiches and a couple of oranges.

Happy to have some free food we began to eat and start to give Samie a very abridged version of our tour. We told her about the Jewish architect, the soccer field, and some other tidbits. As we walked past Leonardo's house, we started to feel a few raindrops. The formerly clear blue sky grew suddenly gray and threatening.

As we approached the Piazza della Signoria again it suddenly began to downpour. Laughing, we ran for cover underneath some scaffolding. We were at the very corner of the Signoria, looking out over the piazza. The rain gathered in pools in the piazza and droplets of water ran down the muscular marble buttocks of the statue in front of us.

I stuck my hand out beyond the scaffolding to feel the rain. It was beautiful to see the streetlights come on and reflect in the puddles. This city, already too beautiful to describe, now looked even better.

When the rain let up for a moment, I ran across the narrow street to the Loggia dei Lanzi, a small open-air galley with a high arched ceiling. There were about a dozen statues in there, all based on classical mythology. Some were very old, but many were just replicas. Inside the gallery, I looked behind me to see the girls still under the scaffolding. They had not seen where I went.

Thinking quickly, I went over to the entrance of the gallery, where two marble lions stood on either side of the stone stairs. Next to each lion were columns which held up the roof. The space between the columns and the lions was maybe ten inches.

Not thinking too much, I put my hand on the back of one of the lions and hoisted myself up, holding onto the column with my other hand.

"Hey I'm over here," I called. The smooth marble was cold and damp underneath my hand. I wasn't on the lion for more than five seconds before a grandfatherly looking police officer started to blow his whistle at me.

He looked furious as he dramatically motioned me to get down. I slid off the lion as the officer waggled his finger at me. These lions were not replicas like I had assumed.

In fact, the lion I had pulled myself up on was over two thousand years old, dated before the birth of Jesus. It was probably made in the 2nd century BCE. I later learned it had been restored in the 16th century and had sat at this plaza since before the founding of the United States. Plus, it even has its own Wikipedia page ('Medici Lions' for the interested). It was definitely a mistake to sit on this statue.

Thoroughly chastised, the girls joined me in the open-air building. We admired the statues as we waited for the rain to break. I saw a heavy-set man with a big bushy white beard walk over to the side of the Loggia, holding a bag with a loaf of bread in it. He leaned heavily on a cane. He rested on the cane and leaned over the short wall. Two little Roma gypsy girls popped up, seemingly from beneath the wall.

"See I told you I would be here," the man said in a raspy, American accent. He lowered the loaf of bread down to their waiting hands. "Come back tomorrow at three for more," the man said.

The girls nodded. "Thank you, sir," they spoke with thick accents and vanished into the crowd. The man then sat on the low slung wall and turned back to face the statues.

"Hey look the rain's letting up," Chloe said, breaking my spying. "Samantha and I decided to get some food at that restaurant." She pointed her slender finger to one of the several restaurants on the piazza, opposite of the Signoria.

Taking advantage of a break in the rain, we dashed across the square, to where the restaurants were. We picked from them at random and were soon seated inside an attractive old brick building, full of fancy tablecloths and flowers.

We should have known better than to eat on the site of a hugely famous tourist attraction. The pasta we ordered was wholly unremarkable and overpriced. I'd eaten much better in much less spectacular places. The waiters placed bread on the table, which we, of course, did not touch in fear of being overcharged. Of all the places the bread scam might happen, it would be in a situation like this.

On the positive side, this place did have free and easily accessible wifi. By logging into Facebook, Chloe was able to coordinate plans with our friends Bill and Bailey. I had seen them briefly while we had checked into our Parisian hostel, but not since then. Chloe had gone to Disneyland with them, taking up most of their time there. They had recently arrived in Florence via Naples.

Chloe and I made plans to meet them at the Uffizi to go to dinner in a few hours. Sam would not be joining us. While we had been coordinating with Bill and Bailey, she had been able to reconnect with her Rachel. Rachel's headache had subsided, so they were making tentative plans to try to meet again for dinner.

We paid our bill and left this tourist trap. They gave us little pillow shaped mints, which was the best part of the meal. Being Americans, we left a tip on the table. Most guidebooks recommended five to ten percent, and we always tipped as much, even though this place hardly deserved it. Some habits die hard.

We were happy to see that the rain had fully stopped when we walked outside. The gray rain clouds had departed, and the bright blue sky was back in full view. Delighted with the weather we walked a few paces over to the Uffizi. We were enjoying how close all the sites were.

The initial view of the Uffizi wasn't anything too eye-catching. It was an ornate building, with a long walkway underneath gothic arches, but did not particularly stand out among the other buildings.

The start of the Uffizi blended in nicely with the Signoria right next to it. Every few arches had much thicker bases. Into these broader brick arches stood beautifully realistic statues of famous residents of Florence. The men were in natural poses, as if they might move a little bit right before your eyes. Machiavelli, Galileo, and Amerigo Vespucci gazed at us.

Chloe and I had a moment of laughter at Amerigo. This random guy somehow got two huge continents named after him. Amerigo, America. Our whole lives were so closely related to this man. The fact that he was just some Florentine schmuck was hilarious.

We thought about going in, as this is one of the most famous museums in the world. Unfortunately, it cost ten euros and had a two-hour wait. Our budget was so tight we could not justify spending the ten euros each.

Instead, we admired the street artists who set up easels all over the courtyard. They sat in front of the statues and were painting beautiful scenes of the city or Tuscan countryside. We went to each one, admiring them as the green Arno River flowed by in the background.

Like numberless people before us, we took a right at the riverbank, walking along a brick wall overlooking the river. Only a few short blocks later, we turned to the left to step onto an old stone bridge. It was relatively wide and full of shops and apartments. There was a mini-neighborhood built onto this bridge.

Most of the shops were high-end diamond and gold stores. This bridge, Pointe Vecchio, was hugely famous, but I did not know this at the time. Instead, I just enjoyed the oddity of seeing so many high-end shops placed on a bridge. I was smug. *What a dumb spot for these shops* I thought. Later I learned these shops were older than the United States.

We took a few pictures between the shops, enjoying a view similar to that Lorenzo Medici or Michelangelo had seen.

It was getting time for us to meet Bill and Bailey. Four hours had slipped by, and they had felt like seconds. Samie waved us goodbye and went back home to wait for Rachel to message her.

Chloe and I went back to the Uffizi. We saw Bill and Bailey standing in the courtyard. All of the artists had headed home for the day, leaving the area nearly empty. We greeted them and went to our restaurant, which was a few blocks to the northeast. The hotel owner had recommended this place, so we were hopeful it would be good. At least, I figured, it would probably be better than our lunch.

Sitting down in the restaruant, we quickly discovered nobody spoke English. They sat us at a tastefully sparse iron-wrought table, next to a yellow plaster wall with green leafy vines growing in pots suspended from the ceiling. When we opened the menus, we instantly discovered the pasta was dirt cheap. I noticed they are selling homemade wine and ordered a half-liter. It was only three euros. Chloe bought an additional quarter liter.

We offered our wine to Bill and Bailey, but they shook their heads and told us they weren't drinking that day. Not drinking today? Chloe and I shared a raised eyebrow. We now had to finish this homemade red wine between us.

We ordered, and the food soon arrived. The waiters placed humongous dishes of steaming pasta in front of us. I ate a delicious penne alfredo with cracked black pepper and fresh oregano. I ate warm bread drizzled with olive oil and drank deeply from my carafe of wine. The meal was incredibly good, and doubly so because it was so cheap.

I was satisfied in other ways. A primary goal of this entire trip was to eat a meal like this. I had pictured eating great food in an authentic Italian restaurant. After spending my entire childhood with the American version, here I was, at long last tasting the real thing. I was most shocked to find that the food tasted precisely as how my mother had made growing up.

As I shook some more parmesan cheese onto my noodles, I realized that this was probably the single best meal I'd had in my entire semester abroad so far. Chloe and I polished off our carafes of wine.

Bill and Bailey entertained us with their stories from Naples and Rome. They told us of crowded cities, majestic ruins and hustlers on every corner. They told us about eating takeaway pizza, and of viewing all of Naples from a secluded hill. I felt like I was in a dream, a feeling no doubt helped by the wine. We finished our fantastic meal and paid our absurdly cheap bill.

We stood up, and I felt a tipsy as we stumbled out of the door into the street. We saw Samie sitting across the road, waiting for us.

"Sam!" Chloe and I yelled as we walked over to hug her. "Dinner so good," we gushed. "It was so good!"

It felt so good to talk to her. I was so happy. I saw Chloe grinning like an idiot.

"And the wine was cheap" she and I cooed together.

"You guys are definitely drunk," Sam said bluntly. Chloe and I looked at each other in surprise, as if we hadn't known.

"Drunk?" Chloe said in an exaggerated voice as if Sam had accused her of something terrible.

"I'm not drunk," I said, slurring my words just a little.

Sam just laughed and shook her head. At our insistence, she took a photo of Chloe and I posing heroically in the street as the sun set behind us. Florence was too perfect.

My night got a little fuzzy as walked through the city at dusk. We crossed over a bridge to the opposite side of the river, wandering around with no location in mind. We passed so many gelato shops it soon became impossible not to visit one.

When I bit into some of the gelatgo, I sighed with pleasure. It was almost too tasty to handle. I knew it wasn't just because I was inebriated either.

Full of gelato, Bill and Bailey went on their way back to their hostel outside the city. We were glad our hotel was so close. Within a few minutes, we were back in our room with the high ceilings and marble tiled floor.

We were getting ready to spend the rest of the night hanging out in the room when Samie finally heard from Rachel. They had not been able to connect all day. Sam had been disappointed about it. Although it was late, ten thirty, Sam was instantly ready to see her.

"Can you please walk me over?" Sam asked me, with puppy eyes. "Please? She said we could bring our laundry."

I groaned and sighed and agreed to walk her over. I was so exhausted that the last thing I wanted to do was walk forty minutes round trip there and back.

Of course, I didn't have a choice, as I wasn't going to let Samie walk alone. We crossed the city to Rachel's apartment. We passed by the famous sights, totally empty of people this time. We reached her building, and before we even got to the entrance, a big heavy wooden door swung open. There stood Rachel, a short girl with long curly brown hair and a piercing stare. We introduced ourselves but I was too tired to offer much conversation.

Instead, I just greeted her and handed her my backpack full of dirty laundry. For the first time since England, we could have it washed in a machine, not in our sinks.

I left the old friends and went home, forcing myself to stay aware of my unfamiliar surroundings. I figured I wouldn't get mugged in the tourist section, but you never know. At one lonely street corner, I saw two men leaning on a light post.

"Marijuana?" they softly called to me, seeing if I was interested. I said nothing and kept walking.

I climbed back up the stairs, exhausted, and fell into my bed. I dozed off for a while until Chloe's phone rang a while later.

"You gotta go pick up Sam," Chloe murmured, barely awake herself. I climbed back down the stairs wearily and walked across the city, half asleep.

I saw the two men again as I passed their street corner a second time. "Cocaine?" they called out to me hopefully. I kept walking past.

I knocked on the big wooden door, and Samie popped out. She was bouncing with happiness.

"Thanks for coming babe," she said, kissing me on the lips. When Samie is happy, she is the happiest person you'll ever see. I was glad to see her pleased, and we went back home. I immediately passed out on the bed.

Florence, Day Eighteen: 14th of April

The morning came early as Chloe shook us awake.

"Come on you two, we have to go meet those guys at the Duomo in fifteen minutes!"

"What?" I groaned, pulling the pillow over my eyes as Chloe opened the shutters to let in the sun.

"Don't you remember? I made these plans last night on Facebook, with Bill, Bailey, Patrick, and Parker".

I had been so groggy when I had gotten back, I did not remember her telling me about these plans.

"Go without us," I groaned again. " I need to sleep."

"Sam?" Chloe asked hopefully.

Samie was silent as a corpse, face down with pillows over her head.

"Fine I'll go by myself," Chloe said, already dressed and heading for the door. When she got there, she turned back around. "Are you guys sure?" she hesitatingly asked.

"Chloe I'm sure, it's just a building," I said and squeezed my eyes shut.

And so, Samie and I slept in for two more hours, missing the views from the top of the Duomo and not seeing the renowned artwork inside. Sam and I only succeeded in sleeping in a handful of times on the whole trip. Usually, Chloe was pretty good in her efforts to rouse us.

Of course, Chloe was right. I missed my chance to see the Duomo, choosing to sleep instead. Traveling is all about compromise, and that morning I skipped beauty and culture for simpler, more earthly pleasures.

Samie and I eventually rolled out of bed, showered and dressed. Being able to relax was glorious. Heading out for the morning, we walked away from the city centre, eager to explore *Firenze*.

It was another beautiful day. The skies were clear, and the temperature was warm. We strolled down the streets, admiring the unique yellow-hued buildings of Florence. It was nice to have an unexpected day just for the two of us.

Not having had breakfast, we were intrigued when we walked past a public market, called Sant'Ambrogio. We went in, going past fruit and vegetable stalls set up outside underneath a metal awning. We bought some fresh apples and then went inside the big building to see the rest of the market.

It was a classic European farmers market. The produce was outside, while the interior held freshly butchered meats, sandwiches, and dry goods. We mimed what we wanted to buy because nobody spoke English. The prices were very low, especially compared with the more prominent tourist markets elsewhere in the city.

Between our gestures and our minuscule Italian (*bonjurno*, *gratzie*, etc.), we picked up some sandwiches and soda to go with our apples. I was standing in line to pay when from the corner of my eye, I saw a man walking up to me.

"Hey how's it going?" he asked, reaching out and shaking my hand before I could respond. He shook with both of his hands, enveloping my own. He spoke in the purest American accent.

"Look, brother," he said to me, putting his hand on my shoulder, "I need to get somewhere, I just need some money for bus fare and maybe a sandwich if you can spare it."

I couldn't believe it. There I was, in a non-touristy market in the middle of Florence, Italy, and I was being hustled by the same smooth motherfucker I ran into all the time in Cleveland, Chicago and Pittsburgh. How did this guy end up here? Maybe the domestic American markets were too saturated with bums already?

I shook my head and shrugged at him. I pretended not to speak English. To his credit, the man left me alone and turned to go after a couple that walked by, speaking with American accents. I was bemused. Oh, the things you will see.

Food in hand, we went over to the nearby Santa Croce, and ate our lunches on the steps of the church. We were pleased with ourselves for having a cultural experience in the market, and also for eating so cheap. So far the day boded well for my budget. After the pleasant lunch, we crossed a different bridge over the Arno, the Ponte alle Grazie. We admired the Pointe Vecchio from this new perspective.

The Germans in World War II had been ordered to destroy all the bridges over the Arno. The commander, who had once lived in Florence before the war, could not bring himself to destroy Pointe Vecchio. Instead, while he blew up the other historic bridges, he 'just' razed all the buildings on either side of Pointe Vecchio. Despite this heinous act, the commander successfully saved this famous bridge

On the south bank of the river, we explored a bit more of the outskirts of the historic city center. This side of the city was no less beautiful than the north bank. We soon found ourselves in front of the sprawling Palazzo Pitti, the ducal seat of the Medici. The palace was massive and handsomely constructed. We had heard the museum inside was well worth the entry fee, but we couldn't justify blowing our meager budget on it.

Instead, we kept walking and soaking up the city, enjoying the pace of life. Everybody was very well-dressed except us sloppy tourists. We browsed some high-end shops back on the north bank. One store sold all sorts of cool things like hand bound books, quills, old maps, and compasses. Sam and I both picked up some souvenirs here, as this is the exact kind of stuff we like.

At about this time, Samie had plans to go back to Rachel's apartment. They had planned this the previous night. I was thrilled to get my laundry back because I had not been wearing socks. Instead, I had worn flip-flops, the ones I typically used for hostel showers. They were not made for walking around a city, and my feet were bruised and dirty from that morning.

On our way to the apartment, located near Santa Maria Novella, we passed again through the Piazza della Signoria and past the Duomo. Florence was so incredible to see. It felt surreal, like a movie or a video game, to actually be here.

Rachel's apartment was up one of the empty side streets. We soon arrived. The entrance to the building was a big heavy wooden door, the kind you see in movies set in medieval eras.

It was surprising to see it grace the entrance of a random apartment block.

We had overestimated the time it would take to us to get here, and so had beat Rachel by a significant margin. Samie and I leaned back against the cool stone walls and admired the architecture around us. Each building, even the most average ones, would have been considered national treasures in the US. But in Florence, they were just apartments.

As we waited, I noticed a white girl with brown hair walking up the street. I had only met Rachel for the first time last night, so I didn't really know what she looked like.

"Is that Rachel?" I asked mostly in jest, as I was pretty sure it wasn't.

Samie discretely studied the woman as she came closer.

"Nah, that's not Rachel," she responded, settling back in against the wall. We thought nothing more as the woman approached us.

Suddenly, the girl stopped directly in front of us.

"Sam? Sam?" she hesitatingly asked as if she was unsure of whom Sam was.

Sam stared at the girl for half a second before it clicked.

"Sara?"

"Sam, what are you doing here?" the girl, Sara, asked, before breaking into a smile and hugging the both of us.

"I'm Sara," she told me, shaking my hand, "I went to high school with Sam."

"Oh," I say, not believing this was happening. "Are you living here with your other high school friend Rachel?"

"Rachel?" Sara turned to Sam. "Rachel from high school? She's living here too?"

"Yeah," Samie said, laughing, "you never ran into her?"

Sara shook her head. It was incredible. Of all the streets in all the cities in Europe, here we were, running into an old high school buddy of Sam's. It turned out Sara and Rachel had been living about five buildings apart from each other. Despite having gone to high school, they had not been best friends nor kept in contact throughout college. They had never run into each other here.

Sara asked us if we wanted to come to her apartment while we waited for Rachel. Sam could then hook up to the wifi and use her phone to contact her. The three of us walked up a few buildings to Sara's apartment.

Sara lived right off the ground floor. It was another beautiful old building, with an elegant interior and pleasing architecture. In America, they would never even let people live in a building like this. In Europe, nobody batted an eye.

It reminded me of an incident in England. We were eating on the second level of a Pizza Express, a sort of fancier Pizza Hut. The windows and floor were slightly askew and crooked, the distinct signs of a medieval building. The wooden walls were black with age, and a few threadbare tapestries hung behind plastic protectors.

When I asked the waiter how old the place was, he just shrugged and responded it was built in the 1400's and once Shakespeare had spent the night here. He then walked away, completely uncaring. This kind of thing is no big deal to Europeans.

We waited around in Sara's kitchen while she cooked some dinner. There was a little green courtyard visible through the window. There were a few cracks in the white plaster on the walls, making the building feel like its age.

Sara told us about her various adventures since she moved here. They were so similar to ours except they swapped out rainy England for sunny Tuscany, cold draft Guinness for homemade red wine, and fish and chips for fresh pasta.

"Oh, and yesterday I was in one of the cemeteries outside of the city, and I saw a bunch of men in suits speaking with American accents. I went up to them and found out they were

Republican congressmen touring the European cemeteries that held American graves from World War II."

"That's pretty crazy," I said, "what are the chances of that?"

Sara shrugged. "Sometimes you just run into people."

It was cool to hang out with Sara, and I still can't believe we accidentally ran into her in Florence. However, we were not over Sara's apartment very long before Rachel called Samie. We hugged Sara goodbye and went back down to Rachel's apartment.

Rachel greeted us at the door again, and this time I finally got to step inside. The foyer was incredible. It was all mosaic tiles and high-quality woodwork. While Sara's apartment felt a little run down, this one seemed like a palace untouched by time. If they hadn't run electricity into the building, you would think you were back in 1450.

We climbed a flight of stairs to Rachel's apartment. It was spacious and even had a little balcony overlooking the cityscape of Florence, although it faced away from the city center. We sat at a short wooden table and chatted.

I could tell Samie was so happy to be spending time with her old friend. Sam is probably the most loyal person to her friends that I've ever met. Although she isn't always good at staying in contact with people, rest assured she is always thinking about her friends and family.

However, our time was limited, and we had to meet up with other friends. Our time with Rachel and Sara had not been long, but it had been very satisfying. We thanked Rachel for the clean laundry she had neatly folded for us and then Sam hugged her goodbye. Rachel was getting married when she got back home and would soon settle into a domestic life marked by work and religion. Sam and her would drift further apart in life, but she would always recall these beautiful evenings in

Italy when it was just them hanging out under the mosaic tiled roof overlooking the skyline of Florence.

For now, though, we were concerned with meeting our friends for dinner. We were supposed to meet up with our friends from England, Patrick and Parker. They were travelling Europe with Jayjay, their friend from back home in Kansas. Jayjay was studying at Exeter, so we were all coming from the relatively same background.

Also joining us was Bill and Bailey again. I was excited to have such a big group together. We met up at the Piazza della Signoria. I easily spotted the group, as it was dusk and the tourist crowds were mostly gone. Chloe's flaming long red hair also made it rather easy to find the group.

"How's it going guys," I greeted them, shaking their hands. They introduced me to Jayjay, a skinny quick witted guy. The three friends were loud and boisterous together. They were some good ol' boys. Bill and Bailey hung out quietly on the periphery of our group as we headed to a restaurant the boys had chosen.

It was refreshing to talk to these guys as we walked. I enjoyed listening to their banter. I loved travelling with Sam and Chloe, of course, but I could only imagine how fun it would have been to tour Europe 'with the boys.' I missed my male friends from back home.

We soon reached the restaurant, a retrofitted a grand old palace. The inside was yellow plaster over brick walls, covered in green vines and reproductions of famous Italian paintings.

"How many?" the host asked us as we entered. When we told him eight, he disappeared for a few minutes.

"Right this way," he said when he got back and led us into a back room with a long wooden table. There were fifteen seats back here, so we had plenty of space to ourselves. We ordered some wine and looked over the menu as the waiters set down bread. Parker and Jayjay grabbed a few pieces and began to put olive oil on them.

"Wait wait wait!" Chloe and I yelled simultaneously. "What are you doing, don't you know they are going to charge us extra for eating those?!" We were both shocked they are eating the bread.

Parker shrugged his broad shoulders. "There are eight of us. Even if they do charge it's no big deal. We'll just split it".

Chloe and I looked at each other, dumbfounded. Just eat the bread? The boys were tearing into it. We had been traveling for weeks with this unreasonable fear of eating the bread. As we watched the boys eagerly devour it, I felt incredibly dumb. I could tell Samie and Chloe felt the same. We joined in. The bread was delicious.

We ordered our food and talked about our travels. The boys told fantastically cool stories about the Parisian catacombs and the papal palaces of Avignon. It was clear they were having the time of their lives.

Throughout our dinner, Bill and Bailey were mostly quiet. Bill went to school back home with these guys but was introspective and shy, especially compared to their extroversion. While the boys mused about good times in Kansas, Bill had nothing to add. As a gay man, I got the feeling he did not want to reminded of Kansas. Not here anyway, not while travelling through exotic Europe.

So, although the dinner was slightly awkward, I enjoyed talking to the Kansas crew. It felt good to not be the only male in the group for once. The pasta was fresh and flavorful when we got our food. We relished the experience, enjoying a great meal in *Firenze*.

For dessert, we went to the nightlife quarter, which was a bit past the famous old parts of town. The streets were buzzing with people going in and out of pastry shops. We saw people standing at coffee bars. We saw others eating cannolis and gelato and stopping into wine bars for a drink. The vibe on the streets was joyous.

We couldn't walk by all those cannoli shops and not get some. We stopped at one where the glass display case faced the street. The cannolis were large and coated in powdered sugar. They called out to me, and we couldn't help but buy one each. Patrick had never before had a cannoli.

"Is this how you eat it?" he asked, moving the piece toward his face as it if were a hotdog. When he bit into the pastry and tasted the sweet cream filling, and powdered sugar he knew had made the right decision. Of course, though, they weren't as good as my mother's.

We walked past the Duomo which was beautifully lit up against the night sky. I wish I had better descriptions to convey the grace and grandeur of this building. I fail to be able to write about it more eloquently.

We wandered through the rest of the city center, walking along the sidewalk above the Arno River. We crossed at Pointe Vecchio and again admired the two-story buildings perched on the bridge. Michelangelo and Lorenzo the Magnificent once strolled here.

On the south side of the river, we walked toward a hill that overlooked the city. We reached it, the Piazza Michelangelo, by climbing a series of endless stairs. It was a strenuous hike for me, tired from my miles of walking already. The stairs went on and on, past quiet houses and the occasional kids playing soccer in the streets. A stray cat followed us up the stairs for a while.

At the top we were rewarded with the city laid out below us. The entire skyline of Florence was lit up across the river. The Duomo dwarfed the rest of the buildings in the city.

The crew who had visited the church earlier were excited about comparing the viewpoints. They had climbed the big bell tower next to the church and seen this hill. I had been napping through that experience.

Conversation died as the eight of us looked over the city. The piazza was empty save for us. The night was calm and still and the lights of Florence twinkled beneath us. It was one of those eternal moments again, the kind you think will never end. While you stand there, you wonder if this is all even happening. How can life possibly be this incredible?

But, as always, the moment did have to end. It was getting cold, and we were worn out. The boys had a full day tomorrow, heading to Sardinia or Geneva or somewhere. We climbed back down the hill and crossed back over the magical Pointe Vecchio.

It was here, right past the famous bridge that we had to say goodbye. We were all going different directions. Although I had not spent a whole lot of time with these guys, it had been nice to hang out with them. It felt very familiar and comforting to hear these guys razzing on each other. I missed my group of friends back home.

We split up. Bill and Bailey were heading to Venice soon, so I knew it wouldn't be long until we saw them again. Parker and Patrick, well, I knew I would see them in Leicester. We weren't the best of friends, but I had enjoyed our time together. I knew I would probably never see them again when this was all over. Travel buddies are like this.

Ironically though, years later, Chloe would run into Patrick as they both were protesting Donald Trump's inauguration in Washington. I promise none of us ever would have predicted that meeting, in that circumstance, on this night in Florence.

Chloe, Samie and I walked back through the dark streets of the city. On the way, the tensions between Chloe and Samie blew up again. I don't know what set it off, but soon they were verbally attacking each other. This time I was able to hang back and not get involved.

It was always a delicate act to balance being a partner to Sam and a friend to Chloe. I could not always do both successfully, as my relationship with Sam often took first priority. Although I couldn't support her attacking my girlfriend, I could at least sympathize with her being the third wheel all day, every day.

We made it back to the hotel in one piece physically, if not emotionally. Samie and I headed right back out to allow Chloe some space. We hung out in the park by our hotel again. Samie was frustrated with the situation, but I was just happy she and I weren't fighting at the moment. For me at least, it was easy to separate our personal fights and the beauty around us. For me, it was easy to compartmentalize our disagreements into one mental box, and the awesomeness of each new day into another. I could easily fight one hour and be awed at some ancient church the next. Samie did not see it this way. For her, our time in Florence was soured by these two days of fights. When I later will speak of Florence in glowing tones, she will roll her eyes and tell me it wasn't that good.

Later that night we entered the room to find Chloe on her laptop skyping her partner. Later, we somehow ended up on some silly website doing personality tests. The three of us read out our results and all of us were described as being 'extremely disliking of direct conflict.' As we read the results out loud, an awkward feeling hung over us.

The results were ironic and true because of our fights were 'resolved' by us just pretending like it never happened. We never really dealt with any of the issues plaguing us this trip. We just acted like nothing had just happened. Exactly true to form, noby of commented the test results.

However, that second fight let off a lot of steam. For the rest of the trip, whenever tensions arose, they would never reach this point again.

We had a fun rest of our night in the hotel room. We watched a kids show in German on TV. If I understood the show correctly, they were explaining black holes and quantum physics to little children. Those Germans sure know how to have fun. Chloe and I discovered that our clothes cabinet was super big. We never hung up anything, so we had not noticed it prior.

"This is big enough to fit two people," I said to Chloe as we stood in front of this fancy cabinet. She looked at me with a raised eyebrow. I nodded. No words were needed. We both hopped in the cabinet and closed the door.

"Sam take our picture," we called out laughing, hiding inside the wooden cabinet. "Sam! Don't ignore us".

We opened the door to see Sam sighing exasperatedly. "You two are children together."

Chloe and I just laughed. Maybe we knew how to have fun better.

Sam and I ended up watching a few more episodes of *Game of Thrones* and went to bed, happy with our day.

Venice, Day Nineteen: 15th of April

We left the hotel at the tender time of seven thirty. We wanted to check out the Galleria Dell'Accademia to see the statue *David*. We couldn't leave Florence without seeing its most famous work of art.

We didn't have a firm time to leave because our railpasses would take us to our next stop, Venice, whenever we wanted. For once, we were in a city that ran direct trains once every hour or two to our next destination. We planned to see *David*, grab our stuff from the hotel, check out and then hit the road for Venice before noon or so.

On our way to Accademia, we crossed the quiet streets, laughing and joking. The ugly fights of the last two nights were finally receding behind us and we were loving each other's company.

We soon reached the museum to see a line already stretching around the block. The museum wasn't even open yet. I was glad we got here so early. Over the next two hours, the line would extend an absurd distance back.

It was a lovely time in line. It was quiet and peaceful as the sun rose over the city and the streets came alive around us. We browsed the tourist stalls cleverly set up next to the line and purchased some dumb souvenirs.

I stepped away from the line for a cappuccino. I went into a brick-and-mortar establishment instead of my usual roadside stall. I was the only person in the store except for the barista, a middle age Italian man with jet-black hair. The coffee was only two euros, but it took him several minutes to lovingly craft it. When he handed it to me, his eyes glistened with pride. I had a lot of coffee all over Europe, and this place had the single best cup of cappuccino I had. I admired how much work the Italians put into their coffee making.

After about two hours in line, we finally entered the museum and walked up the long hallway to where *David* stood. The statue was much bigger than I expected, over seventeen feet tall. It was astoundingly exquisite. I'd never much appreciated statues as a form of art, but *David* caused me to rethink this.

I had seen pictures, of course, but in real life I couldn't help but be in awe of the exceptional skill it had taken to create. Every single inch of the statue was perfectly carved, literally perfectly. I did not expect to be so blown away by the figure. In fact, that morning I had wanted to sleep in.

"It's just a dumb statue," I had groaned from the bed, "I've seen a million statues."

Standing in front of *David* I was glad they had dragged me along.

After *David*, which one sees immediately upon entering, the rest of the museum was surprisingly average. It didn't hold a lot of other pieces, just random pottery and some church art. We browsed for a little longer before deciding to go.

This was where we ran into trouble. We walked around, looking for an exit. We searched near the entrance, but it was one way only. We looked near *David* and by the ends of the other wings. There was nothing resembling an exit.

We crossed and recrossed the museum, looking in vain for a door or exit sign. We desperately needed to get out so we could grab our bags and check out before eleven. If we weren't back in time, they might charge us for another night. During our third lap around the museum, we began to panic.

And then we finally spied it. Hidden away in a room behind another room, tucked behind a tapestry, we finally found the exit sign. We ran out of the museum, feeling like we had just escaped Shawshank Prison. My last memory of *David* was jogging nervously past it, again and again, looking desperately for the exit.

Lucky for us, the city was compact, and we were back at our hotel in no time. We gathered up our stuff and checked out a hair before the eleven o'clock deadline. We thanked the lady profusely for her excellent recommendations and hit the streets of Florence one last time.

Backpacks on, we grabbed some lunch from the little local market Sam and I had found yesterday. We ate as we walked to the train station at Santa Maria Novella.

It was bittersweet to be leaving Florence. I had felt at home here. I pictured myself living in a little apartment, strolling past the Duomo with a coffee in hand, eating fresh pasta and drinking wine by the Arno. I saw myself dodging around tourists and exploring the beautiful sunny Tuscan countryside. Florence was the first city in Europe where I felt like I belonged, or as if I had just gotten back after being gone for a while. Florence, as it had for countless other people over its many centuries, had utterly seduced me.

As we passed the Duomo one last time, I snapped a few pictures. No photograph could catch the scale and grandeur of the church, but I tried anyways. I would love to make it back there one day.

The beautiful yellow buildings of Florence disappeared when we stepped into the train station. The interior of the station was pleasing, with brown and white marble floors and big opaque windows. The station was large enough not to feel crowded. As we got to the electronic ticket kiosk, we discussed potentially taking a short layover in Verona. There, Chloe informed us, we could see the famous balcony that inspired Romeo and Juliet. Bill and Bailey, also traveling to Venice today, had told her about it.

After a brief discussion, we decided to take the direct route. We got our seat numbers and boarded the train when it arrived a little while later.

We boarded the train, passes in hand and looked for our seats. Typically, the ticket people would know you were coming and put a little 'Reserved' sign on your assigned seat. All three seats were right next to each other, and as such, we did not expect the train to be very full. Usually, when it's full, all three seats are randomly spread out.

We walked over to our seat numbers, seeing that they were arranged around a little table with four seats. And, right in front of us, was an asshole kid sitting in Sam's seat, the sign reading 'Reserved' right over his head. He had blue eyes and a bushy red beard. I stared at him in irrational anger. *What the hell*, I thought, *this train is practically empty and this dude is sitting in the only clearly reserved seat.*

We took the three seats around him. I didn't know anything about this guy, as we did not speak, but his face generally annoyed me for the length of the ride.

Checking the route, I saw that there were two similarly named stops, Venezia Mestre and Venezia Santa Lucia. Train stations can be funny like this. Especially in big cities, it is not uncommon for there to be several stations in a row with very similar names.

Right behind us, I saw an unmistakably American couple sitting across from each other on a train. It was a man and a woman dressed like only middle-upper class Americans can, with pastel clothes, cargo shorts, Chaco sandals and baseball caps.

"Is this our stop?" the man asked his wife in a Midwestern accent. The stop in question was one of several with similar names.

"I'm not sure," the wife said nervously, looking around at the uncaring Europeans around her.

These guys must have recently arrived, I thought to myself.

"We need to decide," the man said, panic rising in his voice as the train slowed down. Like usual, the train would only stop for a few minutes.

"I'm not sure if this is the right one," the woman said, sitting half-up in her seat. Having memorized the route in advance, I suspected this was indeed their stop. I always wrote down the couple of stops before mine, so I would always know when we were getting close.

"You need to decide! Right now!" the husband barked at his wife, as the woman broke down underneath the pressure. She groaned in worry. "You gotta pick right now!" her husband demanded.

I leaned back in my seat and smiled as the couple stood up to grab their bags and sprint off the train. Shitty moments like this were all part of the fun. It seems so easy when you are sitting at home in the suburbs.

"Hey let's go to Europe and ride the trains around."

It sounds so romantic and exciting, but then you get here and see only a few things are written in English, and the Europeans could not give less of a shit about you. Nobody cares that you are lost and confused. Each city you come to is crammed with other tourists. Beneath every famous monument, there are men yelling at you, imploring you to buy their t-shirts or sunglasses.

In contrast to that couple, the three of us sat relaxed and comfortable as our station neared. As the train started to slow down, we stood up, grabbed our bags from the overhead compartments and put them on in a single fluid motion. We walked to the doors just as the train stopped and they swing open. With no effort, we sidestepped the people boarding and left the station.

We had long since settled into a very comfortable system of travelling. Every train journey had become routine, as we have adapted to traveling on the rails. These trains have become as comfortable as any hostel. We can sleep, write, eat or just watch the countryside speed by without a second thought. The three of us have adopted the European custom of being very quiet on the trains, enjoying the peace and silence instead of filling it with noise.

Despite becoming so at home with train travel, I never lost the excitement that it brings. Despite the downsides, there is a wonderful romance to traveling like this. I love seeing the rural countryside. I love passing through these tiny European villages and towns. I like when the ticket man looks at my pass and punches a hole in it. I enjoy the adventure of trying to find the bathrooms. I like the guy who rolls the coffee and snack cart. I never buy his chips or cookies because they are way too expensive, but I like him nonetheless.

I like boarding a train in a new country and seeing their style. The Italian and Spanish cars were sleek and modern, with four seats around a big table, while the French ones were two shallow benches and one tiny useless folding table. I love all these little details.

Now that our European adventure was half over, I was noticing another weird side effect. When we first moved to England, being immersed in the culture, we naturally picked up some English elements. All of the Americans I knew, including myself, had quickly picked up English slang and phrasing. In addition to such foreign words like *uni*, *wanker*, and *chunder*, we would often add that unnecessary 'then' at the end of sentences (as in "are you going to uni, then?"). We also gotten used to English manners, like being aloof and hyper-polite.

But, then we hit Amsterdam. On the very first day I was hit by culture shock all over again. The food, the money, and the languages were entirely different. Back in Ohio, I did not expect the night and day difference between England and the rest of the continent.

As we travelled, we found out that the rest of Europe had much more in common with each other than the English do with them. The English fancy themselves a race apart from the other Europeans, and we met very few English people throughout our trip. They don't seem to venture out from their dreary island very often, a sentiment voiced by several English folks back in Leicester. In fact, whenever I heard the English talk about 'Europeans' it was readily apparent they were not referring to themselves. When the Brexit vote occurred, over two years later, I was not surprised by the results.

All of this had the effect of washing away our acclimation to England. By the time we were riding towards Venice we had stopped using British slang and would no longer phrase our sentences as the English do. The rhythms of life in England seemed as distant as those in Ohio.

In fact, by the time our five weeks in Europe were over, we only would have two more weeks in England before returning home. When we did get back, we didn't have as hard a time readjusting as others who never left the U.K. did. We did not return with accents or anything like that because we had so long to revert to our regular, American, selves.

This was all in the future as we walked out of the station at Venezia Mestre. Following my handwritten directions, we found the bus that would take us right to our lodging. Although the instructions were a little unclear, we were not worried as we hopped on the bus. Not sure where or how much to pay, we showed a few euros to the driver. The bus driver just shrugged at us and motioned for us to take a seat.

Later, I will tell this story to a friend from Rome. She will laugh and explain to me that Italians don't pay for buses.

"If a ticket inspector gets on the bus, three-fourths of people will get off at the next stop," she will say to me in her throaty Italian accent.

The short twenty-minute bus ride took us out of an unremarkable urban center and into what felt like the countryside. There were only a few buildings here, and only light traffic on the road. The bus driver announced the next stop, Via Orlando, and we excitedly got off.

Not yet knowing quite how long the Via Orlando was, we stood dumbfounded as the bus pulled away. There was nothing here beyond a road, a traffic circle ahead and empty fields behind us. Across the two-lane road was a swanky looking hotel, no doubt the sole reason for the bus stop.

Having no other option, we walked to the swanky hotel. We walked past a few ponds and through sliding glass doors to enter the hotel. We could never afford something like this. At the immaculate desk, we found that the clerk spoke excellent English. I guess when you pay this much you get stellar service.

Fortunately, the guy was amiable and told us exactly how to get to our lodging. It was only another twenty minutes up the road by foot.

Thanking our savior, we trampled along the side of the lonely road, passing by small car dealerships, empty fields, and gas stations. It was classic exurban sprawl. We seemed to be far from Venice proper, in fact, we weren't even sure where Venice was in relation to us. But soon, across the street from an Aldi's, we saw the brown metal sign welcoming us to our lodging, Camping Rialto.

We walked up the short gravel road into the campground. It was awesome. On the left side there were rows of tiny one-room cabins. On the right side, there were rows of parked RV's, while in the middle sat neat rows of individual tents. Near where we stood, at the entrance, was a small wooden building which contained the reception, a restaurant and general store all rolled into one. You could check in, buy toilet paper, wine and order a burger at the same time. I never saw the employees leave their building.

We spoke with an older woman chain-smoking cigarettes. As we checked in, she explained that a bus would run into Venice each day every few hours. It was already late afternoon and we were too tired to catch another bus right now. Instead, we decided just to stay in the campground for the evening.

We went to stow our bags in our little cabin. The wooden cabin had a electric heater in the middle of the floor between two sets of bunk beds. Samie and I chose the two ground level bunks while Chloe went on top of Sam's bed. Samie couldn't stop a giant grin from spreading across her face. We were far out of the city for once, in a tiny cabin in a campground. She was right at home.

"This is so great," she said.

We walked back to the general store/restaurant area. Despite the number of RV's and tents, Camping Rialto was empty and quiet. Samie's enthusiasm for the campground grew. She was buzzing with happy energy.

The restaurant area had a few wooden picnic benches underneath a plastic tent awning. Beyond this were some smaller metal tables and big flowerpots. Young, small trees gave us cool shade. It was terrific to just relax and do nothing.

After a while, we saw Bill and Bailey walk by. We waved them over. We asked about the Verona balcony and found out it had been a big disappointment. Bill told us there was a huge crowd crammed into the small plaza. Beyond the balcony, there wasn't a whole lot else to see in that city.

The sun was going down and it became time for dinner. We ordered pizzas from the shop. The campground pizzas were pretty cheap and they had a lot of options. Samie noticed an option called potato pizza.

"This sounds good," she said as she went up to the counter to order. Not long after they brought out our food. In front of Sam, the young man set down a cheese pizza covered with random handfuls of French fries. We shared a laugh. At the time I assumed it was a cheap campground gimmick, but later on in Venice, I will see many advertisements for potato pizza. I guess this was a just Venetian thing.

To accompany dinner, we ordered some drinks from the shop. Instead of wine, as everybody else purchased, I bought a big bottle of Italian beer. I was interested in trying all the local variations of alcohol. I quickly discovered Italian beer was not nearly as good as Italian wine.

Leaving Chloe with Bill and Bailey, Samie and I went back to our cabin to start season two of *Game of Thrones*. Later, brushing my teeth in the dark next to the cabin, swigging from a bottle of water, I felt very content. I went to bed with a smile on my face.

A few hours into the night the three of us had a big surprise. Although the day and evening had been warm, the night was freezing. I woke up shaking from the cold. I pulled my clothes out of my back and wrapped them around me. I cranked up the tiny space heater, but it seemed to do nothing to the cold. It would too cold for me to go back to sleep. I shivered for hours in the cold dark.

Around five in the morning, Samie crawled wordlessly into my bunk. Our combined warmth mercifully let us both fall back asleep. As I mercifully drifted off, I saw Chloe's bed in the darkness. I felt terrible for her, freezing in her bunk, nobody to keep her warm.

Venice, Day Twenty: 16th of April

I got a few more hours of sleep before we went to get breakfast at the wooden hut. We didn't talk much, as we were fatigued from the sleepless night. Upon checking in yesterday we had all gotten a single free ticket for breakfast, and we all cashed it in. Bill and Bailey were already there, eating their free food.

We went to the counter and handed over our tickets. The young man accepted them and gestured us to sit. We joined Bill and Bailey and soon our food arrived.

It was a full breakfast of orange juice, coffee, toast, eggs, and bacon. Instead of crispy American bacon, or that hammy English bacon, the meat was prosciutto, paper thin and nearly raw. The meat was amazingly tasty, and our little feast was very satisfying.

Bellies full, we bought our bus tickets from the same building. We paid, not yet realizing only suckers pay for public transit in *Italia*.

The five of us crossed the street to the bus stop and patiently waited. When the bus came, we gave our tickets to the driver and claimed some seats near the back. Within a few minutes, we were on the causeway to Venice.

When I was a kid, my family would always go to Cedar Point each summer. Since the amusement park was on a peninsula, we had to enter via a narrow causeway with Lake Eire on both sides. Driving into Venice was a very similar feeling. Looking out of the window over the green sea, I could see why Venice was built here. It was an easily defensible location and natural harbor.

My excitement grew as the city came into view. I could see tan-colored brick buildings in the hazy distance. The bus slowed down and pulled into a parking lot near a train station. It was the end of the road for the cars, buses, and trains. There was no transportation on these islands except feet and boats. Vehicles cannot go further than this lot.

Once off the bus, we looked a map we got at the campground. Venice was literally the shape of a big fish. *Well, this looks dumb,* I thought, looking at the map. I had a hunch that the glorious and refined medieval Venetians had not built their city into the ridiculous shape of a fish. Later that evening I looked it up and immediately discovered that for most of history Venice had an ovular shape. The 'fins' on the west end of the city were added in the very modern era, in order to turn the oval into a fish.

We were entering near the mouth of the fish, which, paradoxically, is the 'back door' of Venice. The 'front door' was the opposite side, the side that faced the sea. For a thousand years, all visitors entered Venice from the sea, not the modern causeway.

We were short on time so we hurried into the city. We had booked a place on a free walking tour that departed in about twenty minutes. We glanced at the map and picked an accessible route to where the tour began. It seemed simple so we weren't concerned, having done this so many times in so many unfamiliar cities.

Leaving the parking lot, we crossed over a bridge made of frosted glass. From the apex of the bridge, I could see mysterious green domed churches and red-tiled roofs. On the other side of the bridge, we hurried along the street, pushing past heavy foot traffic to the plaza.

Upon first impression, I immediately noticed *Venezia* was like no other city I'd ever seen. Lanky brick buildings were crammed next to each other in front of desperately narrow cobblestone walkways. Often the walkways would veer suddenly from broad plazas into tiny alleys. Other times we will be forced to backtrack when our alley abruptly ended and a canal began. Sometimes the channels had tiny little bridges spanning them but other times not. Sometimes we could walk across the bridges, other times they were locked and inaccessible.

These canals ranged from just a couple of feet across, to the Grand Canal, which was huge and would be a challenge to swim across. The water in the canals varied from a bright baby blue to murky emerald green. The hue of the water was incredible.

The buildings looked weather-beaten and ancient, and all seemed to be in various states of decay. Many of the buildings only opened up to the canals and were not able to be accessed by foot. The canal-facing entrance was always the grand and fancy one, not the unobtrusive street-facing one. Everything was draped in ivy.

Because big open plazas were rare, they were surprising when we would stumble across them. Although the city was packed full of crowds in some areas, there was a strange calm and quiet from the lack of cars. Venice was not a loud city.

Given these navigation challenges, we barely made it to the starting point of the tour on time. We joined the small group and met our guide, a fiery young Venetian woman. She had been called in last minute because there were so many tourists waiting for the free tour. She was excited to show us her insider's view of the city.

"This tour will be about two hours, but we don't have to keep a strict schedule," she told us in a thick accent. Our group of twenty-odd people nodded. We wanted to see some cool stuff. We departed around nine-thirty.

Walking tours are great because they show you a lot of the city for cheap, and usually include excellent recommendations for food and drink. They also serve to orient you around significant landmarks.

Venice was not like that. We got the recommendations but orienting ourselves was utterly hopeless. Each magnificent alley, plaza, and church was terrific but looked so similar. We crossed from the north end of the city to the south, but none of us ever had a good idea of where we were. The streets were numerous and organic, and they had no order to them. One road would run gently into the next, and then the next street would just end and turn into a canal. If we backtracked, we would find ourselves in a new plaza in front of some old stone church, and not the area we just left from.

First, our tour took us to the old Jewish quarter of the city. We stopped in empty stone plazas surrounded by brick walls overgrown with green vines. The quarter had existed for hundreds of years and had even grown relatively prosperous despite the Jews being unable to leave it. The English word 'ghetto' comes from the Italian name of this place, *ghèto*. For a long time, Jewish people worked and lived here. However, in 1944, the Germans emptied it out, and most Jews did not return. Time and time again, we would find that the shadow of World War Two hung heavy over Europe, even all these years later.

A bit later, standing in a rare open plaza, the tour guide asked us if we want to continue the touristy tour, or go on her own 'native' tour.' Our group agreed the local tour would be better.

How wrong we were.

We ended up going down every little canal and tiny side street in the city. We would occasionally catch sight of a famous landmark only to be whisked away before we got too close. We passed by numerous restaurants and bars, all of which looked awesome and all of which looked, from the outside, nondescript. There was no way any of us was ever going to find these cool local spots again.

I learned a lot on the tour, like about how Venice was a series of islands, joined together by brick bridges. The individual islands were impossible to see from the street since they have been built up for hundreds of years. The water wells found everywhere indicated actual ground because people can't drink seawater. Elsewhere, it was possible the street was built directly over the lagoon water. The bricks were built on hundreds of layers of other bricks, all of which are progressively older the deeper they were.

Seeing the remote corners of the city was awesome. At times we would be entirely alone on these beautiful streets, except maybe for the odd old man playing chess or reading a book in the shade. The casual beauty of Venice cannot be overstated.

However, as the sun beat down on us we grew tired as the tour stretched past two hours. People began to slip away clandestinely from our group as we rounded corners, hoping the guide wouldn't see them.

We passed churches were indulgences were once sold. We stopped by a shop that had a mannequin dressed up as a plague doctor, complete with the black robes, a wide-brimmed black felt hat and that long wooden bird nose stuffed full of herbs to ward off the plague. Venice got the plague a lot, so these doctors were once a common sight.

We heard stories of hauntings stemming from murders that occurred hundreds of years ago. We saw fearsome stone faces carved into towers, placed there to scare off the Devil from climbing them and ringing the bells.

We passed apartment after apartment, all covered in vines and leaning drunkenly on each other because the soft sand could not hold buildings straight. We learned that the stone beams between buildings were keeping them from falling into each other.

Eventually, three hours in, we stopped for lunch at a café. It was the same one that Indiana Jones disturbed when he popped out of the sewer in the *Last Crusade*. I was exhausted from walking, and it was hard to enjoy this moment, although I was a huge fan of the film. We bought some sandwiches from the ancient-looking shop. We ate in silence, only breaking it only to discuss escaping the tour.

"Now's our chance," I hissed. "She isn't looking." Indeed, some of the remaining people used the lunch break to get the hell out. We felt too guilty to run off though because these guides work on tips and we didn't want to stiff her.

"Ok let's gather up," the guide called and we restarted our endless tour.

The tour continued down more alleys and canals. We passed a big marble building hosting an aquatic police department, the house of Christopher Columbus and the last remaining place that still built gondolas. The guide, only five feet tall, grew more energetic as the rest of us wilted in the sun. She strode down the sidewalks with us staggering behind her like troops defeated in battle.

At one point, she somehow segued into Italian politics and began to angrily denounce the government in Rome. She spit our venomous accusations against those bastards and advocated Venetian succession as the rest of us stood there with blank, tired faces.

At last, after several excruciating hours, our tour came to an end on the marble steps of Santa Marie della Salute. It was a beautifully decorated Baroque church in a neat square shape, with a big white dome on top. It sat directly on the Grand Canal on the south rim of the city. The view was beautiful, especially with the brilliant blue water of the canal right in front of us. Glad our tour was over, we handed our money over to the guide, and then Chloe, Bill, and Bailey went to sit down on the steps of the church.

About forty minutes prior, Sam had clutched my arm and told me she had desperately needed to pee. Being in Venice, or hell, being in Europe in general, there were no public bathrooms that we had passed. As soon as I handed the guide some euros, Samie and I fled down the Canal, desperate to find a bathroom.

"We'll meet up with you in a little bit" we yelled as the two of us sped off. Bill, Chloe, and Bailey stayed in front of the church as we dashed down the street we just came from. This part of the city was narrow, as we were between the Grand Canal on one side and the lagoon on the other side. The street we were running down was fairly wide for a Venetian street, with a few trees contained by iron boxes granting shade. This was a nifty innovation to allow living trees without having their roots disrupt the fragile pavement. By now, Sam was in physical pain from having to piss so badly.

We turned the corner out of the street to the boulevard that ran alongside the lagoon. As soon as we turned the corner, we heard a shout of surprise and saw three people running at us.

I couldn't believe my eyes as the figures came into view. It was three of our friends from Leicester! There was Jess, a gentle and sweet Australian girl studying law. Sam especially got along really well with Jess. Alongside her was Bogdan, a wiry American son of Ukrainian immigrants with a face that seemed to perpetually frown. Finishing off the trio was Mahala, a skinny artsy white girl who was fearsomely intelligent and had a reputation for sometimes being quite icy. Mahala and Bogdan had come to Europe as a long-term couple but had broken up a few weeks ago. They had already booked the trip across Europe before their breakup and had decided to stick with their original plans.

The three of them, alongside another friend not currently with them, were traveling the opposite direction around Europe as us. Of all the places the both of our groups went to, we ran into them here, a random street overlooking the Veneto lagoon. We weren't even near any of the big tourist sites.

Jess enveloped Sam in a hug. "It's so good to see you!"

"You too!" Samie exclaimed. My mind reeled from this coincidence. After just a few minutes, I saw Sam doing a little dance, obviously to curb the pain from her full bladder. It seemed that the three of these guys might want to hang out with the rest of the group.

"Hey stay right here Samie" I gently tugged at Sam's arm. "I am going to let those other guys know these guys are here." Seeing her head nod, I ran back up the alley to find my group of people. We hadn't made it very far, so I was back at the basilica in no time.

I looked at the stone square in front of the domed church. A few tourists were poking around. A few gondolas floated by in the Grand Canal. My group was nowhere to be seen.

No big deal, I thought, *they must have gone their own way.*

I sprinted back to Samie. As I got back, Bogdan, Mahala, and Jess were getting ready to leave. I came back just in time for a quick selfie, before Sam and I left to search for that elusive bathroom.

We strode up the walkways looking desperately for one. We passed over stone bridges, saw African migrants selling sunglasses and admired the beauty of the decaying buildings set against such bright blue water.

After what felt like forever, we finally found an expensive gelato place with a toilet. Since nobody in Europe let people pee for free, I had to pay an outrageous two euros and fifty cents for a can of soda. I had urged Sam to sneak past the counter, but she had refused to do so.

I sat on the edge of the walkway waiting for Sam, legs dangling over. We were on the north side of the city, so I faced the lagoon. There was another island across from me, and I could see beautiful Baroque churches and brick buildings on it. A few yachts lazily passed between the other island and me. I sipped my coke. The city was unreal.

Sam joined me and we sat for a while on the edge of the walkway, admiring the serene beauty of this place. We were in no hurry because I had told Sam the group had left without us. We strolled alongside the edge of the water leisurely, poking our heads into a few open doors. Some of the smaller churches were open to the public. The insides of those churches were dark and mysterious. It felt like we were exploring an ancient abandoned city, as there was hardly anybody around.

Quite by accident, we found ourselves sometime later back at the basilica where our tour had ended an hour ago. To my pleasant surprise, I saw Bill, Chloe, and Bailey standing in front of the church.

"Oh hey, guys" I said casually. "I see you came back."

They glared at me angrily. "We never left."

Oh. Whoops. I must have missed them when I ran back here. They had been waiting for us the whole time.

Eager to move on and let these guys forget this incident, we led them back up to where Sam and I had just been. Venice is a great city to wander aimlessly around in. No other city felt even remotely like it. Wandering through this magical, surreal city, they soon forgot that I had stranded them on the banks of the Grand Canal for an hour.

We wandered without a goal. The maps we carried were of little use. Something would look so clear on the map, but as soon as we were away from the Canal, it became hopelessly impossible to orient ourselves. As we got deeper into the city, we noticed the crowds, sparse in most parts of the city, grow significantly bigger. Turning another corner, we suddenly found ourselves at the foot of the magnificent and famous Basilica of Saint Mark on the San Marco Piazza. This was the center of life in Venice.

The Basilica is famous for its priceless artwork in the interior and the enormous delicate domes and decorative marble spires on the exterior. The church was easily the most recognizable landmark of Venice and one of the most beautiful buildings in the world.

Unfortunately for us, the vast majority of the exterior was hidden behind scaffolding and screens. As we stood there, looking up, the only art easily visible were the beautifully painted portals above the enormous doors. The church was Byzantine in style.

The only other artwork I could spot was something I had wanted to see ever since arriving in England months ago. Above the painted portals sat the glorious Horses of Saint Mark. These were four copper horses, poised as if they were in the middle of a race. They were built three or four hundred years before the birth of Jesus, most likely for a triumphal arch in Rome. Constantine the Great had them moved to Constantinople, his new Christian capital, around six hundred years later. There they sat until the Venetians sacked and looted Constantinople during the Fourth Crusade in 1204 when they were installed at this church. They have been here ever since, except for a brief period when Napoleon took them to Paris. The history these statues have seen was incredible to contemplate. I wish I could have seen them up close, but the church cost too much for our budgets.

To the right of the church stood the architectural marvel of the Doge's palace. Before my eyes could explore the wonder, they got caught on something red, near eye-level. The church and the palace shared a common wall, and both were built of gray and white stones. This red colored stone stuck out like a sore thumb.

I stepped closer, pushing through the crushing crowd. My jaw dropped. Not but a few feet in front of me stood the *Portrait of the Four Tetrarchs*. I immediately recognized the dull red stone carvings, carved in a proto-medieval style. Four kings with crowns, capes, and chainmail, their hands on the hilts of their sheathed swords, clutched each other in a gesture of solidarity.

The crowd of people walked by the carving, uncaring and unaware that these statues were carved when the Rome Empire was split into four sections, two in the east and two in the west. Each section had its own emperor, one senior *Augusti,* and two junior *Caesars*. Emperor Diocletian instituted this system to better administer the vast Roman Empire. However, the system was inherently unstable and soon collapsed into civil war, ending only when Constantine the Great was able to reunite it under his sole rule. This laid down the foundations for another thousand years of Roman rule in the east and for a long decline and collapse in the west. This statue, now in front of me, represented the end of the Western Roman Empire, the birth of the Middle Ages, and the formation of Europe as we know it. I couldn't believe my eyes, and nobody around me cared.

Realizing I could touch the statues, I reached out my hand only to stop an inch away. I was almost afraid. It felt wrong and somehow sacrilegious. I gingerly touched the foot of one of the four kings. The smooth stone was warm from the sun, and I felt seventeen centuries fall away before me. I felt like the world was rushing around me and like time was slipping back and forth. I pulled my hand off it, in awe of what these statues had witnessed during those long centuries. It was for me, a truly amazing experience.

Next to the church and the Tetrarchs, was the Palazzo Ducale, the Doge's Palace. It was a long rectangular building, supported by symmetrical white arches over two floors. One could walk under them on the ground level without paying to enter. Above the center of the building, facing out over the square, was a small white balcony where the Doge would make announcements and give speeches to the Venetians. I had now seen several such premodern balconies. I always expected them to be grand and imposing and yet they were always shallow and narrow. This one only jutted out about two or three feet.

My description of the palace does not reflect the sublime architecture and beauty of the building. Although we usually wouldn't pay to enter these places I knew I had to get inside this one.

For now, however, we walked to the end of San Marco Piazza, to where the mossy stone steps descended right into the bright blue waters of the lagoon. This was the actual 'front door' of Venice. This is where most people coming to Venice for most of history had landed. On either side of us were two simple stone pillars, one topped with a statue of St Theodore and the other with the Winged Lion, both symbols of the city. That bad boy Napoleon had also looted the lion and displayed it for a while in front of the Hotel des les Invalids I had been at several weeks ago.

Sam, Chloe and I sat down on the mossy steps, the water lapping only a few steps below us. It was from these very steps that the Venetians had rowed out from and conquered the Mediterranean. The lagoon in front of us was busy with various boats sailing back and forth. Venice has had a thousand years of commerce and it is still going strong today.

It was a bit past midday and was quite sunny, especially with the sun reflecting off the water. Samie wrapped her black scarf around her head.

"What are you doing?" Chloe and I asked, laughing.

"Don't laugh at me," Samie said defensibly. "It's so bright, you know I'm sensitive to light."

Tiring of the crowds on the San Marco Piazza, we walked northeast, following the edge of the island city. We wandered until we ended up in front of the Arsenale. This was a naval military base surrounded by high brick walls impossible to see over. The Arsenale was the historic center of Venetian military power, from whence their galleys and navy was kept. Between the imposing walls was a canal flanked by watchtowers. Massive stone lions guarded the closed pedestrian doors. It was still an active Italian naval base, and we could not enter.

We continued to wander even further to the west, towards the very end of Venice, the 'fins' on the fish. There were no tourists there, just empty stone courtyards with uneven grounds and tall crumbling apartments.

On our tour, we had learned that the European Union controlled the rent in Venice. Unless you are fabulously wealthy you cannot buy a home here. Venice is considered a European heritage site. Riches aside, the only other way to live here is to be born into a real Venetian family, with deep roots set into the city.

While each alley, canal and brick building was beautiful and picturesque, we didn't want to wander any further and get lost. We wound our way back the San Marco Piazza to gape at the palace, the beckoning sea, and the bits of amazing artwork that seemed to be everywhere.

We had just rounded the corner of the Doge's Palace when we heard another shout and once again saw a small group of people run to us.

"Ok," Mahala said hugging us again, "this is a small city, that's it." Accompanying them this time was my good friend Phil.

Phil was another mutual friend from Leicester. I had got to know him from a few trips we had taken together. Phil was a photography nut in law school. Like Jess, he hailed from Australia and had a thick Aussie accent. He was a bit eccentric but in the best possible way. We had wanted to Phil to join our little crew around Europe, but it had not shaken out that way.

"It's good to see you guys," he said us with a big grin on his face. He had been staying in a separate hostel from the rest of the group and told us about how he had spent the morning with a bunch of 'obnoxious Americans.'

"They were every stereotype you picture Americans being," Phil told me laughing. Phil had floated down the canals of Venice in a gondola with a bunch of American frat bros. I had to laugh. Of all people, Phil would be the one to end up in a situation like that.

Bogdan, Mahala, Jess, and Phil were on their way back to their hostel for dinner, so we walked with them for a while. The seven of us headed through the San Marco Piazza towards the Rialto Bridge. As we wove in and out of the groups of tourists, Phil told me how happy he was that we ran into them. He quietly told me how their group was being torn apart by intragroup tensions and fights.

I felt a little better knowing other groups were going through the same stresses we were. If anything, it seemed that their group had it worse than us. I couldn't imagine how Chloe would feel if Sam and I were doing this trip as exes. Up ahead I saw Samie deep in discussion with Jess, probably talking about the same thing.

It was great seeing these guys again, if only for a brief time. My happiness was magnified by the fact that this encounter had been entirely random. We didn't even know they were going to be in Venice.

We arrived at the Rialto Bridge, a massive stone and marble arch over the Grand Canal. This was the historic crossing point between the two halves of the city. The street ahead of both sides of the bridge was thick with food stalls and tourist shops and thronged with people. We stepped on the bridge, also loaded down with shops and people. The views weren't as good as they might have been, but we had to take pictures and pose like everybody else around us.

We bid goodbye to our friends on top of the bridge, amid a crush of tourists, all trying to crane their necks over the Canal, and perhaps spit on a passing gondolier. As I shook Phil's hand, I felt a great sense of sadness come over me. I wasn't sad because I was saying bye now, but because I knew in a few weeks, we'd be saying goodbye permanently.

As we crossed back over Canal, I slapped my forehead in surprise. We are staying at Camping Rialto, and right then we were near the Campo Rialto. The name of our campground was a clever pun. Ha!

It was getting to be dinnertime for us too, and we had made plans to meet back with Bill and Bailey at the San Marco Piazza. Meeting them there, we decided to go to one of the restaurants recommended on our walking tour. Cantina du Spade was the name, and it had been open since the Middle Ages. It was located only five minutes from the Rialto Bridge. Our stomachs rumbling, we confidently walked down the streets of Venice. A five-minute walk would not be an issue.

Once again, we were sorely mistaken. This five-minute walk soon stretched on and on. We turned down countless streets and crossed over dozens of little canals. We would turn down a street, sure it was the one we needed, only to find it emptied back out onto the Grand Canal. Or, the street would just turn into water abruptly, or maybe it would just dead-end into a solid brick wall. We would leave one little square, complete with a cistern and old medieval church and then walk for twenty minutes and find ourselves back in the same plaza. It was like a Scooby-Doo episode.

I had a picture of the restaurant in my camera, and we tried to figure out its location by the buildings around it. Unfortunately, every building and alley in this damn city looked alike. We would come across ancient bookstores and tiny shops selling the most splendid masks I'd ever seen. We passed alleys with shiny padlocks over rusting metal grates. We would gather in one street and split up in different directions, inevitably losing somebody in the process. We would then have to split up again just to find the lost person.

It was about at this time I realized *Veniza* was a maze that outsiders have no chance in. I felt like I was in a movie where the maze keeps shifting and changing with each step. Every so often, on the sides of buildings, there were written instructions, with arrows pointing towards 'Per. Rialto' or 'S. Marco'. How people navigated before those signs were installed, I have no idea.

"I know it's here" I insisted to the group. "This looks really familiar, and I think it's just around this corner."

Inevitably, I faced revolt. The group was exhausted from the burning sunlight reflected by the water and this wild goose chase that was taking us nowhere. We settled on the next restaurant we walked by. Not even glancing at the menu, we walked in.

The restaurant, although not the one I had wanted, turned out to be not so bad. Even the prices were only slightly over the top. We drank spritz, a traditional Venetian drink of wine, tonic, and amaretto. For such an odd cocktail, it was surprisingly easy to drink and quite refreshing. My seafood pasta dish tasted fresh and filling and I was happy.

Sam's meal was less stellar. She bit into an entire eggshell that was mixed into her carbonara pasta. When she showed it to the waiter, he just shrugged. In Europe, the customer is never right.

It was time to go home to our cabin after eating. We had walked many miles today and had eaten very little. We joined the actual exodus of other tourists heading towards the city's only parking lot.

As we got closer to the west end of the city, the signs on the buildings now read '*Uscita*' and in smaller letters 'Exit'. Venice literally had exit signs. Even though the exit of the city was clearly marked like this, it didn't mean some tourists weren't confused. We would see people spilling out of alleys and side streets, confused and frustrated as they held their maps up to the dying light of the setting sun. The locals, as a rule, do not help lost tourists

For once in this crazy city, we found our bus with no problem. We stepped on, bodies aching with every step, and flashed our ticket at the uncaring driver. As the bus powered down the darkened causeway I snapped a picture of the girls sitting with Bill and Bailey, slumped over exhaustedly.

The bus dropped us off right in front of the campground. Samie and I watched two more episodes of *Game of Thrones*, before wrapping ourselves in seemingly all of our clothes. Poor Chloe resorted to putting socks on her hands. We were determined to beat the cold tonight.

At five the morning, unable to sleep, I climbed into Samie's bunk, desperate to get warm.

Venice, Day Twenty-One: 17th of April

There was dew on the grass as we walked to the breakfast hut to meet Bill and Bailey. The air was cool damp. It was the kind of morning that is refreshing to wake up to. Having squandered our breakfast tickets yesterday, we ate cheap cereal bars and nursed small coffees. Lorde's new single 'White Teeth Teens' played on a TV hung on the wall near the tables

Near the end of our meal, a woman came up to us and asked if we wanted some celery.

"Sure," we replied after looking at each other, unsure of what to expect. The woman smiled and pulled out a ridiculously big piece of celery. It was the size of my forearm, with big green leaves coming off the top.

Getting on with our day, we crossed the street to the lonely bus stop. It was a single wooden bench. Next to us, seated on the bench, was a Nordic young man reading a *Game of Thrones* paperback. I had been resisting this show and book series for years, and now that I had delved in, I saw it everywhere. This shit was really blowing up.

We hopped on the bus when it arrived. We had discussed not paying for the ticket, but Chloe and I had been too nervous. Sam had no problem being a stowaway and calmly walked onto the bus sans ticket. It couldn't have been easier.

We rode into the city, the bus quieter than yesterday. The sun was rising over the lagoon as we pulled into the parking lot. We didn't have much of a plan for the day, so we began to meander our way into the city, stopping at all sorts of tourist shops along the way.

At one open-air market, I stepped close to inspect a hoodie. The logo, some Italian symbol, had intrigued me. It cost twenty euros, but I did not want to buy it, I just wanted to see what the logo was.

As I stepped away to leave the stall, a big Arab man came after me. "My friend, wait! Fifteen euros! For you, fifteen euros!"

I kept walking, having no interest.

"My friend, thirteen euros! Ten euros! My friend!"

I kept walking away. I was laughing to myself. My accidental haggling skills were unparalleled.

Continuing, we stepped into several little shops set inside ancient brick buildings in tiny alleys. At one point we spilled out from a three-foot wide alley onto a big street, wide enough for four people abreast. To our right was a rusty iron fence covered in thick ivy. The ivy climbed up the small building, covering almost all the fading white plaster on the walls. In the small courtyard of the building was a table with stacks of old books.

Our curiosity piqued, we entered the store. It was dark, with all the light coming from two or three small dirty windows. There were hundreds of stacks of books haphazardly piled everywhere, in no order. A thick, musty smell hung over us, as all these books were antiques. Most were at least a hundred years old.

It was great. We browsed the old books, a fair number of which were in English. They covered all kinds of arcane topics and were arranged without order. We saw old globes and tattered maps. If our trip were a movie, it would be here that we would discover some lost Venetian treasure map or some magic Egyptian scroll. We didn't buy anything, but it was a remarkable moment that stood out in a city full of wonder.

The hours slipped by pleasantly. For lunch, we sat in the shade of a church steeple, in a stone courtyard near a cistern and a canal. A few trees grew in their iron boxes nearby. And naturally, in Venice, that could describe anywhere in the whole city.

We ate Nutella and orange slices. Across the canal was a pretty ornamental church with no apparent sidewalks or bridges, instead just a few little docks for small boats.

Seeing the docks made me muse on something the tour guide had told us yesterday. She had spilled the beans on gondoliers. In Venice, gondolas are an outdated, inefficient means of transportation. They ceased being useful, or profitable, decades or perhaps centuries ago. They were a persevered relic for the amusement of tourists. In fact, if not for EU subsidies, there would be no way for any of these boats to stay in business.

Being a gondolier is a hard and thankless task. Every gondolier I saw looked rough around the edges. I wouldn't want to run into these guys at a bar in any country. The rides themselves were extremely costly, certainly nothing we could afford. The cheap option was to take a gondola across the Grand Canal. Only lasting five minutes or so, the ride cost three euros and was the best way to experience gondolas for cheap.

It was around one o'clock when we made it to the San Marco Piazza. We admired the brick bellower, the Campanile di San Marco, that rose high over the square. The line to see the view was far longer than we were willing to wait.

Instead, we walked underneath the beautiful symmetrical arches of the Doge's Palace. We turned the corner to where the Palace faced the lagoon. There was a modest, unobtrusive entrance. The Doge would have been able to stroll out of the door and directly onto a boat. The ships would sail, from these very stairs to Greece, Constantinople, Egypt and the Kingdom of Jerusalem.

The sign above the entrance only read 'Palazzo Ducale.' There were no tourists in line. We walked in and went immediately to the little wooden both. We simply paid and walked into the interior courtyard of the palace.

Venice never had much space to build, so Venetian architecture tends to be narrow, tall and very ornate. Despite the physical limitations, or perhaps because of them, the palace rose triumphantly around us. It was all airy Gothic arches, brilliant marble and big glass windows cut out of the walls. Behind an impressive colonnade and classically inspired statues, we could see the stained glass and onion domes of the Basilica next door. I was left gaping at the architecture.

The ground floor of the Doge's Palace mainly held archaeological remnants of the earlier palaces. The recovered columns down here were over a thousand years old. Like most historic buildings this one had been ravaged by fire several times, so while it had been occupied since the 9th century, the current form reflected the 14th.

Like a lot of older buildings, the doorways on the ground floor were comically small. I had to stoop way down to pass through them. Even the very wealthy, the very elite of Venice did not eat nearly as good or as balanced a diet as we do now.

To get to the next level, we had to walk up the grandest staircase imaginable. The stone was polished marble, while the walls and ceilings were covered in frescos and set in gilded frames. The words ethereal and heavenly came to mind. The few people ahead and behind us walked in silence, in awe at the beauty and craftsmanship overhead.

We passed through the apartments were the Doges had lived. Venice had a strange quasi-democratic system of governance. The Doge was elected by and from one of the few patrician families. Once elected, the Doge was constantly under surveillance as the families worried that he might seek to seize total power. Given the patterns of history, this fear was not unfounded. So, while the ducal apartments were magnificent and splendid, they must have seemed like a prison at the same time.

Chloe and I had a great time taking pictures with anything related to Enrico Dandolo. In addition to sacking Constantinople and permanently crippling the Roman Empire, Enrico is a playable character in the video game *Civilization*. Chloe and I were both fans of the game in general and of Enrico specifically.

We also kept laughing at the ridiculous Doge hat. Each Doge had to wear a special hat once they assumed power. It was very traditional and a huge deal. The cap in question sort of resembled a misshapen red Santa Claus cap without the white tassel at the tip. Although a symbol of power, it had the effect of making each stiff ducal portrait look rather silly.

As we passed through giant room after room, each one was more impressive than the last. Each room had more beautiful paintings and was trimmed in ever more gold. Venice had been the wealthiest city in Europe for hundreds of years.

Passing through several rooms like this, we entered the Chamber of the Great Council, or the throne room. The informative plaques told me this was the biggest throne room in Europe, and for once I believed it. The room was cavernous and empty aside from the thrones on the far wall of the room. The floors were brown-flecked marble, and the few seats built into the walls were of dark mahogany.

The seats on the far wall were where the council and Doge would sit. The thrones, although also made of high-quality wood and trimmed in gold, were surprisingly plain. The doge's throne sat just a bit higher than the other seats, and all were carved directly into the wall.

Behind the thrones was a spectacular humongous painting with hundreds of figures in robes looking at an ascendant Jesus Christ. The Christ was unsubtly directly behind the Doge, meaning the painted figures, and your eyes, were naturally drawn to his seat. Every inch of the ceiling and wall was likewise decorated with stunning beautiful paintings. Dark colors like black, red and gold dominated the room giving it a solemn air. From the windows, one could peer into the courtyard, or across the San Marco square.

I could easily imagine entering here and having to walk across the massive room to the waiting Doge and his council. It must have been overwhelming. Even empty, it radiated power and splendor. I could physically feel the past here, to the time when the Doge ruled Venice and Venice ruled the world.

Next, we saw a few more spectacular rooms, including a massive cartography room. Maps were a considerable source of Venetian power and were kept strictly secret. From these maps, Venezia dominated trade routes and plundered cities. There were massive eight-foot globes that were hundreds of years old. There were huge unrolled canvas maps with incredible levels of detail. As map enthusiasts, Sam and I delighted in looking at the old maps and their glory.

To wind down the tour, us tourists were funneled into a few more rooms, where Turkish armor and weapons were displayed. Usually, such as in Cleveland, these items are donated from collectors or purchased in auctions. But, these weapons in front of us now had been captured in battle and never left Venice. The distinction was subtle but a reminder that men had died wearing these suits and carrying these pikes.

Near the back end of the palace, there were windows cut out of the stone walls. They had no glass. I could lean out of these windows and gaze over picturesque brown Venetian rooftops and clear blue skies. Across the room, from another window, I could see nothing but the bright aqua green water and distant islands hosting more churches and forts. The blue-green water of the lagoon was passive, with boats zooming back and forth under the clear sky. A gentle and refreshing breeze rolled through the open window while I looked out of it.

The Venetians had called their empire the *Serenissima Repubblica*, or the Most Serene Republic. I felt serene, totally at peace as I beheld everything from this window in the palace. It was one of the brightest highlights of my whole trip.

We walked down the marble staircase that took us back to the interior courtyard. We took a few last photos and exited the palace. We took one more look across the lagoon, at the

Basilica, the bell tower and the old administrative buildings of the empire. We left San Marco piazza for the last time.

We had made plans that morning with Bill and Bailey to meet at Pointe Rialto for dinner. On the way, we stopped into a cannoli shop for a mid-afternoon snack. We ate a lot of cannoli's in Italy and none were ever disappointing. We enjoyed our slow walk over to the bridge, taking in the exotic city around us.

We spotted Bill and Bailey standing near the base of the bridge. We fought our way down to them and headed off to dinner. Where did we head? The same place we couldn't find yesterday.

I had looked up the maps at our cabin and saw how close the restaurant was to the bridge. I was confident we could find it this time.

I should not have been so confident. The next two hours passed in a frustrated jumbled mess. Just like yesterday, we would get close, only to wind up in a square we just left. Bill even asked directions in his broken Italian to an old dignified looking gentleman. He just shrugged and turned his back to us; annoyed we had dared bother him at all.

Once we returned to the same nondescript square for the third time, with the rest of the group staring daggers at me, I gave up. I chalked it up as a mystery of Venice. Earlier, I had seen a shirt displayed in the window of some tiny shop in a darkened alley. It was a black shirt with a complex white maze screened onto it. Below the maze was written, simply, the word *Venezia*.

I should have bought it.

We gave up our search amidst the winding alleys and dead-end streets and ate at the first tourist trap we found. Although the restaurant looked posh, with couches instead of seats, the food was subpar. At least Samie didn't find an eggshell in her food this time.

We said goodbye to Bill and Bailey after dinner, as they were heading back. The girls and I weren't quite ready to leave yet, so we walked around the city until well past nightfall.

We admired the decaying brick buildings lit by the rays of the setting sun. We stopped into a few mask shops. These masks were well made and expensive. They were big heavy ornate objects, covered in feathers and stage jewels. Most managed to look refined and elegant and not the least bit gaudy. Venice was famous for its masks and wild parties of *Carnivale*. Given the whole mysterious, sexy and otherworldly vibe of the city, I was not surprised to learn this.

When we came across a sweets shop, we were amazed to see the whole storefront piled with mountains of delicious desserts. There were cookies, cannolis, licorice rolls, cupcakes and more. We bought yet more cannolis and a bit of tiramisu.

Soon it was properly nighttime. I was surprised that, unlike most cities, Venice didn't look very pretty in the dark. There weren't many lights, and the black canal waters seemed to be invisible. Frankly, there was not much to look at.

We knew it was time to head back, so we decided to bite the bullet and buy a gondola across the Grand Canal. The Canal itself was a bit better to see at night, as both sides of it had restaurants lit up by streetlights. They looked like twinkling Christmas lights as they reflected on the water.

We approached one of the tough looking men wearing the striped shirt of a gondolier. He briskly told us he was closed as we got nearer to him. We had missed closing time by only a few minutes.

We consoled ourselves by returning to the Rialto Bridge, now much less populated. It was fairly quiet and calm as we stood on the famous bridge and looked over the peaceful canal.

All good times must end, and it was our time to leave Venice. We took the long walk back to the parking lot. It was too dark to appreciate the buildings, but down one street we passed an old man in an elegant suit playing moving music from a violin. He had no hat or case open to accept money and did not seem to be advertising for a hotel or restaurant. Belly full of cannoli and pasta, standing by a Venetian canal hearing violin music, I was touched by the moment. It was exactly what I had wanted out of Italy.

We got back to the campsite after getting on the bus without paying. Chloe and I had finally gotten up our nerve to do so. It felt good to join in with the locals for this little tradition.

At the campsite, we saw Bill and Bailey having a drink at the food hut. Not wanting them to drink alone, Chloe and I ran across the street to pick up some booze from Aldi's. We grabbed a bottle of wine, a bottle of spritz and a bottle of limoncello.

Limoncello is a traditional Italian liquor made from lemons. I read later that this can be a high end, fancy drink. What we had was the bottom of the bottom shelf. It tasted like lemon-flavored cleaning fluid. The others refused to drink it, opting for the wine and spritz instead. Not wanting to carry the bottle with us, Chloe and I took shots of it until the bottle was empty.

The night became a fuzzy blur of me going into the store to buy snacks and more beer. Behind the counter was a young man, the son of the owners. He was impressed with my choice of limoncello.

"It is very Italian," he said approvingly. "It's the only thing I drink."

Before I realized it, I was drunk. Chloe and I took one too many shots of limoncello. I said goodnight to Bill and Bailey and wished them luck on the rest of their adventures. The three of us were going to be on our own for the rest of the trip.

I drunkenly stumbled around the dark campground, happy to be here on our fantastic journey. I had been very pleased with the Italian leg of our trip. The campground had been nice too, and I had enjoyed our communal breakfast outside and chatting with the owners.

I made it back to our little cabin to find Samie still awake. She had come back from drinking long ago. We cuddled up to watch some more episodes of *Game of Thrones*. During the show, we piled on more blankets and clothes and went to sleep together afterwards.

Warm and cozy, we slept uninterrupted the entire night.

"Sam, we are not drunk" - Chloe and I, after drinking several liters of wine (we were drunk)

Chapter 5: Central Europe

Vienna, Day Twenty-Two: 18th of April

Although Samie and I had slept soundly, we had to wake up painfully early in the dull light of dawn. We packed in a rushed silence and hurried out to the bus stop. I had only gotten a few hours of sleep, and the limoncello was leaving a hell of a hangover.

We ran out of the entrance of the campground just in time to watch our bus pull away, leaving a cloud of dust in its wake. Great.

We sat down on the bench, shivering in the cold dewy morning. I pulled my leather jacket tighter and tried to forget that the world was spinning around me. Eventually, the next bus arrived and we grabbed our packs and got on the bus. This time we did not pay.

By the time we got the Venezia Mestre train station, I was feeling a lot better. We walked in and reserved our seats on the long journey to Vienna. It was going to be our longest ride yet, clocking in at over eight hours. It took as long to fly across the Atlantic Ocean.

From the ticket kiosk, we walked to our platform. I loved these platforms. They were always long concrete slabs about fifteen feet wide and raised maybe five feet above the ground. They usually had a bench or two and a vending machine. Most of the stations I saw were cavernous depots and were typically pretty empty until right before the train pulled in. I always liked the relative solitude of these big buildings as there was something very zen about them. They always smelled of stone and oil, a very industrial scent. The smell excited me because it meant I was about to embark on some adventure.

Next to the vending machine, there would typically be a coffee dispenser. I would almost always buy a little drink from them as I waited for my train. It was always only a single euro coin for a pretty decent cappuccino. The styrofoam cup would drop into the metal claw and then fill up with liquid. I would sip it slowly, enjoying my mediocre quality but low-cost coffee. Like walking tours, or buying flags and postcards, this became a quintessential ritual of travel for me, and one that particularly brought me joy.

As I drank my coffee in the quiet station, who did we saw walking up the platform across the tracks from us, but Bill and Bailey again? They were heading off to a different city, but it was lovely having one last chat with them. Travel buddies are often not people you necessarily have much in common with, but end up sharing a magical experience. Although I didn't know them very well, I had experienced a big chuck of my trip with me, and will always remember it. Our train arrived and we waved goodbye, this time for the last time.

We settled in our seats, the car almost entirely empty. I pulled out my little laptop and plugged it in. I figured an eight-hour train ride was an excellent time to get some work done on my papers.

We had not been riding for more than twenty minutes when a sudden intense wave of nausea washed over me. Vomit welled up in my throat. I felt terrible. I tried to ignore it, but looking at my laptop made the feeling worse. I closed it and settled back in my seat, hoping I could sleep it off.

Unfortunately, as our train picked up speed, it got worse. Samie looked over at me and noticed I had gone white. I was hesitant to speak, afraid I would puke all over the car. Samie handed me some ginger chews. She had brought them on our European adventure for just this reason.

My stomach felt slightly calmer after eating some, but I was barely holding it together. About an hour in, we got to our first change in Verona. As soon as the train stopped, I ran off, leaving the girls confused. I immediately found a bathroom and puked. We had a fifteen minute layover, and there I was, throwing up into a dirty toilet in the bowels of a train station, full backpack strapped on.

Ever conscious of time, I swigged some water from my Nalgene and ran back the stairs to the girls in the main lobby. The train station was tightly packed and they had panicked looks on their faces.

"What the hell was that?" Sam asked me accusingly. Not wanting to explain myself, I shrugged off the question.

"Do we know what platform our train is?" I asked, changing the subject.

"Yeah, and we have eight minutes until it leaves," Chloe told me. We pushed our way to the platform and boarded the train. On board there were two benches of three seats facing each other, set inside little cabins. Closing the door would leave your group in welcome privacy. It reminded us of the Hogwarts Express.

Our cabin was shared by a young mother and her bratty-ass kid. The kid was probably eight or so and at every stop he would ask the same thing.

"*Sind wir hier jetzt?*" he whined, asking if they were there yet. His mother would frown and answer *nein* curtly each time. The lovely family was with us for hours as we crossed from *Italia* to *Österreich*.

Outside the car, the landscape shifted from the sunny hills and vineyards of Tuscany to charming little villages nestled in the misty green foothills of the Alps. The homes were painted light pastel colors, with steep earthy red roofs. It looked exactly like how movies like the Sound of Music portrayed Austria. It was another scene I never expected to actually exist, but there it was. Mountains rose on either side of the tracks and we rode next to broad green rivers. It was beautiful countryside.

As we neared our destination, I heard some commotion outside of our cabin. I slid the door open and poked my head out. Multiple men carrying assault rifles walked by. The word *POLIZEI* was emblazoned in large letters across their backs. I slid the door closed again. No need to get involved with that.

A bit later, we heard a knock on the door. I slid it open again, this time to see an old granny. She wore a dress that might have been the height of fashion sixty years ago and was small and frail looking.

She spoke to us in rapid German. I didn't catch all of it except for the word *helfen* or help. I stood up and walked next door to her cabin. She pointed up at the luggage rack and spoke some more German. I understood the words for suitcase, help and hard.

I moved to grab the big old-fashioned suitcase. "*Schwer, schwer*" the old lady kept saying.

Schwer, I thought, *why does she keep saying 'hard'*? I pulled the suitcase down and found it to be heavy as shit. *Oh*, I thought as my brain lit up, *'schwer' also means 'heavy.'* The word means different things than I had learned in school.

The woman thanked in the most accented English I'd ever heard. She gathered from my silence that I didn't speak German. I nodded politely, but inside I was elated. For the first time in my life, I was finally hearing German being used in an everyday way. After four years of practicing German in the classroom, I had never been able to interact with German as a living breathing language. I was just barely in the German-speaking world and I was already making new and organic connections.

"*Herzlich Wilkommen in Wien, Österreich*" The train conductor announced, welcoming us heartily to Vienna. I was stoked.

We departed the train station, happy to stretch our legs again. The ride had taken all day, and it was already early evening. We left the Westbahnhoff station and followed Google maps to our hostel. The route took us along a narrow dirt road next to the tracks. The station was on a hill, overlooking part of the city. From what I could see this neighborhood looked industrial and gritty. As we crossed the tracks into the city proper, we shared a moment of fear that we might be in another Madrid-type situation.

Our fears were unfounded as we found our hostel clearly marked on the first street we walked down. We were welcomed by a friendly staff. Beyond the check-in counter were a cluttered lounge and a noisy bar. We were staying in an eight-bed dorm and were a little nervous at the party-hostel vibe.

We were well aware as to why most young travelers prefer places like this. They like the cheap drinks, the camaraderie and the adventurous types of personalities that congregate here. These kinds of hostels often organize pub-crawls and such, so one can easily spend all night drinking with new friends. This wasn't what Sam, Chloe or myself were looking for. The three of us would much rather roam around old castles by day and sleep soundly by night.

Not sure of what to expect we climbed a few floors to our room. It was spacious and clean, with four sets of bunk beds, a big window to the street and an en-suite bathroom with a shower. Three of the bunks were clearly occupied, but our new roommates were not in. We threw our packs on empty beds and headed back out to find some food. We had barely eaten all day.

Lucky for us, we did not have to wander far. We found a charming little restaurant at the end of the street, just a few buildings down. The inside was white and airy, with a high ceiling. The lights were old fashioned and looked like gas lamps, giving the place a refined air. A waiter walked up to us.

"Rauch oder kein Rauch?" he asked us expectantly. I blanked on what he was asking, so I just shrugged. He led us to a big long wooden table where two ladies were already eating. *So, it's true,* I thought, *in German countries, they really do seat you with strangers.* I soon deduced the waiter had been asking us for smoking or non-smoking sections. As I saw people lighting up cigarettes, I remembered Austria was one of the very few European countries that still allowed smoking indoors.

The waiter came over again, handed us menus and starting spouting off German. I was too tired, and he was speaking too fast for me to translate. Literally in mid-sentence, the waiter noticed our blank stares and changed languages.

*"Die Spiesekarte ist-*oh wait you speak English, why didn't you tell me? These are our specials..."

I immediately ordered a big ass beer, a Köning Ludwig dunkel, and a plate of wiener schnitzel. The beer was a classic dark lager, full of malty flavors and easily drinkable. I got a half-liter for a decently low price. The food itself was fantastic. The schnitzel was well made and the potato salad was just right. The place was pretty cheap, and we were quite satisfied. We left, full and happy, to go back to the hostel for an early night.

As we entered our room, we met two of our roommates. As we introduced ourselves, my ears perked up at their familiar, yet slightly off accents.

"Are you guys Australians?" I asked.

"Not really," the brown hair girl said slyly.

"We're kiwis" her blonde haired friend finished for her.

I smiled, thinking of what Phil had told me about New Zealanders. "So, was that fighting words? Calling you Australians?"

The girls laughed, but their response was serious. "Depends on who is saying it. Americans are safe."

The ice broken, the five us launched into a great conversation, standing around our bunks. The two New Zealanders had just come from Prague, our next destination. We chatted about general travel, school, jobs, and all the usual stuff. I was especially struck by their particular use of the word 'average' as in "she was quite average really" or "yeah it's a really average place." In kiwi slang average meant basic or not good and I can't but smile when I think of those girls saying it in their thick New Zealand accents.

During our conversation, our final roommate came in. She was a black-haired American girl who had been travelling Europe for a few months. She said hello, introduced herself, then crawled into her bunk and immediately went to sleep with the overhead lights blazing and us still talking. If that's not some hardcore travelling, I don't know what is.

Vienna, Day Twenty-Three: 19th of April

I woke up feeling refreshed and rested. After a meager breakfast of stray snacks from the train ride, we went down to leave. Next to the front door was a coffee machine. I was delighted and put my euro coin in. The machine ate my coin and gave me no coffee. I left the hostel dejected and caffeine-free.

We had no idea what to do in Vienna. We had added it very late in our planning when we dropped Nice in France. We had picked Vienna solely because it was halfway between Venice and Prague, and we had not wanted a sixteen-hour train ride between them. We didn't have the slightest idea of what Vienna could offer.

We began to walk down the street, with vague plans to see some museums. Our kiwi friends had told us Vienna had a ton of world-class museums not far from the hostel. I had grabbed a map of the public transit in the hostel. Looking at it, I saw there was a *Straßebahn,* or S-Bahn, track right near us. The S-Bahn is like a slow tram that crisscrossed the city. Unfortunately for us, we could not decipher the very confusing map of the S-Bahn routes and opted for the familiar subway, which was called the *Unterbahn* in German.

The U-Bahn, proved to be easily navigable. All metros are basically the same, so we bought our tickets from an electronic kiosk. But, to our surprise, there was no gate or turnstile to feed our tickets into. From the ticket machine, one simply steps onto the platform. All the metros I had ever used, including in America, had some system designed to block non-paying riders.

Looking around stupidly, we clutched our tickets as we boarded the spacious and clean metro cars. As we rocketed towards our stop (the straightforwardly named *Museumsquartier*) we watched for somewhere to put our tickets. Our stop came, and the conductor called out *"Aufsteht am Links,"* telling us to exit on the left.

We exited the U-Bahn and climbed the stairs out. No gates or turnstiles again. We finally realized it ran entirely on the honor system. Unlike in Italy, I got the feeling people followed the rules in Austria.

We left the metro and took a look around downtown Vienna. The roads were wide, and telephone wires were thick over our heads. There wasn't as much traffic as I'd expected, and tramcars glided by. The buildings were elegant and the color of organic eggshells, full of big windows and arched doorways. They were only lightly decorated and not gaudy. Especially coming from colorful Spain and Italy, Vienna looked much more drab, cold, and Germanic.

The museums were only a stone's throw away. Multiple huge buildings housing the museums were spread across a well-manicured lawn. Formerly the Hapsburg royal palaces, these impressive buildings had long since been converted into various museums covering every subject under the sun.

In the middle of the grounds was a tower with a giant statue of Maria Theresa. Chloe split up with us here, because she wanted to gaze upon the immaculate Venus of Willendorff. The Venus is one of the oldest works of art by humanity and a precious piece of our human story. I wanted to see it but was overpowered by an empty stomach and desire for coffee. With a meeting time agreed upon, Chloe headed into the *Naturhistorisches*, natural history, museum while Sam and I searched for food.

We didn't need to go far before, to our delight, we came across a stall in the park selling sausages. We ordered *auf Deutsch*, and the man asked us *"Senf oder kein Senf?"*

Not understanding what he was asking, I answered *"Ja,"* and he put spicy brown mustard on my bratwurst. I was suddenly transported to my sophomore year in high school German class where Frau Hahn was teaching us the word for mustard.

This experience would often happened in Austria. I was remaking connections I learned years ago and forgot because I had never used them in real life. I smiled, happy to be working on my second language.

We ate our *Wurst,* drank our *Kaffee* and had a nice long chat while sitting in front of the grand old Habsburg palaces. Samie and I were enjoying each other's company in the warm spring Viennese air.

In no hurry, we walked around the massive palace. A Hapsburg once sat on almost every throne in Europe at various times. Since the main building of the palatial complex was so big, it was split into many self-enclosed museums. One smaller wing was labeled as a museum of ethnology. Being good anthropology students, we decided to go in.

Despite being relatively compact, the rooms and lobby were specular. European royalty certainly knew how to live in style. I cannot write yet another description of white marble, gold trim and painted ceilings. Suffice to say, it was a beautiful place for a museum. After centuries of stomping on the little people, I am glad these buildings are being used in this public manner.

We saw interactive exhibits on Southeast Asian dances and some other exotic cultural activities. We also saw a cool exhibit on the travels of Franz Ferdinand. Franz is only really remembered for being assassinated and kicking off World War One, but here I learned he travelled the globe extensively collecting oddities, in classic 19th-century anthropology style. Anthropologists in those days loved studying the 'savages' of the world. Anthropology was simple then, as the world was either civilized or savage, with little middle ground.

Franz had been relatively liberal for a monarch, and it was interesting to see that the museum painted his death as a tragedy. We admired his rows of artifacts from African ceremonial masks to carved tusks from India. It was a great collection of antique anthropology. A collection like this would never fly in the USA.

What really excited me was something else though. I was amazed and astonished I stumbled across this object. Hidden deep in the back of the museum, in a dark empty room patrolled by a guard it laid, quietly and calmly. It was the headdress of Montezuma II.

I couldn't believe it. It was the headdress worn by the Aztec emperor as Cortez, and the conquistadores rode into Tenochtitlan and utterly destroyed Native America. The quetzal feathers making up the headdress were brilliant green. This particular shade of green was sacred to the Mesoamerican people as it represented the primordial sludge from whence the world, Turtle Island, arose. The priests and kings who wore this color had a special connection to the all-important spirit world. Little old me, just a kid from the suburbs, was now looking at it.

The room had a long wall of German text describing how the headdress ended up, improbably, in Vienna. The story was long and convoluted and involved royalty and bloodlines and all sorts of German dynastic terms I couldn't understand. The story of how the Mexican headdress ended up in Austria remains unknown to me.

Pleased with our impromptu visit, Samie and I strolled back over to the statue of Maria Theresa to meet with Chloe. She had also enjoyed her museum visit. Chloe and I then had to snap some pictures of the statue. We were no doubt some of the only tourists to be interested in Maria.

In addition to being a character in our beloved *Civilization* video game, she was a powerful queen of the Austrian Empire at its height. Although her modern legacy mainly is to have been the mother of the unlucky Marie Antoinette, she was a transformative ruler.

I had a personal connection to Maria Theresa. Soon after assuming the throne of Austria, Maria wanted to repopulate the lands recently retaken from the Muslim Ottoman Empire. They had ethnically cleansed the area and wanted good German Roman Catholics there. Whether by order or voluntarily, my ancestors left their homes in southwest Germany and trekked to a small settlement in present-day Romania.

My ancestors came from several places, including the city of Rastatt. The name 'Rastatter' does not predate this move. They have picked it up during their time in Romania. It would not make sense to be known as somebody from Rastatt unless Rastatt was far away.

The Rastatters moved to Romania around 1750 or so and stayed in their little German enclave for the one hundred and sixty years. During the first decade of the 20th century, the Rastatters left their homes and settled in Cleveland, Ohio. They still practiced their Roman Catholic faith and spoke their dialect of German. They left at a choice time, for not too long later, two world wars ripped through this region. The ethnically German population did not fare too well during the years of Soviet domination.

History can seem dull and far-off until you know stories like this. When you pay attention closely, you see how everything connects, and this is never more apparent than in these European capitals. The Rastatter family history was directly impacted by decisions made in a palace I now stood in front of, by a woman whose statue I stood beneath. Those Ottoman weapons in Venice? Those were the spoils of the victories that led Maria to resettle Hungary with Germans. Maria's daughter then helped to spark the French Revolution, which is why most old churches don't have stained glass. Angry mobs destroyed them during the Revolution. The same Revolution led to Napoleon taking power, and I had stood in his magnificent crypt. Everything is always connected, past and present, and it is always just a matter of merely seeing the connections.

Chloe brought me back to the present time.

"I'm glad there weren't too many people in the museum," Chloe told us. "Because I stood in amazement in front of the Venus of Willendorf for a long long time." She laughed. "I'm a good archaeology student."

Our kiwi roommates had told us about a flea and farmers market nearby, so we went to check it out. It was only a couple of blocks over. The market was cool, but not as crazy or hectic as the one in Madrid. Being the experienced travelers we were, perhaps we were starting to get jaded?

We walked around to the different stalls, browsing slowly. We bought a big bag of candy from some friendly Arabs.

Among the usual treats, there was also, strangely enough, candied hibiscus. It looked weird, like exactly how a candied flower would. Despite our trepidation, it tasted terrific. It was like a sugary gelatin snack that had a faint smell of flowery perfume.

We checked out some more stalls. They were selling everything from trinkets to sausage to beer. I was able to buy an Austrian flag for my collection at one of these shops. I smiled to myself when the store owner greeted me with '*Gruß Gott.*'

In German class, we had been taught this was a regional greeting used only in Austria and Bavaria and is akin to something like 'howdy y'all.' Northern Germans, we had learned, scoffed at this. Hearing German in reality was kind of jarring. For so many years it had been an almost a secret language, one that was only spoken by a few friends and me. We would sometimes talk in German if we wanted to keep something secret or on the downlow.

To balance out our bag of candy, we also bought some groceries and boarded the metro to go back home. We were short on time because we had made plans with the New Zealanders to go to the opera. We had almost gone to the opera in Madrid, and our kiwi friends told us Vienna had the same kind of deal. For only three euros we could go to the very worst seats and see a genuine European opera.

At the hostel, we ate quickly, showered and met with our roommates. They were as excited as us to go. We rode the metro back into the city, as a light rain began to fall. The Staatsoper building was another architectural marvel. Yellow floodlights lit the beautiful classical columns against the dark and rainy evening. Outside the doors of the building were tickets being scalped by men dressed like Mozart. We had been warned not to buy from these guys. However, I could not help but be impressed. Vienna was so classy the scam artists dressed like Mozart.

The cheap tickets were only sold first come first serve. We had arrived a couple hours early and found the line quite long already. We joined the queue and sat down to wait on the cold hard marble floor. Soon after, the line snaked out of the building and those poor people had to wait in the rain.

The time passed quickly as we chatted with each other and with the New Zealanders. Before we knew it, we had our tickets in hand and were climbing yet another set of beautiful marble stairs in a beautiful old building. The opulence of these royal buildings was too magnificent to truly describe.

Our spots were at the very top of the building. The stage was far below us, and there were no seats for us poor folk. Instead, we just had a railing to grip. Luckily there were little screens for every three or four spots attached to the railing. These showed the lyrics in English or German, so we could follow the show.

The lights went down and the curtains went up. The opera called *Ariadne auf Naxos*. It followed a person in modern times writing and directing an opera, so there was a story-within-the-story dynamic. Interspersed with the classic opera themes of Greek mythology and whatnot was a troupe of clowns performing slapstick antics. The electronic screens were of great help, for I wouldn't have been able to understand the old-fashioned German lyrics, all which were sung.

At the halfway break, I went down a few floors to check out the snack station. I was pretty hungry, as we had eaten only a little before we left. There were waiters wearing vests and bowties behind the glass counter. I discreetly checked out the price and saw that tiny pieces of cake were eight euros and a bottle of Heineken was ten. I went back upstairs empty-handed.

As the opera began again, I had an out of body experience. I stood there, tired and smelly, weeks into backpacking around Europe, standing in the elite opera house of Vienna, watching a play sung in German. Far below sat rich Austrians and other Europeans, dressed so smartly with pearls and expensive suits. Standing in that place, watching hours of operatic entertainment was one of the most surreal moments in my life. Despite my prior doubts, I found I enjoyed the experience and could appreciate the beauty and skill it took to do this kind of theater.

The opera went on for hours, and we applauded enthusiastically at the end, thoroughly impressed. As we walked down the central staircase, I had to take some pictures of the interior of the beautiful building to remember it by. We stepped outside and immediately got drenched by the pouring rain.

The three of us were desperately hungry. Across the street we spied another *Wurst* vendor, so we ran over. We bought street sausages in the rain and devoured them right there. When I ordered this time, I confidently got mine *mit Senf*.

We got back to our hostel no problem. The girls got ready for bed, while I went back out to look for more food. I had been hankering for a good kebab. In Europe, you can't swing a dead cat without hitting a kebab stand. True to form, I found one only one block over.

I ordered in German, determined to get things right on my first try. All was going smoothly until they asked me which toppings I wanted. *Zweibel* I knew meant onion, but then the man asked me if I wanted *Rotkohl*.

Rotkohl? My mind drew a blank, and I hesitated. Seconds later, the young man asked me, in English, if I wanted cabbage on it. He did not switch back to German. Both here and in Germany this would often occur. If you fuck up one time, the German speaker would change effortlessly into flawless

English and refuse to return German, even if you keep going on in it.

Laying in my bunk later, stomach full of kebab, I thought about how awesome Vienna had been so far. I was excited to see what tomorrow would hold. I fell asleep to the muffled sounds of the hostel bar far below me.

Vienna, Day Twenty-Four: 20th of April

After sleeping in, we ate our normal homemade breakfast and headed out to the Schloss Schönbrunn, the old summer palace of the Habsburgs. It was a short two-mile walk.

Outside the palace there was a big Easter market set up. The market was right in front of the vast Baroque palace. At the entrance, were three human-sized colored Easter eggs. Beyond, there were lots of little wooden vendor stalls and people eating and drinking merrily. It was all framed by the colossal palace.

We walked around the gravel footpaths, buying souvenirs, big creampuffs, and hot cider. I was able to order several times in German without the speaker switching to English. In one corner of the market, a band was playing jazz. Later that evening I would post the one picture on Facebook from my whole trip, of us in front of the Easter eggs. My high school German teacher will immediately comment on it, praising my excellent choice of place to visit. *Danke Frau Hahn.*

While the palace itself was too expensive to go in, around the back were massive public gardens. These formerly royal gardens had been opened to the public for almost a hundred years now and were loved by the locals. The grounds were well maintained and the paths were big enough across that, despite the amount of people around, one never felt crowded.

We came across a reflecting pool, set underneath old tall trees. There was a big, perfect set of Roman ruins, overgrown with vines and shrubs. A sign told us these 'ruins' were built in the 18th century during a fad for all things Roman. These faux-ruins were meant to evoke the never-ending splendor of the Austrian Empire.

Near the ruins was a big hedge maze interspersed with fitness stations. Naturally, the Austrians and Germans loved it because it combined two of their favorite things, physical activity and mental exercise.

The maze was built for kids, but I had an excellent time running around in it. One of the activities involved climbing a straight metal pole and ringing a bell at the top. Although I tried, I could not get up very far. Samie made it all the way to the top, but couldn't quite reach out and ring the bell. Turning another corner in the maze, we came across a group of full-size mirrors facing themselves. We had great fun taking pictures of our endless reflections.

Outside the maze was a big playground full of little carousels and teeter-totters. Upon seeing these, Chloe immediately jumped onto one of the spinney carousel cars and spun around. I have never seen such looks of pure joy cross her face as I did then.

"Don't judge me," she said, stepping off the ride, her face glowing and red hair askew over her black leather jacket. I wasn't.

To get back to Vienna, we stowed away on the metro and rode to the city center. We walked around only briefly. While pretty, downtown Vienna, in my opinion, was just another big European city with the same pedestrian streets, lights strung up across the streets, big advertisements and large chain stores. In contrast to the Italian cities, Vienna had long ago lost any medieval charm it might have once had. *I didn't come to Europe to see modern cities*, I thought to myself, *I want to see some old shit, dammit.*

One medieval landmark still in the heart of the city was the Stephansdom, a grand Gothic cathedral that has stood since the

14th century. We felt like tiny ants standing in the shadow of the single massive Gothic tower attached to the church. Somehow the cathedral had miraculously survived both Nazi and Russian sieges during the Second World War. Since our trip would not spend much time in the Germanic countries, it would be one of the few real Gothic churches we would see, and the sight was quite impressive.

Sometimes these kinds of churches are free to tour and they always hold amazing stained glass and old statues. We stepped inside through the big heavy wooden doors. I was sort of surprised to see a lot of people milling around the little lobby until I looked into the central nave of the church.

I saw a priest swinging a traditional Catholic incense ball. I watched the clouds of frankincense wafting up to the rafters hundreds of feet up, past the glorious stained glass and looming statues. Smelling the frankincense, Chloe and I were instantly transported back to the dark and haunting beauty of the Catholic rituals of our childhoods. I hadn't realized that today was Easter Sunday.

We left the magnificent ancient cathedral, feeling it wrong to take pictures of a mass in action. We left the city center to go back to the palaces that been turned into museums. These buildings, unlike the modern downtown, had much more character. They recalled the golden age of Vienna in the mid-18th century, the Vienna of Mozart and Schilling.

Samie needed to go back to the hostel to work on her school papers. All three of us were realizing that our trip was soon coming to an end and we still needed to finish our essays. Samie left Chloe and I to explore more of the former palaces.

Chloe and I saw some cool Baroque buildings, big decorative fountains, and the ever-present statues of Roman gods. We stopped in a huge bookstore that was set in a rotunda. There were piles of books and endless shelves all arranged around the checkout desks in the center of the room.

Finally growing hungry, Chloe and I went to find a restaurant. After going back and forth for a few minutes, we found a restaurant hidden inside a small courtyard, overgrown with vines and ivy. We sat at a little two-seat green wicker table and had a pleasant meal sitting outside. Everything here felt so civilized.

Going to back to the hostel, we found Sam chatting with the lovely kiwis. We had another amiable conversation and then the three of us went to eat some strudel for dessert. Sam, Chloe and I walked back over to the restaurant we had first ate at when we arrived in Vienna. We ordered three pieces of strudel, one salad for Sam, and a beer for me. The waiter was genuinely confused as to why we were eating dessert and a salad with no food.

"Are you sure?" he kept asking, perplexed by our unorthodox order. We were sure.

As somebody who has eaten a lot of strudel I was very impressed by what Vienna could offer. It was sweet, fluffy and delicate. Other countries need to step up their game.

We stopped at the hostel bar after dessert. Our beds had come with one free drink, so we got some beers and sat in the relative privacy of the hostel kitchen. The bar was full of backpackers trying to play beer pong, get drunk and screw each other. Ugh.

In the kitchen, we talked about how we had loved Vienna. We had had no expectations for this city and had been blown away by its high-quality museums, opera, and little coffee houses selling cappuccino and strudel. We enjoyed the elegant feel to the city and the fact that it was steeped in the culture of Mozart, Freud and countless other poets and musicians. Vienna represented the very best of Germanic culture. It was clean, modern and classy.

We climbed the stairs back to our room to grab Samie's phone that had been charging. We skyped my family as they were celebrating Easter at my sister's house in Akron, Ohio. I spoke them for a while, feeling weird that it was the only afternoon there. We had already had a long and adventurous day.

"What are you doing after this call?" asked my mom.

"Going to bed," I replied, "it's late." I guess I wasn't the only one thrown off by the time difference. I said goodbye to everybody and hung up the phone. I was surprised I didn't feel too homesick.

Before going to bed, Samie and I watched more *Game of Thrones*. Samie has an infamous adversity to all things horror. Even the mildest of scares will keep her up for days. The episode ended with the White Walkers riding their undead horses, leading their frozen zombie horde to some unseen goal. I grinned at the hokeyness of it.

"Holy shit," Sam said in a hushed voice and eyes wide. "That was intense!"

Prague, Day Twenty-Five: 21st of April

It was another early morning as we left Vienna. It had been a whirlwind tour of the city and we were heading to Prague.

We had heard so much about Prague from the kiwis, the girls in Spain, from Phil, and from the Kansas boys. Everybody had raved about the city. We were excited about how cheap we had heard it was, our budget always on our minds. The train ride was to be another journey that would take all day, so we settled in for the long haul.

Our car was very comfortable, as we had a private room with a sliding door again. I liked these cabins. Europeans take privacy pretty seriously, and I enjoyed this aspect of life. Public bathroom stalls, for example, were made of brick, with real doors to them. It was a far cry from the flimsy sheet metal with gaping holes I knew from America.

As we rode across Austria and crossed briefly into Bavaria, I wrote my school papers. It was slow going. I had no wifi, so I was stuck using the couple of academic articles I had downloaded before leaving the UK.

Tiring of writing after a while, I took a walk around the train. I liked to watch the countryside from the windows. As we got closer to the Czech Republic, the mountains faded and turned into open pastures. We had crossed from Western to Central Europe.

Now in Bohemia, the villages looked different somehow. They seemed less organized and more ramshackle. For the first time we were behind the former Iron Curtain, into the old Soviet sphere of influence. These countries had been free hardly longer than I have been alive.

Wandering around the train, I crossed from car to car, trying to reach the very rear. It was an older train model, one where the passageway between cars was not enclosed. Instead of walking through a small connecting room, there was a shaking metal walkway with only a short railing to stop one from falling onto the tracks. I soon found myself in the last car of the train. I could go no further and watched the train tracks disappear behind us.

I watched the tracks for a while, reflecting on how much of Europe I said seen on these rails. To me, these rails meant freedom and adventure. I walked back to our car, moving smoothly with the motion of the train. Once upon a time walking like this would have nearly knocked me to the ground as the train rolled over bumps and around corners, but now I stepped with ease.

Back in the car, I slept when I could. I placed my flannel shirt over my eye and positioned my head on the neck rest. I slept sitting straight up, gently rocked back and forth by the swaying train.

I awoke as we neared Prague. Maybe because I was dazed from my long nap, but I had a moment of panic as we pulled into the central station. They didn't even use the euro here. I gulped as we departed the train, nervous to find what this city had to offer.

But, before anything else we needed to withdraw money. We quickly found an ATM and got some cash. When we did so, the bills were all five hundred and one thousand denominations. It felt like monopoly money. We walked out of the train with thousands of Czech *korunas* between us.

We walked to the hostel along the main roads. Cars whipped by on big four-lane highways. The city immediately struck me as less beautiful and refined than Austria or Italy. Here, buildings were tall and black with age. We saw a golden dome in the distance, atop a sooty black palace.

To me, it seemed that *Praha*'s architecture reflected, at least to some degree, it's Slavic roots. I couldn't say what exactly, but something just felt different. While Italy and Austria had seemed deeply familiar in some ways, Prague felt seriously foreign.

Our hostel was located on the main street Sokolska, a short journey from the train station. The exterior was quite plain, just another building on a busy road, one of the several brick high rises on the block. The interior was much more substantial than it looked from outside. There was a whole kitchen, stocked with spices and a few leftovers from previous travelers, complete with two wooden picnic tables for eating. There were a small courtyard and a big common area with books and two computers. As we checked in, the man told us the breakfast area would be reached by going through a tunnel. That sounded intriguing.

As always, our room was a couple of floors up. This was no problem, however, because our room was superb. There were three twin size beds in a row, each with a little nightstand. We had a big window overlooking the street. The big window gave us plenty of room to hang and dry our wet clothes if needed. We had not washed our clothes since Florence. There was no private bathroom, but the showers and toilets were located directly across the hall. Overall it was an excellent room for a so-so price.

Our empty stomachs rumbled. We had been recommended a nearby Mexican restaurant, so we decided to check it out. I was curious to see how that would be, as Europe has very few people from Mexico. The route took us off the main drag, to where the side streets were a lot prettier. The tree-lined streets were peaceful and devoid of traffic.

I had been craving Mexican food for months. While England had its share of spicy food, including Portuguese peri-peri and Indian curry, nothing can ever replace cheap, delicious Mexican cuisine. Inside the restaurant, it did indeed feel like we were back home. The restaurant had perfect Mexican décor. Mariachi music played over the speakers. So far, it was quite promising.

We each ordered a big margarita. I had a mango chili one, which was delicious. Or, at least the few sips I had were tasty until I accidentally knocked it all over the floor. You can't take me anywhere.

We ordered our food, and some chips and salsa. Strike one against this place, charging for chips and salsa. When the chips came, they consisted of four or five corn chips and a spoonful of salsa, arranged as if this was a gourmet dish in a fancy restaurant. It was like a bad joke.

When the entrees arrived, one of the girls got the wrong dish. This being Europe, the waiters did not give a shit. Say what you will about the American tipping system, but at least it ensures prompt and good customer service. Here they get paid the same regardless, and it shows.

My enchiladas had no spice in the slightest. I've never had blander 'Mexican' food in my life. I was looking forward to a comfort meal. It tasted like somebody had read about Mexican food, but had never ate it before. The girls, however, loved their meals, so perhaps I was just in a bad mood.

When we got the bill, we carefully counted out the money we each owed. I mentally converted the Czech korunas to euros. One euro was roughly thirty korunas, and my bill was five hundred and forty korunas. I frowned. That was eighteen euros or about twenty-one US dollars. Prague wasn't any cheaper at all.

Damn. My disappointment was complete. The koruna, pronounced 'crown,' being weaker did not mean anything. All the prices were just higher. I would find out that the costs of food and everything else in Prague would be only the slightest bit lower than the rest of Europe. I had been looking forward to saving some money so I could do more museums and tours and such but it seemed like it would not be. Given our terrible service, we did not tip and left the restaurant in a hurry.

We walked right back to the hostel to work on our papers. As we entered the building, a young Czech man at the desk stopped us.

"I do not mean to be rude," he said in good but accented English. "But here in Czech Republic, we have a tradition where we spank the girls with palm leaves to get good luck for the year."

I looked at his friend, who had glasses and waist-long blonde hair, holding a palm leaf, the kind you get on Palm Sunday, looking eagerly at Sam and Chloe.

"Normally we are supposed to run up and just hit them, but since you are foreign we wanted to ask you first." I looked back at the girls. I was ready to support this ancient fertility rite, this national tradition. The girls, however, both looked horrified.

They politely declined to take part in such a hallowed tradition and we turned to go to our room. The blonde hair guy ran excitedly out of the front door, having seen a pretty Czech girl crossing the street or something.

Safely back in our room, we googled the tradition. We found it to be a real thing. Young men do in fact use the palm leaves from Palm Sunday to spank young ladies. The tradition has deep pre-Christian roots and has been practiced for a long time. I also read that more and more younger Czech females are rejecting the custom, as it is sexist and symbolizes violence against women.

I just thought it had looked kind of fun.

Prague, Day Twenty-Six: 22nd of April

We met that morning in the lobby, eager to see what breakfast would be like. From the lobby, we entered a wooden doorway that led into a subterranean tunnel. The walls were stucco white and held a whiff of dampness.

We entered into the basement of a restaurant at the other end of the tunnel. It was entirely underground with no windows or natural light. It consisted of three rooms with several picnic tables. The walls were covered in movie posters from the fifties and sixties. Big heavy wooden beams held up the ceiling, and the flickering yellow lights gave the whole room a decidedly medieval vibe. It was a fabulous place to eat breakfast.

And how was the breakfast? Fucking amazing. The spread consisted of dark and wheat bread, rolls, cereal, oatmeal, smoked meats and cold cuts, yogurt, jam and brown sugar cinnamon cake. For drinks, we could choose from chilled water, fruit juice, and coffee. The feast was neatly arranged on the table facing the hallway we exited from, with the other rooms splitting off in either direction.

My jaw dropped upon seeing the food. For weeks we had been scraping by on bites of Nutella sandwiches and bits of fruit. We counted ourselves lucky if our hostel only provided coffee. Each day I would come down here and stuff myself with sliced meat on dark bread, drink two cups of coffee and then eat of a bowl of cereal mixed with yogurt. It was decadent, and I loved every minute of it.

As I ate that morning I considered the price of our room, only thirty-five US dollars or so. It was really cheap, especially considering we had a private three-bed room, not a dorm. Now that I saw the glorious breakfast I realized that our hostel was a great deal, the best one of our trip. Perhaps I had judged Prague too harshly yesterday. For this much free food, I would be saving considerably by skipping buying breakfast, my coffee, and most of lunch. We'd be saving money after all.

If it seems like I have been getting excited about eating it's because I definitely was. Traveling on a limited budget meant I usually couldn't eat very well or very much. If I squandered my meal money on a lousy meal or got small portions, then I went to bed hungry. Chloe was stick thin and Samie was a foot shorter than me. A meal that left them full would leave me hungry. Food was never far from my thoughts.

Pleased with our sumptuous meal, Chloe and I went off to go on a free walking tour. Samie, of course, opted to stay behind. She claimed she wanted to write her papers and do laundry, but Chloe and I knew she just hated these tours.

The tour started in the Old Town Square. It was a short twenty-minute walk away. We found the tour group nearby a cluster of bronze statues turned blue-green with age. Our tour guide was a tall, skinny Prague native. He had studied architecture and was struggling to find full-time work, so he did these tours to make ends meet. He was very friendly and was one of the best tour guides I have had.

The tour itself focused on the older parts of the city. He began by describing the square itself. The statues were of Jan Hus and the Hussites. Jan had believed in reforming the Catholic Church and preached against its abuse of power. In response the Church executed him in 1415. His followers, the Hussites, subsequently rose up in revolt. The Catholic authorities then launched several bloody crusades to crush the uprising. Over the next five hundred years of oppression, Jan became a symbol of Czech resistance and national identity.

The Old Town Square itself was quite large, probably the biggest premodern plaza I have seen. Around us was set up dozens of red cloth tents, selling all kinds of treats, sausages, beer, and trinkets.

"You should avoid this Easter Market," he told us. "It's run by the thieving Russians and is not Czech at all." Our guide had come of age under the Soviet rule and did not think kindly of Russians. "The square is much prettier when there are no Russian booths."

Grand churches and buildings surrounded the Square. Of those, one stood out. It was an imposing cathedral, with two giant Gothic towers rising from it. The *Týnský chrám*, Tyn Church, looked like it was out of a Dracula movie. Age had discolored the bricks into a dark tan color, and the multiple spires of the tower were jet black. It looked almost sinister.

On the other side of the square stood a big white Baroque church. The towers had green bulbous copper coverings, and a red tiled roof. No longer an active church, it now hosted concerts.

Across from this church was the Old Town Hall. It consisted of a big Gothic tower, which was not quite as fancy as the ones of the Tyn church, and the stub of a two-story building coming off of it. The attached structure was oddly shallow, and there was a grassy area fenced off next to it.

The guide told us the Town Hall used to be a much larger fancy old building. At the end of World War II, the Czechs rose up to fight the Germans as the Soviet army surrounded the city. The Germans and Czechs fought a bloody battle, while the Soviets deliberately stalled their advance. During the fighting, most of the Town Hall was destroyed. After the war, the building was never rebuilt. Instead, the Czechs turned the grounds into a green space, as a reminder of their bloody battle for liberation.

The guide was stoked about the architecture of Prague. His enthusiasm was infectious as he talked about the buildings and their history. We would soon be seeing a dizzying array of styles, from early medieval to Gothic, Baroque, neo-Renaissance and even Stalinist and cutting edge modern.

After learning about the square, we crossed to the other side of the Old Town Hall to check out the Astronomical Clock. The Clock was attached to the Gothic tower of the Town Hall. It is a huge tourist draw and for good reason.

Completed in 1410, the clock face had multiple arms pointing at several overlaid circles, telling people both the astronomical cycle, the month, the time, and what saint's feast day it is. The clock even told us the cycle of the moon. That would be impressive by itself, much less what came next.

Once an hour, twelve moving figures, representing the Apostles, filed by, each looking out of little windows above the clock face. The four statues next to the clock would shake their heads back and forth. They represented different motifs. A figure of Vanity gazed in a mirror. Lust played a mandolin, while Greed grasped a bag of gold. The fourth figure was a skeleton that raised his arm to ring a bell and remind us that death was always near. At the end of the procession, a golden rooster perched above the whole scene would spread its wings and caw.

The entire spectacle was magnificent. We would return to watch it many times. Each time a large crowd would form and everybody would clap and cheer at the end of it. It was amazing to see something so intricate and so old still work. It was impressive now and must have been jaw-droppingly astounding back in the 15th century.

From here, we walked up the inviting Wenceslas Square. Despite the name, it was a spacious double boulevard shaded by leafy oak trees. It led up a hill, at the top of which stood an equestrian statue of St Wenceslas, the patron saint of the Czech Republic. The well-known Christmas carol is named after him.

Behind Wenceslas stood the black and golden dome of the National Museum. It resembled the US Capitol Building. Lining both sides of the road were shops, department stores, and a few wooden vendor stalls. The street was bustling with business and foot traffic. The guide told us that these shops were mainly empty during the Soviet period and that the first McDonalds in Prague opened here right after the Wall came down. Wenceslas Square was about halfway between our hostel and the Old Town Square so we would be passing through it frequently.

The tour headed north. Near the Vltava River, we came across an imposing and featureless Stalinist apartment complex. It was as ugly as the rest of Prague was beautiful. It was only a few blocks from the Gothic and Baroque churches of the Square and looked hilariously out of place.

Across the river, we saw an empty pedestal where a massive Stalin statue had once stood. It had been one of the largest statues in the world but had towered over Prague for less than a decade before Khrushchev tore it down.

Our guide told us stories of growing up under communism. It was not a great time. They would wait in line for hours for food and wait years for a car.

Our guide had been in middle school when the Wall came down, and communism collapsed. He laughed as he recalled his teachers throwing away their Russian language lessons and immediately trying to teach English. We chatted as we walked and I found out he had passed through Cleveland and Akron several years ago. It's a damn small world.

We went into a wealthy residential neighborhood to learn about Franz Kafka. For centuries Germans had dominated Prague. The Prague of Kafka was a German, not Czech, city.

Regardless, the modern Czech nation is proud of this towering literary figure. In the center of the neighborhood was a weird statue of a little Franz Kafka riding on the back of a headless, anamorphic suit of clothes. What does the statue represent? It's Kafkaesque.

Next to the avant-garde statue was am old synagogue built in the lofty Moorish style. It was jarring to see such an old-fashioned, Arabic-Spanish style building in the heart of Prague. The guide explained that after the Spaniards had expelled the Jews in 1492, a lot of them had immigrated to Prague. This explained why they were built in this style, as it reminded them of home. It certainly looked like a lot of the older buildings we had seen in Spain.

As we walked, Chloe and I made friends with some other members of the group. We met a middle-aged couple from the Midwest and a traveling nurse from Colorado.

As an American abroad, any other American is instantly your friend. It's like being a part of some secret club. As soon as you hear the unmistakable American voice coming out of their mouth, you smile and extend your hand, and immediately you are welcomed as a friend. We Americans are friendly in general, and being abroad amplifies this trait.

The traveling nurse was lovely. She told us a story about how she once worked with the father of Reese Witherspoon in rural New Mexico. The nurse, a bubbly blonde woman in her late twenties, would work for a few months at one location, then go travel for a month abroad. It seemed like a neat way of life.

The guide stopped our group in the courtyard of a restaurant. It was a quiet stone courtyard with vines and trees overgrown on the edges of it. We were to head downstairs to the basement to eat an optional lunch. The building was an old Prague establishment, all wooden panels and stone walls. As we entered, the guide recommended the pilsner beer.

"It's a little sharp, but you will find it to be very good," he told us. I made a mental note to try it later. Chloe and I didn't eat but enjoyed chatting with the nurse and the older American couple.

The two older folks were in their sixties and were traveling across Europe for the first time. They were going by cruise ships along the Danube. They had just come from Vienna and were very excited about their travels.

"We saw the actual blood of Jesus Christ in Vienna!" they told me, eyes alight with wonder. Much like the relic in Bruges, the Viennese also had some of the 'blood of Jesus'. These relics were common in medieval Europe.

"I didn't believe it, but there it was! I am not a Christian but holy cow." The wife beamed at the memory.

I enjoyed talking to them. Unlike a lot of younger travelers, these guys were utterly unpretentious. Their enthusiasm was infectious.

From the restaurant, we went to the Powder Tower, one of the last big Gothic gates that once served as the entrance of the Old Town from the New Town. Now, the gate stood alone in the middle of an intersection, the differences between the Old and New Town long since erased. Frederick the Great had damaged the tower when he sieged the city during the Seven Years War, which is called the French and Indian War back in the States. The tower itself was black with age and had the same spired grasping roof that made me feel like I was in a vampire movie.

Our group toured some of the newer buildings in Prague, before tour ended in front of the Czech Philharmonic building, the Rudolfinum. The building was a striking neo-Renaissance concert hall. In the movie *Eurotrip*, it had doubled as the Louvre. In fact, rewatching the movie a few weeks later, I would recognize most of the scenes as having been filmed in Prague.

The name of the Square was Jan Palach Square. Jan had self-immolated himself to protest the Soviet occupation of his land. His subsequent death had sparked the brutal and bloody 1968 Czech Uprising. It seemed like every building and square here in Prague had some monument to a murdered protestor or some sign of a conquering army.

We chatted with our tour guide for a while after the tour. He was frustrated with his job search.

"If you tour guide for ten days or ten years it looks the same on your CV," he told us sadly. However, he took pride in showing tourists around his home city. The tour had taken several hours, but unlike in Venice, the guide had kept it interesting the whole time.

Chloe and I took a long way home, following the Vltava River south. We walked along the sidewalks overlooking the river as we discussed philosophy. Chloe had been reading a lot of Foucault but I never had much use for these theorists who never seemed to do much in the real world.

With the river on the right, the buildings were on the left of us. One building stood out in particular. It was a rounded eight-story building, seemingly perched on two legs. It looked expressive and poised. Next to that was a curved glass building a floor or two higher. It was twisted as if it was an elegant woman leaning in and dancing with the partner building.

These are aptly called the 'Dancing House' or sometimes 'Fred and Ginger' for us Americans.

It was so interesting, and a bit jarring, to see such slick modern buildings nearby Slavic Gothic churches, which were adjacent to 19th century buildings with bullet holes from Nazi guns. The history in Prague was incredible.

We made it back to the hostel and found Sam. She had hung our laundry up to dry and was writing her papers. Happy to see Chloe and I, the three of us went across the street to a local grocery store. We bought rice, corn, ham, tortillas, and beer. Our total bill was only two hundred korunas or eight euros.

We went back to the hostel to make dinner. Samie fried the ham and warmed the tortillas as Chloe made the rice. I had not yet blossomed into a cook, so I read a travel book and drank my Czech beer. The beer was great. Of course, I did not yet know nor appreciate that the Czech Republic was one of the best countries for beer in the world.

The tour guide had told us the Czechs were first in the world for beer consumption. They also ranked the highest for meat eating and cigarette smoking. The guide laughed at that but then frowned as he informed they also had the lowest life expectancy in the EU.

When the meal was ready, Chloe and Samie brought out some peas, corn, black olives and salsa. We stuffed our tortillas and ate our dinner like one big happy family. We were the only ones in the kitchen/dining room area.

Happy and full, I washed the dishes while Samie and Chloe retired upstairs. After they were washed, I looked around the empty kitchen and dining area and felt pretty good. It had been a good day. I turned out the lights in the kitchen and climbed the stairs back to our room on the second floor.

Upstairs we got to work on our papers. Poor Chloe had to type on her phone. Later that evening I had to shower. I crossed the hall in my sandals and went to the communal showers. They were empty, so I picked a random stall and got in. Halfway through my shower, the lights went out, leaving me complete blackness. The room did not have windows.

I sighed. More motion activated lights. I finished my shower in the dark.

Prague, Day Twenty-Seven: 23rd of April

We woke up and had another sublime, wonderous full breakfast. After eating, we promptly went off to the Old Town Square to check out the Easter Markets run by the thieving Russians. Samie had not yet seen any of Prague so we showed her around, pointing out what we had learned.

The first part of the walk was through heavy traffic and involved passing a lot of sex shops. Then, we turned left and were suddenly atop of Wenceslas Square, looking down at the city unfolded beneath us. It was neat to see the old buildings popping out over the spring leaves of the trees.

On the way down the hill, I thought again how the street reminded me so much of Paris. The wide boulevard, the trees giving off shade, even the architecture of the buildings were reminiscent of Paris. There was even a replica of the Eiffel Tower on the outskirts of the city.

Near the base of the hill, we stopped to watch some street performers. They were tattooed shaven-headed men wearing monks robe and playing an energetic mix of rock and medieval music. They were acting like they were performing in front of a vast sold-out crowd, not a group of fifteen tourists. They were excellent, and we tipped them well.

We walked the rest of the way to the Old Town Square and showed Sam the Gothic churches. We walked around the Easter Market and checked out the different stalls. They sold all kinds of different things, most of which weren't worth our time. The sausages smelled pretty good, and I made a mental note to come back later to eat some.

We went to the edge of the square where the clock tower was. We had arrived just a few minutes before the end of the hour, so we did not have to wait long. The show happened and we watched with the crowd, clapping at the end of it. Sam was delighted with the clock tower. Both the Tower and the Old Town Square in general, were really appealing and we ended up spending a lot of time here during our stay in Prague.

From the Tower, it was only a five-minute walk to the old Jewish quarter. It was once cramped and crowded but was now open and airy and felt very Parisian. Prague once had the highest concentration of Jews in the world. The Golem legend originated in Prague. Now, there were very few Jews left.

Besides a couple of historic synagogues and town halls, the main attraction in the Jewish Quarter was the Jewish Cemetery. Founded in the 15th century, it was used for hundreds of years by the Jews of Prague. Having no other space for their cemeteries, they would heap dirt on the old graves to bury the new bodies on top of the old ones. Stone walls ran along the length of the cemetery. The cemetery was six to twelve feet higher than the streets on the other side of the walls, due to the multitude of bodies buried over the centuries.

We walked along the outside edge of the cemetery. We found ourselves on a quiet dead-end street. The cemetery wall was on one side, shaded by trees. A row of modest houses stood across the narrow street. Next to the wall were about fifteen wooden stalls selling handmade crafts. All the stall owners were Jewish. I noticed on the handwritten signs displaying the price, these vendors accepted Israeli shekels in addition to korunas and euros.

The prices were fantastically low. As Sam walked ahead of me, I quickly bought her a little red rose made of steel. I got it for her birthday in June and managed to secretly travel with it for the rest of the trip. The whole street was charming. It was nice and calm next to the cemetery, nearly empty except for a few Orthodox Jews. This little hidden corner of Prague sticks out in my mind, and I can sometimes picture it in the warm afternoon sunlight of that day, blue sky above us, as I stood watching Chloe and Sam look through the stalls.

This quarter had apparently been saved from Nazi destruction because Hitler had wanted to preserve it as a kind of museum for the extinct Jewish race. In our European travels, we came across a lot of places like this. The Nazis had emptied the old Jewish quarter of Venice. The Catholic Monarchs had cleansed the Jewish population of Toledo. Anne Frank's apartment was empty and cleared out. How many cities in England had once held Jewish subjects before King Edward got rid of them? Europe had not been kind to its Jewish children, and we had not even seen the worst parts yet.

From the Jewish cemetery, we walked over to the wealthy adjacent neighborhood. These tall Parisian-style apartments were built only a hundred odd years ago, quite new by European standards. *How expensive it must be live there now*, I thought. According to our tour yesterday this had been the blue-collar part of town at one point. It was home to thousands of Germans who were crammed into squalid tenements and worked dangerous, dirty industrial jobs.

Franz Kafka had been one those tenants. We had the joy of looking at Sam's perplexed face when she saw the statue of little Franz riding on the headless suit. Not too far from the statue was a sculpture made of small metal blocks, stacked in a way that they resembled a pregnant woman on her knees. The blocks were coated with mirror-like reflective paint and were big enough that the whole statue looked like a pixilated image from the old days of the internet.

Tired from our weeks of walking, we headed back to the hostel for rest and dinner. We ate leftovers, and I was able to utilize some cayenne that other tenants had left. Very little European food contained much spice. We finished eating and went back to work on our dreaded papers.

As the sun was setting, we decided to go back out and explore the city at night. The streets much calmer and quieter and we soon arrived at the Old Town Square.

The Square had a magical quality at night. The churches and buildings look like they are from a fairy tale. The gothic spires rose into the inky black sky while low yellow lights bathed their elegant, brooding forms. The lights on the inside of the Russian's booths make the red tents look like they were glowing. The old-fashioned streetlights and cobblestone plaza only added to the feeling.

We bought some sausages from the Russians in the square. When I paid them, they returned to me the wrong change. It was only fifty cents worth so I didn't say anything. Thieving Russians indeed.

We enjoyed the piping hot sausages and then bought some mead to wash it down. It was my first time drinking mead, which is fermented honey. It was served hot and warmed our bellies nicely.

The Prague Castle overlooks the city from the west bank of Vltava River. It is a large imposing structure always present and visible from most places in the Old Town. Having seen it from afar all day, we decided to check it out now. To get over the river, we crossed the famous Charles Bridge.

The Charles Bridge, or *Karlův most,* was a medieval era pedestrian bridge. The gate to the bridge was a huge, three or four story gothic tower. Like all old buildings it seemed, the gate was dark, nearly black, with age and soot. A few golden statues of kings and bishops looked down at us from above.

The disastrous Thirty Year's War had begun in Prague when the Protestant Elector of the Palatinate tried to wrestle the crown of Bohemia from the Catholic Hapsburgs. The revolt failed, and the twenty-seven Protestant ringleaders were executed en masse in the Old Town Square. Three decades of war followed. Twenty-eight years later, the final battle of the war was fought on this bridge. The Swedes held the west bank and charged across where we stood. The Swedes could not breach the Gate and died in large numbers, ending the massively destructive war only a few blocks from where it began.

During the day the bridge was thronged with tourists. It had been so full we did not even attempt to cross it. Now it was practically empty. Dozens of statues of Czech monarchs and saints stood on either side of the bridge. They were also black, but not with age. The original figures, added in 1700, were replaced with replicas under the Soviets. The black soot was added to make them look old. We crossed the medieval bridge while chatting amicably.

On the west bank, the streets were likewise. The roads sloped upward. The city felt spooky and mysterious as we trudged along. Between the few streetlights, empty roads and old buildings I felt like I might suddenly be transported back in time. I glanced in the window of one building and saw the interior was made of rough-hewn wood and had big wax candles. It looked like it was from another century.

We entered the castle grounds alone and unnoticed. The castle was so big it's actually a series of buildings and grounds. We found ourselves in front of the St Vitus Church, the heart of the castle. The church was the structure that was visible throughout Prague.

We stood in silence and awe while looking up at the flying buttresses and twin spires. Gothic architecture was meant to emphasize, among other things, vertical height and grandeur. Worshippers were supposed to crane their necks in wonder as they saw the church rise high above them. They were meant to be blown away by the decorative details and complex interlocking exterior features. All of this was intended to reflect the magnificent nature of God. I can't speak as a religious person, but the grand architecture still exuded the intended effect on me.

The church was closed, but we stayed there for a while, enjoying the warm spring air and our conversations. We sat on the edge of a fountain, alternating between looking at each other and up at the grand building.

On our way back down to our hostel, Chloe and I swapped ghost stories, much to the dismay and horror of Samantha. This was a girl who had been strongly affected by the White Walkers, after all.

"Please stop," she pleaded with us, panic in her eyes. "I want to be able to sleep." Chloe and I reluctantly acquiesced

Our route home took us past the Old Town Square again. We stopped by the clock to watch the hour change and then headed up past Wenceslas Square. My impression during the day had been one of peaceful friendliness, a lovely centerpiece of the Old Town. I was not expecting what we encountered at night. It was wild bacchanalia of drunks staggering around, blaring music and open-air drug sales. People offered us heroin and cocaine. Skinny half-dressed girls with taut cheeks and sunken eyes beckoned to me. Pimps were more direct, shouting out and advertising for their 'girls.'

Drugs and prostitution were legal in Prague, just like Amsterdam. However, the Netherlands had felt somehow sophisticated and urbane. Here, it felt sketchy and uncomfortable. We got the hell out of Wenceslas Square as fast we could.

As I brushed my teeth in the hostel bathroom, I reflected that we were doing less sightseeing each day. Our weeks of traveling and endless miles of walking were beating me down. I felt exhausted all the time. I collapsed into my twin-sized bed after changing into my basketball shorts and fell asleep instantly.

Prague, Day Twenty-Eight: 24th of April

This morning, after our usual jaunt down Wenceslas Square, the three of us split up. The girls wanted to do some shopping while I was more interested in the Museum of Communism, something they were definitely not into. The museum had eye-catching advertisements all over town, featuring sinister Russian cultural icons like a bloody Father Christmas or a snarling nesting doll.

I found the entrance off Wenceslas Square and paid the modest entrance fee. The museum was actually just a converted apartment stuffed full of artifacts salvaged from Czechoslovakia S.S.R. after it collapsed in 1989. It was cramped but informative and eye-opening. It was located, ironically enough, between a McDonalds and a casino.

As I looked over the artifacts, I was struck by stylized Soviet propaganda posters, which were full of heroic smiling peasants. It served as such a contrast against how threadbare the lives of people actually were. The fantasy and reality were very different.

The most sobering moment came when I sat in a small room to watch a short video. The VCR tape was a grainy late 1980's quality, the kind I had grown up watching. Except, instead of family movies, the footage showed the Communist police ruthlessly beating protesters on Wenceslas Square. Unlike the black and white Nazi footage that felt ancient, this footage felt startlingly new. Wenceslas Square looked almost exactly the same. I had been on that street less than an hour ago.

The museum was a good peek into the lives of everyday folks under communism. It was pretty crappy for almost everybody. Everything was uniform. Food selections and even alcohol were limited. The exhibits on the brutal 1968 revolt were also eye-opening. While Americans were dancing at Woodstock, Czech youths the same age were being gunned down. It was hard to see Americans as anything but spoiled.

At the same time, the museum would stray into far right-wing territory. 'Many Czechs wished for their own General Pinochet' is a line that stood out to me. The idea that a people might yearn for a bloodthirsty dictator was foreign to me at that time. Little did I know that only a few years away conservative American politicians would quite literally be parroting this very line.

Most of my generation thinks of the Cold War as ancient history, if they think of it at all. Historically speaking though, it was only a blink of an eye ago. Thirty years is nothing. At the museum I thought about how Russia had just forcibly annexed the Crimea. I did not yet fully understand that our world was just starting to slide back into something similar to the times documented in the museum. Looking at the propaganda, rigged elections and fake news of the past, I had no inkling that I was living in the final twilight of the post-Cold War era.

My generation had grown up at the 'End of History', when the collapse of communism meant that liberal democracy was going to spread everywhere. It's naïve now, of course, but in this museum, I would never have thought these techniques would make a comeback, much less in my own country.

I walked out of the museum feeling down about man's ability to be so cruel to each other. I walked around the Old Town with my hands in my pockets. It was hours before I was to meet up with the girls. I trudged to the Square to buy some food from the Russians. They ripped me off again, but this time I just felt sorry for them. They looked miserable and well aware that the locals hated them. But, even counting the scam, the sausages were still the cheapest around.

I wandered out of the Old Town into the New, feeling tired and sad. I felt more like a rat in a maze every block I turned. I was getting burnt out. My prior admiration of Prague was forgotten as I decided the city was shit and did not impress me.

I wandered alone down old streets, past churches and bustling intersections. I was acutely aware of how far away I was from home and how alone I was. Nearly thirty days of constant walking and my legs groaned with each step I took. I was exhausted, both mentally and physically.

I reflected that the streets I walked had seen horses, carriages, festivals, cars, the laughter of a million children, the Nazi's and the Communists. I thought about the endless waves of blood that had been spilled here by papists, Hapsburgs, Germans, and Russians. Who was I to walk these streets? I felt utterly insignificant next to such history. I felt very much like a foreigner, trespassing on somebody's land, like I wasn't supposed to be here.

I looked up at the blue sky between the buildings. I had only heard amazing things about Prague, but now I just wanted to be somewhere else. I couldn't take any more crowds or museums or scammers trying to get my money. Like London or Paris or Madrid, it was just another big city with expensive meals and cheap souvenirs. I would have killed for a nice cold Guinness in a quiet pub.

I wandered through more streets, spilled onto a four-lane road, and walked past jewelry vendors. I heard shouts in Czech, Russian and Hungarian. I had felt a weird foreboding angst when the train had entered the city, and I didn't know why. Here, alone in a strange city in a strange country on a strange continent the feeling returned stronger than ever. As I walked, I wished I were lying in bed. I had no energy yet kept moving, as if in a trance.

I entered a sleek modern mall. I rode the escalators up and down several levels, wandering into bookstores, desperate to read something in English. For the first time since January, I felt uncomfortably foreign. I am not sure why it hit me here. Maybe it was the museum of cruelty I had just seen, the thieving Russians or perhaps I was just tired.

I don't remember getting back to the Old Town Square, but I sat down near the Clock. I watched a couple take wedding photos. I was too close to them, but I was too tired to think or care. I felt numb. All of a sudden, Sam and Chloe rushed out of the crowd and grabbed my arm, hissing at me to move.

"You are in their pictures," they said as they hustled me away. Maybe this melancholia had hit because I had been alone all morning? After all, I had had no time to myself in four weeks. All day and night I was with these girls. The dark cloud continued to hover over me for the rest of the afternoon.

Part of the reason I felt weird was because of a newfound awareness of being American. I never expected this identity shift when I came Europe. Like most young liberal people who came of age during the Iraq War, I never considered myself particularly patriotic or proud of my country. Yet, here in Europe, people identified me as an American first and foremost. Having my nationality be my first layer of identity was entirely novel to me.

A year or two later a German friend will tell me that she loved America because "there is energy in the air that you can feel." Here in Europe, I felt proud of my country for the first time. Sure, we have terrible violence and a broken healthcare system, but damn if we aren't charming and friendly. I missed people asking me how my day was. A lot of Europeans consider this to be rude and fake when they visit America.

"They don't even care" they moan, confused as to why every shopkeeper and waitress asks them how their day was. But I think there is sincerity when we ask this question. We want to hear that you are doing 'awesome' or 'super.' We want to be upbeat and confident. I missed the comfort of America as we crossed the Charles Bridge to the west bank of the city.

Unbeknownst to me, we were embarking on a very long and hot walk across the other side of the city. Near the Prague Castle, there was an interesting monument. It was larger than life Czech flag being ripped into different parts. It was nominally to commemorate the dismantling of the country on the eve of World War II, but could also serve as a memorial to any of the many times the country had been invaded and dismembered.

We climbed up the steep hills of the city to admire scenic Prague from the old walls of the castle. We bought smoothies and drank them as we overlooked the red roofs and curving river. Turning around, we found and entered the St Vitus church we had admired last night.

Inside the church, we gaped at the massive stained glass windows as they flooded the church with dark green, red and blue light. Gothic architects thought that light was divine and sought to make their churches diffuse as much sunlight as possible. I truly enjoyed seeing these old royal cathedrals, admiring the gold and marble and hearing my voice echo across the vast halls.

Outside we once more admired the black stone exterior. I don't know why all the old buildings in Prague were black. Whether it's from age or soot, it had an interesting effect. It made Prague seem brooding and dark. It made it seem mysterious, sexy, and possibly dangerous. It certainly made Prague stand out among the other European cities in that regard. Leaving the castle, we threw some pennies in a beautiful fountain for good luck.

Winding our way north and then east, we passed through a few miles of empty gardens. They were pretty, but I was too tired to care about them. At one point we passed a trainer holding huge birds of prey. For only a dollar or two, the trainer would have these giant eagles and raptors sit on your arm. Some of these birds had a six-foot wingspan. I almost did it, but in the end, their sharp talons and fierce beaks were too much for me to risk.

Eventually, the gardens ended and emptied us out into a rolling field covered in white dandelions. A warm gust of wind blew and the dandelions took flight. They were so thick that we could see nothing but white. We stood there, lost for a moment with white dandelions falling around us, green gardens behind us, a gleaming blue river to our left and beyond that the red tile roofs of Prague.

We continued. Samie and I were openly complaining now. We were hungry and wanted to go back to the hostel. Chloe, however, insisted we complete our walk by going to the Metronome at the north bend of the Vltava River. Chloe always pushed to do more, to see more and experience more. At the times, like this, Sam and I would try to push back, often to no avail. And, now, I am deeply grateful for her in doing this. Travel is a precious thing and Chloe realized this well before I did.

The Metronome was where that great Stalin statue once stood. It had been the largest stone statue in the world, before it was torn down shortly after Stalin's death. For decades the pedestal had simply been empty until eventually, somebody installed an eight-foot metronome. It looked comically small on the giant pedestal and was flanked by two humongous steel drums. They once were lit with bonfires that had cast a sinister red glow on Stalin's face. Now they were covered in graffiti and skateboarding youth.

Crossing back over the Vltava on a footbridge, we re-entered the city on the north end, passing by the classic Stalinist buildings. Communist architecture is large, featureless and ugly. It's as if they tried to make it unappealing. Picture the worst of 1970's cheap plywood and faux-wood paneling and make it worse; the result is Communist architecture.

At long last, we returned to our hostel, finally free from the endless walking and glaring sun. We ate some pasta that Samie whipped up, and then went work on our papers. It was nice to relax after a long day, but I soon lost focus. I laid in my bunk trying in vain to concentrate as the sun set outside our window. As a traveler, I could be very inconsistent. That afternoon I had desperately wanted to return to my room. Now that I was there, I was looking up stuff to do in Prague, unable to concentrate on my work.

"Hey Chloe" I asked softly. "Wanna do a ghost tour with me?"

Chloe looked up excitedly. "Yeah, of course!"

I had been rereading a few of my favorite Reddit ghost stories the night before, after our conversation at the church. My paranormal interest had been piqued. We asked Sam if she wanted to go, but of course, she politely refused.

And so, Chloe and I found ourselves on a side street near the Old Town Square right after sunset. We stood gathered with a couple of other international travelers. We were a group of about ten. When we bought the tickets from the store, we asked the cashier how we would identify the guide.

"You will know when you see him," the ticket seller said mysteriously.

Outside, we waited and looked around. Nobody else was on the deserted street. Although we were only a block or two from the Russian markets, all the shops on this side street had closed. It was just us who stood there on the narrow cobblestone street, bathed in the orange glow of electric streetlights.

To our left the street curved gently out of sight. On this far wall of a building, a shadow appeared. The shadow was long and oddly shaped, like as if they were Dracula in an old movie. My brain was puzzled by the shadow until the dark figure turned the corner and came into view.

It was a man wearing a tall black top hat, a flowing black cape and a cowl that nearly reached his ears. Beneath the cloak he wore an old-fashioned suit. In his outstretched arm, he held a gas lantern, the flickering light from it casting his caped shadow in all directions

On this street, all the modern neon lights and signs had been turned off. For a moment I was utterly transported a hundred and twenty years back in time as the man approached us, striding down the elegant old street.

The guide came up to us and grinned a toothy smile. "Hey guy's how's it going?" he asked with only a slight accent. Despite the outfit, the guide was not the least bit sinister or scary. He was a jovial young Czech man. He told us he was a little embarrassed by the costume he had to wear it but enjoyed his job a lot.

Our group was full of paranormal skeptics and so nobody took the tour too seriously. Instead of bone-chilling stories, the guide took on a comical tone as he discussed the local legends surrounding the old buildings.

We crossed around to a few of the famous Prague sites and heard some predictable stories of ladies-in-white and hexed kings. We saw the exterior of an old tuberculosis ward, supposedly haunted by dead children. We did get to see some spooky abandoned buildings on quiet cobblestone streets. It was creepy to peer inside the boarded up windows in these dirty old buildings. Sometimes, the guide told us, homeless men will gaze back and scare his groups.

The tour had been fun, and our guide was a joy. It was nice walking around the Old Town at night when there was absolutely nobody else around. It was also enjoyable to get such a different take on the European monuments and buildings we saw every day.

Our tour wrapped up after an enjoyable hour. Chloe and I went back to the hostel, amped up from the tour. It was still early, and the three of us wanted to cut loose after working so much on our papers.

Back in Madrid, we had a gotten a tip that there was a particularly neat bar named U-Sudo. The girls who told us about it had made it sound awesome. The bar was supposedly located in an underground bunker. It seemed different and interesting, so the three of us went to check it out.

We found the bar quickly as it was nearby. Inside it looked like a typical hole-in-the-wall pub. It seemed ok, but certainly nothing special. We stood near the bar, disappointed.

Then, we saw people walking to the back of the room and disappearing. The room was tiny, and the people were going in without coming back out. A feeling of excitement grew as we walked over and found a big heavy wooden door. We swung it open and saw a steep set of stone stairs that descended downwards, into darkness.

We followed the stairs down. They took us into a big dark underground room full of tables and chairs with a bar on the far end. The Clash was bumping over the loudspeakers. U-Sudo was perfect. Looking around the room, we found there were, in fact, multiple rooms upon rooms accessed through narrow concrete doorways. Electric candles dimly lit the seemingly endless rooms. A thick haze of cigarette smoke hung heavy over everything. Unlike a regular bar, there was no ventilation, since we were underground.

We settled in a room with a ceiling so high, we couldn't even see it through the dark hazy smoke. As the girls claimed a well-worn wooden table for us, I doubled back to buy some drinks. Like the rooms, there were multiple bars scattered around the place. I went up to one and ordered a beer.

"Three beers, pilsner" I yelled over the music, holding up my fingers and miming drinking. I was too tired to try the challenging Czech language. The bartender rolled their eyes at me, just another foreigner ruining a bar for locals.

During the walking tour, I had been told that the Pilsner style, named for the Czech town of Plzen, was a traditional Czech beer. I wanted to try the local brew. They handed a big mug of Pilsner for twenty korunas. The beer was just under a US dollar. I raised my eyebrows in surprise. Beer in the Czech Republic was amazingly cheap.

The beer I was drinking was called Pilsner Urquell and may be the single best beer I had in Europe. It was a pure, clean lager with a fresh bitter bite and smooth finish. It was incredible. This pilsner ('Urquell' is German for 'original') started a beer revolution in the 1880's. I could see why. This beer style dominated all beer sales for over a hundred subsequent years and continues to do so today.

A lot of beer snobs dismiss lagers out of hand. I have drunk Pilsner-Urquell in America and have found it a bit flat and disappointing. But, damn, on tap and fresh in Prague it was mind-blowing.

I drank nearly two liters for less than five dollars or so. Sam and Chloe switched back and forth between mojitos, pilsners, and cider. Soon we were very drunk. As we sat drinking in the smoky bunker, Chloe opened up to us about her rough childhood. Sam and I both felt a bit guilty. We would often overrule Chloe when we voted on something. Typically, Sam and I would vote together. Her stories made me reflect on why Chloe might have been mad at us on and off at various points on our trip.

Chloe and I have an unusual relationship. We had been thrown together by circumstance and had very similar personalities. Sam had been afraid this would lead to us butting heads, but we got along better than not.

Deep underground and knocking back drinks the three of us had a real heart-to-heart conversations at our little wooden table underneath the clouds of cigarette smoke. We moved from room to room, bar hopping within the same bunker.

After a few hours of revelry, we left U-Sudo and stumbled back home, laughing drunkenly and in good spirits. It had been a long day, but we each felt good from our heartfelt conversation.

Our mood grew more somber as we got ready for bed. Before I had booked the ghost tour, we had come across a different one and had decided to book it. Tomorrow, the three of us would be heading to a concentration camp.

Prague/Terezin, Day Twenty-Nine: 25th of April

We woke up with muted spirits and ate breakfast in silence. We had a strange feeling about going to Terezin, a concentration camp. We wanted to see it but it felt inappropriate to be excited about it.

Without fanfare, we packed our lunches and walked to the Old Town Square meet our group. The tour was to last all day. We chatted with the tour guide as the sun began to rise over the square, casting a golden light. The Russians had not yet opened their shops, and the Square was quiet and peaceful.

"It's not really a fun tour," he told us as we filled out the waivers, "but I think it's really important." Our guide was tall and blonde with a serious face.

Our group was maybe only twelve people, including us. The camp itself was over an hour away by train, so we walked over to the central train station. On the way, we took a detour to see the Jubilee Synagogue. It was built in a Moorish style with bulbs and flying arches. It was gaudily multicolored, with bright pink and blue hues that looked like candy cane stripes. I was surprised that it had survived the Nazis. Apparently, they had used the building for storage.

From the synagogue, we got to the train station and boarded the train. The car was old, from the 1950's. The model was, coincidentally, very similar to the models the Germans and non-Jews would have ridden on. The prisoner, however, would have been packed into cattle cars. Because they were so old, the toilets emptied directly onto the tracks.

"This is why Czech fields are so green and healthy," the guide said, laughing.

The cars were cramped. Inside the cabins, two benches faced one another. Across from us sat an old man with a bushy white beard. With his legs crossed and fingers interlaced, we made small talk.

He was an American from Boston. One of his direct ancestors had been put on trial during the Salem Witch Trials. He was a bit eccentric, but his bright blue eyes were warm and kind. The topic turned to travel, and then to Barcelona. We told him how we liked that city.

"I was beaten and robbed in Barcelona," he said gently, as if discussing the weather.

"Oh no," I said, "Was that a long time ago?" assuming it had happened many years ago.

"It was last week," he said softly and then chuckled sadly.

I didn't know how to respond to that, so I told him I found Barcelona to be lovely and immediately felt like an asshole. The rest of train ride was awkward as we tried to make more small talk after that revelation. The man seemed remarkably well adjusted for having been beaten and robbed last week.

Soon enough our train pulled into Terezin. It was the saddest, most run-down station I have ever seen. There were no benches or lights or even a building. Instead, there was just a sagging wooden platform one would climb onto to board the train. Overgrown weeds pushed through the rotting wood planks.

The dilapidated station set a grim tone as we walked a short distance on a gravel road. On both sides of the street, tall trees and shrubs made us feel isolated, as if we were in the wilderness. When the tree line ended, we arrived in an open field where about nine thousand people were buried.

The cemetery was fairly compact. The tombstones were squat bricks stretching out before us. In the middle of the open field was a ten-foot menorah. Although not quite everybody in the cemetery was Jewish, most were. Beyond the tombstones and the menorah was a small brick building.

"This is the crematorium," the guide told us. Inside we saw bleached white stones and drains in the floor. There were only three rooms. One was for autopsies and still had some old medical equipment in it. Most of the time however, especially during the war, bodies were just laid on a metal bed and incinerated in the oven. Thirty thousand people, in addition to the nine thousand bodies buried outside, had been cremated here during the Holocaust. The bed and incinerator were preserved for us to see.

From there we trudged in silence to the town itself. Terezin had been a city for hundreds of years. During the war, the Nazis had emptied out the Czechs and used the town as a big ghetto for the Jews and a few other dissidents. When the Russians liberated the town in 1945, some residents had come back to rebuild their lives.

And so, the town was still lived in today. The buildings were old and poorly maintained. They were crumbling and run down, and there was nary a soul around. I could feel the weight of the past hanging over this place and couldn't fathom why anybody would live here now. It just felt shitty.

There were a few museums about the ghetto. Life had been cramped and unsanitary. Poles, Russians, Czechs and even a few British prisoners had been held here. The Jews had had it the worst. Many were just here temporarily before heading to Auschwitz and other death camps. We went through the little museums quickly.

Our group left the depressing village and headed to the concentration camp proper. Terezin itself was a military fortress. An aerial view of Terezin would show a vast eight-point star moat around the village. There would have been walls beyond the moat. The modern town was known as the Big Fort. The defensive layout was preciously why the Germans had used it. With the moat and walls, it was a natural place to keep thousands of people trapped.

Just outside the town was the Small Fort. It was a citadel and built in the same style as the Big Fort, in a big seven-point star. The star design was to deflect cannonballs back in the 17th and 18th centuries.

We crossed the river and stopped in front of the walls of the Small Fort. There was a big Christian cross, and a Star of David in front of the entrance. Concrete slabs about a foot long were laid out in neat, endless rows. They signified the number of dead. It was mind-numbing.

Directly inside the Small Fort we learned how Terezin was built by the Austrians, ironically enough, to keep the Prussians out. In German, the name of the town was Theresienstadt, after our old friend Maria Theresa.

The Small Fort had been used as a prison for a long before Nazis were involved. After the assassination of Franz Ferdinand, his killer Gavrilo Princip had been imprisoned here. Gavrilo lived the rest of his life here, dying from tuberculosis in 1918. Our last stop had been the home of Franz Ferdinand, and now we stood in the place where his assassin had died. These two men, a prince and his assassin, were connected by fate and history and millions upon millions had died because of it. A chill passed over me.

Outside of the museum, we saw where the 'ordinary' prisoners lived in ramshackle huts. Beyond this was a walled section of the fort. The walled section was topped with barbed wire and had the bone-chilling words ARBEIT MACHT FREI written in giant letters over the entrance.

The walled section of the Small Fort was a prison, in a prison inside a bigger, town-like, prison. It had started as a barracks for seven thousand Austrian soldiers but ended up holding over seventy thousand political and ethnic prisoners of the Nazis. The featureless brick buildings had no furniture save for hard wooden bunks. Tens of people were crammed into each bunk every night. The cramped rooms were suffocating.

Next door to the barracks were the showers. The nozzles would have sprayed water from the ceiling. In other camps, they sprayed gas. Terezin was 'only' a concentration camp, not a death camp, so here only water came out.

But, at our last stop, we saw the worst cell. It was the size of college dorm room and built entirely of concrete. The room was dark and dank. There was one tiny window twenty feet above the ground. It had been made to house one or two prisoners in solitary confinement. The Nazis had stuffed a hundred Jews in here at a time. I shivered. I could feel the horror in the pit of my stomach and the back of my neck. I felt physically ill in the room.

We left the walled-off portion of the Small Fort and sat down to each lunch. We sat in front of buildings where ordinary people had suffered extraordinarily. We hadn't planned it on purpose, but we had ham sandwiches. It felt wrong to eat them here.

Later, the tour group filed into a theater to watch a short film about the camp. As horrible as it was, Terezin was one of the least deadly camps during the Holocaust. Compared to the people at Auschwitz or Buchenwald, the Terezin prisoners lived a life of quality. Because of this, the Germans had used Terezin as a propaganda tool.

'Look the Jews are treated well and are happy' the Germans would say while showing footage of Terezin. Late in the war, the Germans forced the Jews to put on a musical, complete with an orchestra, child actors and beautiful backdrops. They filmed the musical and used it to show the Red Cross that the Jews were so happy they were doing stage plays.

Once the Nazi's were satisfied with the propaganda film, they promptly sent the director, the actors, the orchestra and most of the children straight to Auschwitz. They were killed upon arrival.

We filed out of the theater and walked back to the sad train station.

"Why would anybody live here?" an American woman asked our tour guide.

"They always lived here," he told us with a shrug. "To them, the events of a few short years don't matter because they've been there for hundreds of years."

"And," he continued, "the rent is really cheap."

The experience at the concentration camp had been grimly enlightening. Like all Americans, I had read and been taught about the wooden bunks, the empty showers, and the endless tombstones. Here I learned knowing and seeing were different things. It had been an eye-opening experience.

On our train ride back, we sat with a friendly American couple from Houston and an Indian-British couple from Singapore. I think all of us were eager to move past the darkness we had just seen, so we made lighthearted discussion. We talked about food and beer, and our train ride passed quickly.

Back in Prague, we thanked our guide and bid farewell to our tour friends. We went back to the hostel for another homemade pasta dinner. We were still a bit too bummed to work on our papers, so after eating, we went back to the Old Town Square again.

The square was charming at night. The red tents were muted against the dark night and the few streetlights. We strolled around the square. The statues looked mystical and mysterious when they were shrouded in darkness.

Leaving the girls behind for a moment, I decided to pay the two dollar entry-fee and climb up the Clock Tower. I had seen the view so many times from the ground that I wanted something more. Inside the tower, I, along with other tourists, slowly made our way up metal catwalks and ladders. Inside the tower, we could see the massive gears and pulleys that controlled the animatronics.

At the top of the tower, I was rewarded with incredible views. I could see the Prague Castle, the Metronome and the little tops of the red tents in the square. The whole city was gently lit up beneath me. I felt serene up there, far away from any darkness I had experienced earlier. Although the top of the Tower was crowded with tourists, everybody was quiet, hushed by the majestic view of the beautiful city. I could have looked out over the city for hours, far away from the sounds of traffic and street performers.

Eventually, I reluctantly climbed back down the Tower and met again with Sam and Chloe. We bought some sausages and pilsner from the Russians. By now we knew to hand them exact change. There were no chairs in the square, but there were small high-top tables we could set our drinks down on and lean against. We huddled around one to eat and drink. Each bite of my Russian sausage was better than the last, and each swig of pilsner seemed smoother and more soothing. I felt at home. I felt wholly at ease with myself.

Prague, Day Thirty: 26th of April

I opened my eyes to the sunlight peeking through the closed curtains. The early morning traffic outside was going at full blast. I couldn't believe it was our last full day in Prague.

Early on in the trip, Bruges and Amsterdam felt like they stretched on and on. We only had a single full day in each city, but both had felt like eternities. We had been in Prague for a week, and it had flown by in the blink of an eye. Maybe we had just become too comfortable in our travels. Meet the locals, see beautiful churches and eat strange food. Wash rinse and repeat.

After our fantastic breakfast, Samie and I somehow convinced Chloe to explore on her own. As soon as she left, Samie and I promptly went back to sleep. We were napping gloriously when a knock came on the door. I dragged myself to the door, thoroughly bedraggled. There stood a laughing maid telling us we needed to change rooms right now.

I was confused for a moment before I remembered we had tacked on another day in a separate booking. I had assumed the room would stay the same. It would not. Sam and I went down to the lobby and swapped keys with the attendant. Our new room was down the hall and around the corner from the old one.

We swung the door open and were surprised to find that the new room was even better. Instead of three twin beds, it had a king and a double. Even better there was an ensuite bathroom and shower. Best of all, the room was the opposite side of the building, away from the street, meaning it was much quieter. We were quite pleased with the new set-up. Not wanting to lose Chloe we decided to hang out until she came back.

Now, Chloe had been gone when we switched rooms. When she left, our things were spread out all over the place.

Wet clothes were drying in the windows, school papers were spread out, and laptops were plugged in. When she got back to the room, she turned the key in the lock and opened the door.

Inside, to Chloe's horror, she saw three neatly made beds and an empty room. Chloe immediately got weak in the knees. Her worst nightmare was coming true.

They left Prague without me. They stranded me in Prague, Chloe thought to herself, panic rising in her chest.

Chloe walked down to the reception, white as a ghost and tears welling up in her eyes. Before she could even explain herself, the receptionist handed her the new keys and told her what room we were in.

Back in the new room, Sam and I were sitting on the bed when the door opened, and Chloe walked in. She was pale and trembling.

"What the hell guys," she said in a shaky voice. Samie and I started laughing. After a moment, Chloe joined in. The situation was too ridiculous not too.

Once Chloe caught her breath and calmed down, the three of us walked down to the Old Town Square. At the square, we poked around, and then watched the clock show. We must have seen it over a dozen times but it honestly never grew old.

Ready for a change of scenery, we crossed over the Vltava River. At the far side of the Charles Bridge, we turned in the opposite direction of the castle. There was an old monastery on top of a hill we had heard about. Jess and Mahala had recommended it to us when we were in Venice. They said it was an excellent spot for lunch.

We walked up the narrow street towards the monastery. The hill the road was on was steep with tall buildings on each side. Between some buildings we could look over the slope to the city below.

There was a short brick wall on top of the hill. The former monastery stood behind the wall. We had gorgeous wide-open views of the scenic city. The grassy hillside went all the way down to the river far below us. Between the warm air and bright blue sky with puffs of white clouds I was reminded of summer in Ohio.

It was peaceful. Prague was beautiful to look at. The castle and cathedral stood proudly on the other large hill, dominating the city. Few cities had such a prominent fortress like this anymore. Turning my eyes across the river, I followed the multiple stone bridges that spanned it. Past the river, I could see the Old Town Square with the magnificent churches and spires rising high above it. Beyond that, over the red-tiled roofs, I could spy the gold dome of the National Museum. Even further away I could see modern skyscrapers. Fifteen hundred years of history and progress lay before me.

We gazed for a long time. When we finally turned away, we checked out the monastery. It had been converted into a four-star restaurant, and the prices were far higher than anything we could even remotely afford. Disappointed we walked back down the steep hill lined with shops.

Halfway down the hill were a bunch of restaurants. Their posted prices were far more affordable, so we stopped in a random one. The server took us to a tiny secluded courtyard out back. There were only two or three tables and the stone courtyard was thick with vines and potted plants. The tall old buildings around us shielded us from the sun.

The restaurant served delicious and straightforward traditional Czech food. I ate a big bowl of Czech goulash and washed it down with a hoppy pilsner. I was very content.

Samie had purchased a glass of water instead of beer. Of course, water was not free in Europe. We paid and stood up to leave.

"Wait a minute," Samie called to us, looking around furtively. With our server nowhere in sight, Sam pulled out her purse, where I could see the top of a water bottle. She carefully poured her glass of water into the water bottle hidden in her bag. It was so ridiculous I had to take a picture of it. It's one of my favorites.

"Well, I paid for it," she said, semi-embarrassed.

Later, on our walk home, we came across a public bathroom. I had to go badly, so I walked over to it. It was a squat gray concrete low-slung building. Outside of the doors sat a scruffy looking man in a hat and sunglasses at a folding table. There was a basket on the table and a sign saying how many korunas it cost to use the bathroom. It was a low price, but I couldn't shake the feeling that the guy had no authority to charge people. The whole set-up looked a little too ramshackle to be official. Either way, I dropped a few korunas into his basket as I walked in. If it was a scam, he was making a killing.

We returned to the hostel pretty early. As usual, we worked on our papers for a while. The sun set and we soon grew weary of writing.

"Hey let's go find another bar," I suggested, and the girls readily agreed. We had a handwritten list that compiled all the suggestions from the girls in Spain and our friends in Venice. We had steadily worked our way through it.

There was one last bar on the list. We had heard it was a bar with cheap cocktails and a bouldering wall. Sam had worked at a climbing gym for years, and I had a little rock climbing experience. Drinking and bouldering sounded like a fun evening.

We got dressed and hit the street. The bar was about two miles away. We could have ridden a bus, but it felt good to walk.

Our decision turned out to be a mistake, as we struggled to find the bar in the dark. After much wandering, we finally found the address. Instead of a cheap bouldering bar, there was an expensive cocktail bar and no rock wall in sight.

We walked back to our neighborhood. It started drizzling. I was tired of walking and angry we couldn't find the bar.

"Let's at least go to U-Sudo" Chloe pleaded with us, as Sam and both turned to go to the hostel.

"Please" she begged us.

We refused. In retrospect, we should have done so, as it was our last night here. But instead I was tired and wet and in no mood to sit in a smoky bar.

With an unhappy Chloe in tow, we made it back to our hostel, showered and went to bed. Our last night in Prague ended with absolutely no fanfare.

"I paid for this!" – Samie as she deftly pours water into her purse

Chapter 6: Germany

Berlin, Day Thirty-One: 27th of April

We awoke early and headed down for one last meal. I loved that we had to go through a tunnel to get to the breakfast area. It was so medieval and different than anything in America.

We took the short walk to the central train station. At one of the corners, while we were waiting for the heavy traffic to stop, a Google van drove by. For months afterward, I would obsessively check that street corner on Google Streetview, desperate to find myself. I never had any luck.

Then I forgot about it for a few years. Much later, after I had moved to Wyoming, I was killing time at work. The memory suddenly popped into my head. I pulled up Google Maps and found the street corner from memory. I pushed the timeline back.

Then, clear as day, I saw myself standing on that street corner, leather jacket slung over my arms. Chloe was looking into her purse. We were frozen in time, on a busy street corner on a beautiful Prague morning.

We boarded the train and relaxed in our seats. It was going to be a long ride. I looked out the window as we pulled into the countryside. I absentmindedly wondered about our hostel in Berlin when the thought hit me like a ton of bricks. *Our trip was almost over.* My stomach sank.

Riding trains gave me a lot of time to think. I thought about being at home in Ohio. I had been twenty-two and had practically never left home. I always had a severe case of wanderlust but had never acted on it. While other people had at least gone to college in other places, I had stayed at home and went to a community college. While other people got new and exciting jobs I kept plugging away at the gig I started in high school.

At night, back in Ohio, I would take walks around my suburban neighborhood and think about how much I wanted to get away, but I kept hanging out in the same places with the same people.

Then my life completely changed. Just over a year ago, I went through a nasty breakup. Before that had happened, I had known where my life was going. I had a plan. My then-girlfriend and I were going to get married, settle down and have kids. I knew this was going to be my future. We were shopping for a wedding ring.

Although obvious in retrospect, I was blindsided by the break-up. It occurred on New Year's Eve.

I'll never forget it. I was sitting at my friend's house about two hours before the ball dropped. The girlfriend and I had been on 'break' for a few weeks. I naively thought we might still be able to work it out. But then, she arrived at the party with her new man in tow.

As soon as they walked in together, I felt sick. I stumbled out of the house in a daze. We had started dating on New Year's Eve going into my senior year of high school. That night would have been our third anniversary.

I ended up leaving a certain group of people I had been running with for a while. I made new friends and made new connections. I quit my old job and experimented with new lifestyles. I was well into my third year of college but was finally experiencing new things for the first time.

Outside of the train window, we sped past flowing rivers, green hills, and quaint little villages. The last year had been tough, but by that autumn things had begun to change. For the first time in a long time, I started feeling really good. I had made new friends and met Samie. My new relationship with her was going great, and now I was five weeks across Europe.

As I looked out of the train window, I felt like my life had turned around. I was heading into my last semester or two of school. I had come of age in England and Europe. I could feel that I was growing immensely. Here in Europe, I saw a version of myself I could be proud of. Instead of dreaming about my best self, I was living it.

And so, I was nervous about this grand experience ending. Would life go back to normal in Ohio? Would these experiences wash away like chalk drawings in the rain? Would I be doomed to revert to my former self?

I pondered this as our train chugged over the German border. Neat, precise German towns replaced the red-tiled cottages and haphazardly laid out Czech villages. We were riding alongside the Elbe River. The Bavarian villages looked like they were out of a fairytale. They were nestled between the tall peaks of the Alps and a rushing blue river. The landscape was green and vibrant, well-manicured and wealthy.

We shared our train car with a bald, tattooed muscular man and his blonde-haired pre-teen daughter. They quietly munched on some cookies. As we got closer to Berlin, the father turned to us and gestured for us to eat some of his cookies. He was very nice.

Our appetites aroused, Samie and I left to explore the dining car. We followed the signs until we arrived. Pulling the door open we saw a swanky room with tables already set. They had crisp white tablecloths and crystal glasses. There was a chandelier above us. We went to the bar to order. Stealing glances at the menus on the tables I knew there was no way in hell we could afford anything. We ended up splitting a bag of chips.

Later our train pulled into the central train station, the Hauptbahnhof. We grabbed our things and hopped off the train. Our hostel was near the East Train Station, Ostbanhhoff. From right inside the station we were able to get onto an S-

Bahn. We were familiar with these from Vienna and found our way with no hassle. We rode across the city center, the *Mitte*. It was all giant skyscrapers. They were brand new as the area had been a no-mans land during the Cold War. So far Berlin looked nothing like the other European cities.

We arrived at Ostbanhhoff. That much was easy. Our hostel was located on the street Straße der Pariser Kommune. Try as we might, we wandered around the outside of the station looking for the street in vain. I was nervous to ask for help, but we had no choice if we wanted to avoid hours of wandering. We went back into the station, with much trepidation, I went to the help desk.

"*Sprechen Sie Englisch?*" I asked nervously, and the middle-aged man shook his head no. I would soon learn that older people in the former East Germany did not usually speak excellent English.

I took a breath to steady myself and asked: "*Kennen Sie wo der Staße vom Pariser Kommune ist?*"

It was incorrect grammar, but the man nodded. He was probably just happy I spoke a bit of German.

"*Ja,*" he said, speaking loudly and slowly. "*Links, dann links wieder.*" He gestured turning left twice.

"*Links dann links wieder,*" I repeated, and then thanked the man profusely. Left and then left again.

Should be easy, I thought.

We followed his directions and found the hostel immediately. I was over the moon that I had been able to communicate successfully in German. Despite my terrible grammar and conjugation, the man had understood me. The encounter gave me the confidence to speak more throughout my time in Germany.

The hostel itself was quite interesting. We were in the former DDR, East Germany. The different between East and West Berlin was still noticeable. The west side of town felt sleek and modern, while the eastern part was rundown. The buildings in the east were tall, imposing and featureless. The sky seemed perpetually gray.

I also sensed a kind of hopefulness here, the kind that can only be found in places like this. I liked East Berlin. It reminded me a lot of Cleveland.

I, like anybody from the Rust Belt, grew up surrounded by the ruins of the past. I grew up seeing empty factories and desolate industrial areas. I always knew something significant had been here once, but no longer. For me, a city isn't complete without some rusting factories, broken windows and graffiti-covered walls. Even though Cleveland is no longer like that, I will still feel most comfortable in cities where the past is as strong as the present. East Berlin felt like home.

We entered our hostel and checked in. The building was a large complex, several stories high. It was once a Jewish dormitory for girls back at the turn of the century, before becoming Communist apartments. The old wooden railings and stairs, and high vaulted ceiling still held a trace of its former glory.

Our room was three floors up. We walked up the stairs and checked it out. There were ten bunks and not much else. No complaints from us. We chatted with two of our roommates, both Americans on spring break, just like us.

We claimed our bunks by throwing our stuff on them, went to the bathroom, then hit the streets. It was early afternoon, and we only had a few days in Berlin. We grabbed a map from the lobby and headed out.

Our hostel was located very close to the East Side Gallery. The Gallery once formed the interior of the Berlin Wall. It was one of the few large parts of the Wall still standing. Artists had covered it with large paintings.

The paintings were meditations on art, violence, division, and world peace. People walked by, gently touching the wall as they passed. There was construction happening around the wall, and I later found out that we had missed a protest of thirty thousand people here only a few weeks previously. A new apartment complex was being built in an empty field near the wall, and people were protesting, wanting to preserve this remaining part of the Wall. Oh, how times change.

Right past the end of the Gallery was a handsome red brick bridge, named the Oberbaumbrücke. It was faux-medieval style with red Gothic inspired towers and small castle walls. The bridge was delightful now but once formed the border of the two Berlins. The Spree River below us had been heavily mined and patrolled by border guards within my lifetime, only twenty years ago.

We got off the bridge and entered West Berlin. Everything was just a bit nicer. The green spaces were better manicured, there were more trees, and everything felt more vibrant. Children were running around and playing on the sidewalks. One was lowering a basket down from his balcony for his friends to fill with rocks.

Not too far into western Berlin, we found a restaurant for dinner. It was on an attractive shaded street with little traffic. The restaurant was painted red and gold, and mostly empty. It was an eatery run by Indians and served traditional German food. I ordered the wiener schnitzel and a dark lager.

The portions were huge and tasty. My beer was large and frosty. My first meal in Germany was everything I had expected. Samie and Chloe were both drinking something called a Berliner Weisse. The menu had been advertising the drink heavily.

"Red or green?" the waiter had asked, and the girls both picked red. Why not?

When the drink arrived, it was in a goblet that looked like a martini glass but much thicker. The glass had gold trim on its rim. The liquid itself was fizzy and was a dark pinkish color. Sam sipped it tentatively, then looked up in surprise.

"Wow it's really good," she said.

Tomorrow, on a walking tour, I will learn all about the history of the Berliner Weisse. It is a traditional sour beer, the kind popular in Belgium. It's a wheat, or white, beer, hence the name. When Napoleon had occupied Berlin, his troops had taken to adding their own herb mixes into the local beer. The French influence had the effect of making it more champagne-like, bubbly and sweet. Over the years the herb mix evolved into a sweet grenadine syrup now used to flavor the beer. It was not as popular as it once was, but it was still considered the drink of Berlin.

The beer was tart and refreshing. Back in the States, I will try a lot of beers done in this style. Unfortunately, Americans think that adding syrup to beer is an unfathomable tragedy and refuse to do it. It's a shame because the modified drink is so tasty. Also, adding the syrup is what makes it a Berliner Weisse and is the proper way to drink it. Sadly, I have not yet had an original Berliner Weisse since Berlin.

Germany had always been atop of my list of places to visit. I never once thought I might study abroad in England, rather, I had always assumed it would be in Germany. I had never much thought about England one way or another before I signed up to come there. Germany, on the other hand, always fascinated me. I studied the language on and off for years, met German exchange students and watched German movies. This country felt right for me.

We finished our meal and strolled back home. On our way, we noticed the strange pedestrian symbols. The 'stop' symbol was a man in a red wide-brimmed hat with arms outstretched in both directions. The green 'go' symbol was the same little man, now happily turned to the side and jovially telling us to cross. They were cute little twists on the dull red hand, and white stick figure one typically sees.

We got back to the hostel and decided to call it an early night. These papers wouldn't write themselves. As we walked up to grab our computers, we admired how damn big the building was. Each room was named after a figure in Greek mythology. Naturally, Chloe loved it. There was a bar attached to the lobby, so we staked out a few tables to do our work.

Soft music played in the dim bar. It was a warm evening, and summer was in the air. As a consequence, all the hard-drinking hostel travelers were in the spacious courtyard, leaving the bar nice and quiet for us. The courtyard was nestled between the tall apartments that blocked out the sunlight during the day. There were a lot of picnic tables, and the kitchen was located out there, in a separate building.

I sat down and got to work. I was putting the finishing touches on one of my papers. I felt a sense of relief as I clicked the save icon. It had been my hardest paper. I was hoping the next few would be easier.

While I worked, I chatted on Facebook with my good friend AJ. He was saying how pumped I must be to be in Germany. Although I write about great sights and moments, at the time I was exhausted and stressed. Some of these papers were due next week, and I still had several to go.

In retrospect, all my travel memories became bright and vibrant. I rarely recall the stress of my papers, the constant search for public restrooms and places to fill my water bottle. I tend to forget how I needed to wash my clothes in tiny hostel sinks and hang them in windows, praying that they dry in time to pack. I tend to not recall my empty stomach from when I was too poor to buy a meal, or couldn't afford to see a famous museum. Traveling can be hard and stressful work.

Like all of us, in my memories, I only recall beautiful moments of joy and pleasure. I recall grand buildings and sweeping views, not the sounds of traffic and dirty sidewalks. I remember the romance of riding trains and not the untold hours of boredom on them. Like all of us, I remember my European adventures almost exclusively in glowing terms.

I closed my laptop and went upstairs to go to bed. I greeted our other roommates in there. In addition to the two Americans, I met two other students from the UK, an elderly Indian couple and an African businessman. Luckily everybody was reasonable and agreed to turn the lights out so we could sleep. For being in a full ten-person dorm, I fell asleep quickly.

Berlin, Day Thirty-Two: 28th of April

It was painfully early in the morning when an incessant jangling sound awakened me. It went on and on and on. I lifted my head after about ten minutes to find out what the hell that noise was.

Looking down from my top bunk, I saw the old Indian couple from last night. The woman was getting ready for the day and packing up her things. She was trying to move quietly, but her silver bangles kept knocking into each other. I couldn't be mad at a little old lady like her whatsoever.

The three of us got up shortly after. We went about our morning routines, bustling around the small room. Right in the middle of the room was a little card table and a folding chair. The African businessman from last night sat in a suit, quiet and unmoving, the entire time.

Then, as Chloe walked in from the shower, drying her long red hair with a towel, the man looked up and asked if he could borrow her shampoo.

"Uh, yeah?" Chloe said quizzically, handing him the bottle. She looked us with confusion on her face. It was apparent she had been put on the spot and had not wanted to give it over.

The man nodded his thanks and took the shampoo bottle. He set it on the table and resumed sitting completely still. The man was bald.

The three of us went down for breakfast. We saw a buffet lined up on the bar and it looked good, but upon closer inspection, we found it was not free. Unwilling to pay for breakfast, Chloe and I decided to skip it and head out for a walking tour. Sam, as usual, opted to stay behind.

Chloe and I walked up the street to the S-Bahn, which was located next to the train station. Rough looking teens were kicking a soccer ball around next to some derelict buildings. If it had been basketball, I would have mistaken this for Akron.

Chloe and I rode the S-Bahn to the famous Friedrichstraße. The ride from East Berlin to the city center was illumining. The closer we got to the heart of the city, the newer and more impressive everything was. When we stepped off the S-Bahn, we were surrounded by towering modern glass skyscrapers. Active construction sites buzzed with activity. The city center was utterly different than any other European city I had been too.

From the S-Bahn stop, we made our way the Brandenburg Gate. The famous stone arches looked over a pedestrian square. These 18th-century pillars, topped by bronze chariots, overlooked some of the swankiest buildings I'd seen on this continent. The Gate itself was indeed impressive to see, although I was a tad disappointed, as usual, by its size. It looked huge in pictures but in reality was only a little over two stories tall.

Not being too familiar with the geography of Berlin, I hadn't realized that the Berlin Wall had cut directly through this area. For the whole Cold War, the platz had been forgotten by the public. It had been heavily guarded on both sides and was a no-go zone. I soon learned that Nike in her chariot was a replica because the Soviets had shelled the old one. I was shocked to learn that the Gate wasn't even fully repaired until 2002.

We didn't have too much time to admire the Gate before our walking tour started. As far as famous pedestrian squares go, this one was on the smaller side and not too crowded. We found our guide quickly, as he was holding the big red umbrella the company always used.

Our guide's name was Craig, and he was from Scotland. All of our other tour guides had been locals of the city, so it was somewhat jarring to hear his animated Scottish accent describe the culture and history of the city. Because almost none of Berlin survived the Second World War, our tour focused on the Cold War-era Berlin. Our tour began where we stood, on Pariser Platz, under the Gate.

"This is the American embassy," the guide said pointing towards a modest building with a few American flags fluttering in the breeze. People nodded politely.

"And this is the hotel where Michael Jackson dangled the baby over the railing," the guide said, pointing in the other direction towards a sleek hotel. An excited gasp rose out of the crowd and everybody began snapping pictures.

We began a to walk in a large circle, weaving in and out of the city center. We would pop through the western and eastern sides, but mostly stayed in the Mitte. As we walked, I was again struck by how new everything was. It felt like I was in Chicago more so than Europe. Most of Berlin was built after World War II, and here in the Mitte, it was all built after my birth.

The entire city center had been an open-fire zone until 1989. Like American cities, there were few relics of the past. Instead, Berlin seemed intently focused on the future.

Not far from the Gate, we came to the 'Monument to the Murdered Jews of Europe.' It occupied a sizeable area right in the heart of the city. The monument consisted of dozens of black granite columns, placed on uneven ground and of varying heights. The stones start at chest level but soon tower over your head as you walk into the forest of black slabs.

"Are they gravestones?" the tour guide asked rhetorically. There was no answer as the monument was purposefully abstract. They were meant to be walked around in and mediated on. It was a tasteful monument.

"The Germans are one of the few peoples to openly confront their past," the guide said, proud of his adopted home. So far, every other country we had visited was all too willing to try to bury it.

The guide told us the Jewish Cemetery in Prague inspired the monument. Of course, we had just seen that cemetery a few days ago, so the comparison was especially apt for Chloe and I.

We walked a bit further and ended up in front of a vast, imposing building. The building was fiercely symmetrical. Not a stone was out of place, and there were no frivolous decorative features. The guide explained that this was one of the only buildings from the Third Reich left in the world.

The building had, ironically, been the headquarters of the Luftwaffe. We were standing right outside the office of Hermann Goering. Miraculously undamaged during the utter destruction of Berlin, it had fallen inside the Soviet half. Since there were few intact buildings in the new DDR (*Deutsche Demokratische Republik*, or East Germany), the Soviets had converted this into the capitol building of their new satellite state. A Stalinist mural across the bottom of the buildings showed a montage of glorious workers and peasants united in communism.

There had been only one single uprising in the DDR during the Cold War. In 1953 the people rose up against the Soviets. Perhaps they were inspired by the fact that nobody had offered real resistance to Hitler. Regardless, the Soviets brutally crushed the uprising. Their reaction was so intense that the

Germans never dared to resist again. So, after the Wall came down, the Germans put a plaque to commemorate the uprising next to the mural. On the ground in front of the mural, there was a blown-up photo of the rebellion set under glass, offering two contrasting views of the DDR.

Not too far from here, we saw some standing stretches of the Wall, or *Die Mauer*. People had died attempting to hop this wall. It was situated right next to the old Gestapo headquarters. Although the building has been destroyed in the war, archaeologists had recently been uncovering the basement. A museum was built adjacent to it. Chloe and I made a mental note to visit this place later.

Nearby was the infamous Checkpoint Charlie, or rather a mock-up of it. The real one had been dismantled after reunification. Now they had a phony replacement staffed by actors in American Army uniforms.

"It's all fake," chirped the tour guide.

Around the corner from the faux-Checkpoint Charlie, there was a museum for Traubis. These were notoriously ugly East German cars. They were reviled during the Communist era, but have since become something of a kitschy nostalgic item. Memories of the DDR are surprisingly bright for many former East Germans.

Throughout our tour, we saw the little Ampelmännchen over and over. These were the green and red foot traffic signals. The guide told us that many East Germans did not see Germany as being 'reunified' after the Cold War. Rather, they watched West Germany engulf and replace all aspects of East German life. Everything from food and drinks, to statues and cultural practices, disappeared within months and were replaced by their West German equivalents.

When the *Westies* finally tried to remove the Ampelmännchen, the *Osties* stood up in protest. They fought to keep this one little part of their heritage. Being a cute little guy, the Ampelmännchen were soon reinstated and even spread into the former West Germany. Now they were a ubiquitous symbol of Berlin.

As the tour wound down, one of our last stops was in the courtyard of a very posh apartment complex. They were precariously close to the border with West Berlin, so only trusted Communist elites were allowed to live in them. These apartments had been built directly over the Fuhrer Bunker, where Hitler had shot himself.

"In fact," the guide said as we turned a corner to face a small playground with a slide in the shape of a silly dragon's head, "this playground is roughly over the spot Hitler ended his life."

Two young children had been on the tour with their parents. Upon seeing the playground and slide, they gave excited shouts and ran over. They happily slid down the slide and jumped around on the dragon's head. It was an odd juxtaposition to see uncaring children playing innocently on the spot where Hitler died, but I'd like to think it kind of symbolized victory over fascism or something.

Our tour ended back at the Brandenburg Gate. We thanked and tipped our guide. Just then Chloe received a text from Samie, who had just arrived at the Starbucks underneath the Brandenburg Gate.

Once we located Sam, the three of us crossed under the Gate and over to the Bundestag. The Bundestag is the German seat of government, like the White House and Capitol building rolled into one. It had hosted the government for a hundred years before the War had destroyed it. It wasn't used again until after Reunification. The iconic dome, seen in all the World War Two movies, had been replaced by one made of glass and steel.

Like usual, we took Sam on an abridged version of the tour in reverse. We passed by Roma gypsies who were begging in the shadow of a monument to their ancestors that were killed in the Holocaust. It felt like a cruel irony to see them there.

For lunch, we ate in a no-frills kebab shop. The spicy gyros were always good for a quick, cheap meal. During our tour, our guide told us Angela Merkel often came here.

"You'll become strong like Merkel if you eat here," the guide said, flexing his arms. Indeed, the portions were large and tasty, although we did not see the Chancellor.

Done with lunch, we went to the Gestapo museum we had passed earlier. It was every bit as informative and heart wrenching as I expected. The basement of the old headquarters was open to the air. There wasn't much down there, but near the perimeter, we could see the tiles of the cell walls. It was surreal to stand there, in broad light, and look at the bits of cells where the Gestapo had tortured people.

Upstairs, in the museum proper, was a rotating display of Nazi victims. The exhibit currently on display was about the T4 victims. These were the mentally unstable, the dumb, the mute and other 'undesirables' the Nazi's had gotten rid of. This action predated the Holocaust slightly and is not well-known. The whole idea of eugenics was popular at the time, including in the US. In fact, as the museum pointed out, Hitler was at least partially inspired by similar contemporary movements in the US. The museum was sobering, and we toured it in silence.

Leaving the Gestapo headquarters, we were quiet and solemn. Then we passed by an entire store dedicated to our friend, the Ampelmann. Overjoyed, we entered. It was the ultimate capitalist victory over communism. Inside they sold everything from gummi Ampelmännchen, to postcards, to sweaters and shirts. It was the perfect pick-me-up after the museum.

We bought a few souvenirs and left the store. We were getting pretty tired, so we decided to go home. We rode the S - Bahn back to Ostbahnhoff. The S-Bahn was just an above ground subway. This meant the seats faced each other. Usually, that would be no big deal. However, in Germany, it is not rude to stare directly at somebody. When I looked up from my seat, I saw a large German man just staring right at me. I flinched instinctively. As an American, I found it was very discomforting.

We got off the S-Bahn at the train station and got on the main road back to our hostel. We stopped at an Aldi's to buy some food for dinner. The store was uneventful until a young boy approached me.

"*Können Sie Bier für mich kaufen, bitte?*" The legal drinking age for beer is sixteen in Germany. How old was this kid? I shook my head no. I was not buying beer for a kid that young.

As we bought our food and a few beers for ourselves, we saw a young lady checking out in front of us. She was paying the cashier for a few cans of beer as the same kid stood eagerly nearby, bouncing with excitement. It could not have been more obvious what was going on here, but the cashier did not seem to care.

Back at the hostel, we went to cook our dinner. The kitchen was accessible only through the courtyard. It was a strange set-up. The kitchen was modest, like the size of an apartment kitchen. Only one group could prepare food at a time.

I sat outside as the girls cooked. The buildings around the courtyard blocked out direct sunlight, but it was warm and pleasant. When the girls brought the food out, I cracked open a nice cold German lager. Immediately the beer spurted up and spilled foam over my hands and shirt.

I heard somebody laughing. At the picnic table next to us was the old Indian man and his wife.

"In India, that means you'll have good luck" the man called to me and held up his drink in a toast as his wife nodded and smiled. I laughed and thanked them as they got up to use the kitchen.

Our meal felt homey as we sat on a picnic bench in the courtyard. The smell of curry drifted out of the kitchen. Across the yard a group of blonde Swedes joked and laughed. We finished our food and just sat out there, happy to be in the moment.

As the sun went down, we took the short ride to Alexanderplatz, back in the heart of the city. We had heard there was an Easter market set up there.

Stepping off the tram, we were directly in the middle of the platz. Streetlights twinkled and were reflected in the glass buildings around us. The platz was broad and felt uncrowded despite hosting a decent number of people. It was a massive space. The TV tower rose up a short distance away. Visible from all of Berlin the silver ball-shaped broadcasting tower was an icon of the city.

In one part of the platz were set up the wooden booths we had become familiar with in Prague. The goods and food offered there were the same overpriced touristy things we had seen in other Easter markets, but it was still lovely strolling around the historic square. It was such a strange feeling to be surrounded by so many modern buildings.

We finished with the Easter Market and wandered west. The platz naturally funneled us towards the Spree River. We followed the broad empty road into a dark courtyard ahead. We were now in the actual center of the city. It was too dark to see, but we were right next to the historic Red Courthouse. For most of Berlin's history, this was a critically important area, the center of power. The historic palace of the Kaisers was once located here before it was destroyed.

There were dark reflecting pools and tree-lined walkways, wooden benches and quaint old-timey streetlights. The plaza was open but rectangular, focusing our gaze in one direction, further west. We found a bench right next to a beautiful Gothic cathedral, no doubt a replica of the destroyed original. We sat on the bench to admire the night and the city lights. Only a few people walked by and it was surprisingly empty for being in a big city.

Unexpectedly, fireworks began to shoot up on the other side of the river. We looked on with delight. Just over a neo-classical dome across the river, were brightly colored explosions in the sky. It was awesome. I won't forget that moment, sitting in Alexanderplatz, just the three of us, in the dark on a bench watching fireworks burst in the sky above us. It was a beautiful private show.

After the fireworks ended, we went back to our hostel, ready for bed. Back in our room, we bumped into a new roommate, an excitable Australian.

His blanket was a giant Australian flag design and he was having the time of his life exploring Europe. Despite their reputation for being loud, obnoxious drunk tourists, I have only had the very best experiences with Australians abroad. They always come across as a very warm and friendly people. Perhaps Europeans, who also view Americans as loud, obnoxious drunks, invented that stereotype too. I have found, culturally, Australians to be very similar to Americans, except that they have free healthcare and no mass shootings.

Tonight, unlike yesterday, we only shared the room with this guy. It was quiet and peaceful, and I fell asleep quickly. I do not know if Chloe ever got her shampoo back.

Berlin, Day Thirty-Three: 29th of April

We did not have much of a plan for the day. As such, we got ready slowly, appreciating the calm morning and quiet hostel. After a breakfast of Nutella sandwiches, we walked over the Ostbahnhoff and rode over to Alexanderplatz.

As we patiently waited for our S-Bahn in the station Chloe and I noticed a sign in German. It told us not to buy tickets from unlicensed vendors and only to use the machines.

The English translation on the bottom of the sign was much more descriptive. In big white letters, the sign read 'Beware of Tricksters!'

Arriving at Alexanderplatz, we walked back over to where we had been last night. The square was charming in the sunlight. It was broad and inviting. We admired the Berlin TV Tower, better able to see it now. It was one of the only communist symbols the West Germans had respected enough to keep around. It was a giant metal ball on top of a white tower that was raised far up into the air and visible from anywhere in the city. When sunlight reflected on the tower, two intersecting sunbeams formed a cross shape. This infuriated and embarrassed the East German government to no end. The locals called it 'The Pope's Revenge.'

Across the way from the tower was the Rotes Rathaus, the Red Courthouse. It was a lovely 19th-century courthouse and administrative center. The red stone made it stand out among the other buildings. We stopped inside, primarily because it was free. Inside there wasn't much to see besides the beautiful marble floor, vaulted ceilings and the busts of famous German artists.

We soon left, as the Courthouse did not much interest us. We walked a single block north, to the banks of the Spree River. The map told us there was a place named Museeninsel or Museum Island. With a name like that, the three of us were intrigued.

We arrived at a bridge, overlooking the Spree River. Just up the river sat a beautiful old building with a giant green copper dome. There were a few smaller spires and domes just below the main one. It wouldn't have been out of place in any other European city, but stood out among the glass and steel skyscrapers of Berlin. Further intrigued, we started to head north, towards it.

We didn't get far before we stumbled across a delightful little park where a giant statue of Marx and Engels stood. Karl Marx was seated, while Friedrich Engels stood beside him. They were about eighteen or twenty feet tall. We had a blast sitting on Marx's lap and holding Engel's humongous hand. I was surprised such a vivid reminder of communism still stood in the center of the city.

We crossed over the Spree just past the Marx statue. On the other end of the bridge was a massive construction site. At the time, I did not think twice, but later I learned it was the former palace of the Hohenzollern Kaisers. The palace fell into disrepair under the Nazi's, was utterly destroyed in the War, and then built over by the Communists. Just a few years previously, a lone German man had advocated for rebuilding the palace. Through a tenacious courting of Berlin officials and the general public, the rebuilding had just been approved when we were there. I have no doubt the palace will be a grand sight when it is finished.

Speaking of wonderful sights, arriving at Museuminsel, the beautiful old museums awed us. There were several fancy old museums placed around a green lawn. Unusual for Berlin. these buildings were actually pre-war. Most of the neo-classical pillars and facades had bullet holes and shrapnel scars. I put my finger in some, amazed at this vivid reminder of the bloody final battle of the War.

The green domes we had seen from down the river belonged to the Berlin Cathedral. It looked even more beautiful than the museums. As usual, none of us had the money to enter any of these wonderful sights. Still, the island was very cool to see.

From the island, we kept following the main boulevard we were on, Unter Den Linden. The eponymous trees provided shade as we leisurely strolled through this sector of Berlin. For a long time, this street represented the best of Germany. The street was synonymous with higher education, class, and culture. That was before the world wars, Hitler and communism wrecked Germany. Euclid Avenue in Cleveland had been modeled on this very street. During the Cold War the area was more or less abandoned, but since the Wall came down, it's been going through quite a revival.

We walked down the street, stopping into coffee shops and yard sales in front of prestigious centers of learning. We browsed bookstores near the universities and admired the urban beauty of Berlin. For the first time in a hundred years, we could again respect Germany, just like they did before the First World War.

We came across the German Tomb of the Unknown Soldier. We had seen a lot of these across Europe and all of them valorized the unknown man. France and Britain both draped flags and flowers on the grave, heroically remembering the soldier that died in service to his country.

Not in Germany. The exterior was plain, a smallish building with neo-classical columns and triangular façade. Inside was one single room, empty and cold. There was nothing inside except a grim statue of a wailing mother holding the lifeless, broken body of her fallen soldier son. It was a simple and moving piece, and I recall it the most vividly of all these monuments. War here was not glorified but instead shown, as it is, a horrible affliction to humanity.

Soon, we were back at the Brandenburg Gate. Directly to the west was the sprawling *Tiergarten,* or deep park. Despite the name, it was no longer home to wild animals, but rather a massive natural park in the center of the city. We split up, so Sam could wander alone and get some mental distance from all the cities we had been visiting. Not used to being in them for so long, the noise and people were getting to her.

Chloe and I wandered together, stopping at various Holocaust memorials. The park was massive and felt very empty, despite the people walking and jogging through it. It was a nice change of pace to walk under green trees and besides little streams. The park was so big I couldn't even hear any cars.

In the dead center of the park was a large column topped by a gigantic golden angel. This was the Victory Column, *Siegessäule*, built by the Prussians during the Unification Wars. As a candidate, Barack Obama has given a famous speech here. Chloe was excited to climb to the top to look over Berlin, but my legs were too sore to do it. Looking at the thousands of steps I had to climb, I opted to stay behind and meet Chloe after she climbed it. She later told me the view was excellent and I felt a little dumb for missing out.

We had agreed to meet Sam at a specific time, so when Chloe got down from the tower, we made our way back to the Gate. On the way back, we stopped by a statue of a giant Russian soldier with golden Cyrillic letters on the base. Artillery pieces and Soviet tanks flanked the soldier. I was impressed by the size and splendor of the monument but also at the fact that the Russian monument still existed. It was physically within eyesight of the current seat of government. Imagine if a towering memorial to British Revolutionary War dead stood a block from the White House.

The Soviets had built the statue right when the war ended. Ironically enough, it ended up within the boundary of West Berlin by accident. Although the memorial was heroic and of massive scale, no East Germans could come to see it.

I later read that it is a somewhat controversial memorial with some locals calling it the 'Tomb of the Unknown Rapist.' No other country in the world would have kept such a humiliating memorial to its invaders. The Russian's weren't even here anymore to stop the Germans from taking it down.

Germany, however, has a history, unlike any other nation. As such, the statue will probably never come down.

We didn't have much time to stay there as we were late to meet Sam. We hurried past the memorial and back to the Brandenburg Gate. Germans never cross during red lights, so we waited at an intersection right next to the Gate.

As we waited patiently, I turned to my side. There I saw an older couple posing for a picture. To my surprise, the photographer was a four or five-year-old boy.

"Take the picture Christopher," the couple said through their gritted, smiling teeth. "Take it!"

The boy held the camera up in confusion.

The light changed, and we crossed the street. We found Sam at the same Starbucks from yesterday, enjoying a coffee and a muffin. She had been there for a while waiting for us.

The three of us went to the hostel for another home-cooked meal. When we finished eating, we worked on our papers in the common area, until Chloe and I both started to get antsy.

"Nate, do you want to go back downtown?" Chloe asked me. I impulsively said yes. It was our last night in the last major city of our grand tour. We couldn't spend it writing papers all night.

As the last rays of sunlight disappeared, Chloe and I walked down Friedrichstraße one last time. In a random souvenir shop, I bought a small piece of the Berlin Wall for my dad. The spray paint on the piece was undoubtedly added later, but some enterprising entrepreneur had purchased several huge sections of the border wall during the fall of East Germany. He then broke them up into billions of tiny pieces and sold them, like this, for a few euros each. Apparently, he has made billions this way and is poised to have his stock last for twenty more years. It was a neat piece of history to have.

Chloe and I walked over to the Brandenburg Gate one more time. It seemed that every city had a focal point to which we returned over and over. From the Notre-Dame in Paris, the San Marco Piazza in Venice, to the Old Town Square in Prague, each city had one place we loved.

Although we didn't plan it, we found ourselves naturally only exploring small parts of each city, like the Old Town of Prague, or the north side of Florence. In Berlin, it was the Mitte. We found it much more enjoyable to see a lot of one part, rather than a little bit of everything. I feel like I'd miss all the small details by rushing from point to point, pausing only to snap a few pictures. It was much better to go slow and let one or two areas sink in. There is always so much more right below the surface.

I find travel to be much more enjoyable when I sit back and tap into the natural pace of life. We had long since stopped planning our days; instead, we would just sort of see where our feet would take us.

In Madrid we saw daily life unfolding in Lavapiés, with parents and children playing, old men perusing anarchist bookstores, and young drug dealers trying to make a living in a dead economy. In Florence, we drank coffee in cafes while young, well-dressed fashionistas rushed by on their way to work. In Barcelona we joined the locals and hung our laundry to dry on the lines between the tall apartment buildings, adding our socks and shirts to numberless sheets drying in the summer air. In Bruges we sipped beer seated on a patio, enjoying the lazy pace of life of a medieval city.

The ability to just stop and observe the world around you, to see how other people do things, is one of the greatest joys of traveling. I love letting the rhythms of life wash over me.

Chloe and I do just this. We sat on a bench and watched life unfold around us. We watched tourists take pictures. We watched guests check into the Michael Jackson hotel and saw young German professionals get their Starbucks fix. We took some more pictures and admired the Gate as it was lit up. The monument was much more appealing at night. With the spotlights trained on it, it looked much grander.

Satisfied we had not wasted the last big night of our trip we took the S-Bahn back to our hostel. On the tram, we sat up stiffly when several punks boarded the car. They had beaten up leather jackets and pierced faces. The other passengers on the car shifted a bit, almost unperceptively, but warily. Like us, nobody moved, but everybody was aware of the punks.

One punk with a purple Mohawk slung his legs over several seats. He mimed smoking a cigarette at a businessman who sat across from him. The businessman withdrew a pack from his jacket and handed the punk a cigarette. The punk smiled and threw his arms around the businessman. The businessman looked shocked and then hugged the punk back. Everybody on the car visibly relaxed, as these were the famous good punks of Berlin.

We got off at our stop, laughing to ourselves about the encounter. Later we found our room to be empty, except for our happy Aussie friend. We chatted a little, but he soon left to party. Berlin was one of the best party places in the world, but we would be having none of that. Instead, we turned out the lights and went to bed.

Bielefeld, Day Thirty-Four: 30th of April

Our last morning in Berlin started uneventfully. Sam and I awoke early to work on our papers. Next to the common room was, bizarrely enough, a video game arcade. We sat on long black couches and balanced our laptops on pinball machines. The early morning sunlight shone through the wide windows facing the street. It was nice and quiet.

After a while Chloe came downstairs, and we moved our bags down to where we sat. We continued to work surrounded by a small fort of backpacks. As we worked, the sound system came blasting to life. *I Follow Rivers* by Lykke Li thumped through the room. Chloe had stepped out to buy breakfast down the street, and when she came back, we switched spots with her. I wasn't hungry, but I craved some coffee.

Samie and I walked south on Pariser Kommune street. Just a few blocks over was a coffee and pastry shop, right near the Aldi's from the other day. We walked in happily and found a woman in line in front of us. The interior was cozy, with yellow painted walls. It reminded me of the unpretentious working class joints I'd frequent in Cleveland or Pittsburgh.

The customer was dressed for business and looked harried. Behind the counter stood a frazzled looking woman with black hair and a white apron.

"Coffee with milk," the woman said with urgency in her voice. "Coffee with milk!"

"*Milchkaffee?*" the worker asked, with a confused look and the pained expression all food service workers know.

"Coffee with milk!" The woman raised her voice more, her American accent heavy with frustration. She balled her hand into a fist on the counter. The lady must have thought that the worker would understand English if she spoke louder.

As this went on, Sam and I initially hung back in true European fashion. After a few more exchanges, we knew we had to intervene.

"*Sie wollen Kaffee mit Milch,*" I told the worker. The lady wanted coffee with milk, not milk-coffee.

The worker looked at me quizzically and asked softly "*Milchkaffee?*"

Sam spoke up. "*Nicht Milchkaffee, schwartz Kaffee....mit Milch.*" The barista nodded, finally understanding. She poured the American woman black coffee and then added a little bit of cold milk to it.

'Milk Coffee' refers to a coffee drink with hot milk added. The customer had been using the wrong term, confusing the poor barista. The woman slammed some euro coins on the counter, grabbed her coffee and stormed out.

Sam and I ordered some coffee and pastries in German. The older woman looked so grateful that she did not have to deal with English, despite our noticeable accents. She made our drinks with extra care and thanked us profusely for getting rid of the last customer.

Coffees in hand, we walked back to the hostel. Sam had been practicing German only since the start of our trip. She was understandably ecstatic to have helped translate and communicate with a native speaker like that.

At the hostel, we grabbed Chloe and checked out. We were early for the train, so we bought cups of fresh fruit from a vendor and goofed off for a while. For being a major train station in a major city it always seemed to be empty.

The train pulled in precisely on time. We boarded and left, also precisely on time. The trains in Europe ran more or less on time, but the German ones never seemed to be even twenty seconds off.

A few years ago my dad's twin sister had moved to Bielefeld. Her husband was setting up a Christian church there. They had four kids. My older two cousins were both married with a couple of kids each, and their families had moved as well. My younger two cousins, their sisters, soon followed.

Two hours later the train slowed down as the station approached. I felt a pang of nervousness in my stomach. Although this was the family of my father's twin sister, I had never spent much time with them. My aunt Marie had married her husband Greg at a young age. Soon after, they experienced a religious awakening and dedicated the rest of their lives traveling around the world preaching the good word. The Rastatter clan is wholly Catholic, to varying degrees of devoutness. I don't think the rest of us ever truly understood the evangelical brand of Protestantism that Greg and Marie believed.

Of course, in other families, this might have caused some irrevocable break. My family wasn't like that. Instead, there was only a slight awkwardness at family gatherings. I just did not know what to say to them, believing we did not have much in common. Despite being twins, Marie had had her children much younger than my dad. Even the youngest of my cousins were several years older than me.

I was understandably nervous about spending a few days with them. I was especially unsure how the whole religious angle would play out. These were people who preached the Bible in countries where it was illegal and dangerous to do so. They were not shy about their faith.

At the station, there was a hallway to the lobby, and I instantly recognized my Aunt Marie waiting at the end of it. My aunt has a head of curly grey hair that I'd recognize anywhere. Her face had the familiar angular lines that most of my father's family, including me, share. I walked over, and we hugged. There was a familiar, although not personal, intimacy to it.

I introduced Chloe and Sam to Marie as we walked out to her car. Getting into the car was a slight shock. It was the first car that we had been in since January that was not a taxi.

The town of Bielefeld was mostly modern and unassuming. After being in such famous and recognizable cities, it was kind of strange to see an average nondescript city. I was reminded that most people live normal lives in normal places. We drove out to the small town to where my family lived. Immediately outside of the town were golden wheat fields and rolling green hills. Unlike American towns, there was little suburban sprawl.

As we drove, Aunt Marie told us a few stories about my cousin-in-law Paul getting lost in Spain and my younger cousins trying to find jobs in Germany. Greg and Marie had four children, all daughters. The oldest, Stacy had married Jeff, an American. Together they had three young girls. The littlest one had only been three or four when they moved to Germany.

The second oldest daughter, Jeanne, had married an Englishman named Paul. They had two boys, and Jeanne was heavily pregnant with their third child.

Lastly, there were my other two cousins, Lydia and Grace. Grace was about five years older than me while Lydia was seven or eight years older. Marie told us about how complicated their immigration process had been.

She explained that to get the German 'green card' you needed to provide a service ordinary EU citizens couldn't do. By starting a church Greg and Marie both gained them easily. Jeff worked directly for his father-in-law, so he also got the green card. By proxy, his wife and children got them too. Paul was an EU citizen because he was English. At the time it was pre-Brexit, so his wife and children were also EU citizens.

Unfortunately, Lydia and Grace were unmarried, unemployed, and too old to get their green cards through their parents. They had been struggling to get legal residency in Germany for a few years without success. They had to leave the EU every ninety days to renew their temporary visas. Although their futures looked uncertain, Lydia had just been hired as a hairdresser. For the moment, the family was feeling tentatively hopeful.

Marie explained this to us during our half hour drive to their home. Occasionally the road forked, and Marie would point down the road we did not take.

"That's the village where Stacy lives" or "Jeanne lives down that way." I had not realized the family lived spread out like this. We pulled into the village were Marie and Greg, and the youngest daughters lived. It was tiny, but everything was brand new. It was a little suburban subdivision that looked like it had been picked up and dropped into the middle of cornfields. There were maybe thirty or so houses. They were so new that some were still under construction. The road was not even fully paved and ended about fifty feet before my aunt's house.

The home itself was a three-story white house. It was homey and cozy, and surprisingly compact. Aunt Marie gave us a tour. The living room and dining room were linked together, with a large wooden table with multiple seats sitting near the couches, armchairs and a coffee table.

Next to these rooms stood a small but functional kitchen. It was spotlessly clean. There were a little table and three chairs right next to the kitchen counter. Beyond that was a glass sliding door. The door opened out to a small patio overlooking a large wheat field. Far beyond the wheat field was a lonely country road where an odd car drove by every so often.

Back inside we walked up a staircase near the living room. The stairs were made of polished dark wood and had open-backed spaces between the steps. They twisted around in a spiral, to take up less space.

"Be careful here," Marie said, "You can slip down these really easy."

Up the stairs, there was a short hallway. "You'll be staying here," Marie told me and showed me the furthest room. She opened the door. Inside was a comfy looking queen bed. There were a nightstand, a dresser and a closed closet.

"This is Grace's room when she is in town, but she offered for you to stay here." Marie flicked what looked like a light switch.

"These are automatic blinders," she said as the window blinds closed, leaving us in complete darkness. "The girls love these." She chuckled and touched the switch to let the sunlight back in.

Marie showed the girls their room, which was adjacent to mine. Sam and I would not be sleeping together.

"And there is the bathroom," she told us, pointing to a room at the end of the wall. I needed no more directions. Within in a few minutes, I was stepping into the shower.

The hot water sprayed over me. I let it soak in. It was the first actual house shower I had used since January. Most hostel and dorms showers were too cold or too cramped to be enjoyable. The shower was brand new and felt glorious.

As I showered, I looked around at the bathroom. It was huge, at least as big as some of our entire hostel rooms. When I reached for a towel, I found it to be fluffy and warm. My aunt must have just set them out. It felt fantastic to clean myself in such luxury.

I got dressed in my room, and then came back downstairs to see what was going on. On my way down I almost slipped on the wooden stairs. With socks on, there was no traction or friction. I promised myself to be more careful.

I spied Marie out on the porch. I sat down in a deck chair opposite her. Behind her, the waves of grain looked like gold in the late afternoon sunlight. The sky was bright blue and off in the distance were endless rolling hills. I told Marie that she had picked a beautiful spot to settle down.

She smiled. "It's really an amazing world, isn't it?" I concurred.

The girls joined us after they showered. Marie told us that her husband Greg had just left on some urgent business in Vienna. I was a little bummed because I had not seen him in a few years. For some families, this might sound like a weak excuse, but this branch of the family traveled at a dizzying pace. They took their religious duties very seriously.

Luckily for me, I had had years of training in being around evangelical Christians. I knew how to communicate and not step in any cultural landmines. Between friends and exes, I had been around this culture for a long time. Chloe, however, had not.

"And where do you live?" Marie asked Chloe nicely. Marie had lived in Northeast Ohio for many years and was familiar with all the small towns.

"Oh well I live in Kent with my boyfriend," she said in a chipper tone. Her posture indicated she was making friendly conversation.

Sam and I both winced in our seats. We knew not to say something like that.

Marie's body stiffened, and her eyes narrowed. There was a moment of heavy silence. To her credit, Marie responded by deftly changing the subject. Pre-marital cohabitation was not something this community promoted. Chloe looked confused as the conversation changed so abruptly.

We went back inside for some coffee. Inside I ran into my little cousin. Kaylee was a bright-eyed little girl in a black skirt and headband. All the people on this side dressed impeccably. She could not have been older than seven, and I couldn't recall seeing her since she was a baby. Since she had been the youngest cousin when they moved here, she had been enrolled in German schools essentially her entire life.

"Hi Kaylee, I'm your cousin," I said to her. She was shy at first but soon warmed up.

"I was playing with my friends *Hund* earlier. He has big fluffy ears," she said sweetly. She had paused on the word *Hund*. From her face, I could see she was trying and failing to think of the English word for dog.

Marie told me the youngest cousins had trouble speaking English sometimes because they were growing up surrounded by German-speakers. My aunt and uncle had the opposite issue. Greg and Marie both struggled with the language. Picking up a language in your fifties is hard, but they went after it with gusto. My older cousins spoke it with varying success, Stacy and Jeff being the best while Lydia and Grace struggled but still spoke it.

The kids, however, were entirely fluent. They spoke perfect, unaccented German. The throaty growl that English speakers struggle with came as naturally to them as the 'th' sound does to Americans. Marie told me that Greg and her would sometimes ask them what road signs meant in English.

"Then they just roll their eyes and sigh exasperatedly," Marie told me. "'Can't you just read it yourself' they groan."

It was a funny story but made me wonder. These girls were going to grow up in German school with German friends. They will probably speak English only at home. Will they even think of themselves as Americans?

The family did their best to keep an entire 'Little America' going. There was a stock of peanut butter and American cereals in the pantry. They had to special order these things. They spoke solely English at home to foster our culture on the kids. But, like any immigrant family, the kids wanted to be like their friends. If your friends all spoke German, why would they think of English as anything but an annoying outdated custom?

Kaylee was at the house with her mom, Stacey. We were going to go with them to her home for dinner. I greeted Stacey warmly. She is a tall, fiercely intelligent woman with a big smile and bigger heart. She has always reminded me a lot of my oldest sister. Stacey and her family lived one village over. As we pulled into their driveway, I saw the home was just as cheerful, and the village just as quaint as my aunts.

As the first one in the door, I ran into my cousin Faith. Faith was the oldest of Stacey's kids and had been about eight or nine when they moved over here. As such, English was still the natural first language for her. We chatted a bit. Faith was very mature for her age and remembered me from Ohio.

Faith began showing me the house when her uncle Paul entered the home. Paul was from Southampton, England and was a real gentleman. I had been at Paul and Jeanne's wedding several years ago. It was one of the few times I met the guy.

Paul, Faith, the girls and I sat down in the lovely unpretentious living room. We talked with Paul. He spoke amicably about our travels and of England. We were soon deep into discussion about the mundane basics of English life.

"Ah yes, Asda is brilliant!" Paul exclaimed at one point. He hadn't lived in England for a few years, and obviously enjoyed talking about British life. We touched on everything British from Wetherspoons to Sainsbury. The girls and I were soon 'homesick' for England.

"Dinner's ready," Stacey called from the dining room. We walked over to the dinner table and saw tacos and taco fillings laid out. "I wanted to make something you can't find in Europe," she said with another big smile. She was right about that, I hadn't even heard the word 'tacos' in months.

Jeff, Stacey's husband, joined the three of us at the head of the table. The girls and Paul sat in the living room, eating and goofing off. We chatted with Jeff. Like the others, I had never spent much time with him. I know they had been married years ago, and I had always seen him around at family functions. It wasn't until here in Germany we found ourselves in an actual conversation.

"There is no Mexican food on this continent," Jeff said, cracking jokes left and right. He was dressed, as usual, in a powder blue polo shirt and khaki shorts, his hair slightly spiked. Jeff manages, somehow, to stay utterly ageless.

We piled seasoned ground beef into our hard taco shells and happily ate. I was delighted to be making new connections with this branch of my family. My cousin Jeanne briefly came by, but immediately went upstairs to sleep. She was nine months pregnant.

The house was soon filled with joy and laughter. I was discovering that I had missed my family. I somehow was surprised by how familiar this scene was. I had always seen these guys as an independent branch of my family, people I shared blood but not culture with. Instead, I was being shown I was dead wrong. They acted in the same ways and idiosyncrasies the rest of my dad's family did.

We finished off the meal with a traditional German dessert, Welfenspiese. It was a delicious chocolate pudding layered with lemon juice and egg whites. Right as we finished a friend of the family entered the house. The man was about my height with slightly messy brown hair and wearing a brown leather jacket. He must have been about ten years older than me. He was Christian, a friend who had just driven in from Kiel. That was a very long journey for Germans, clocking in at four hours.

Christian immediately greeted us with a hug and a warm smile. He was the kind of guy who instantly made you feel good. We did not have much time to talk with Christian because soon my last two cousins showed up. In their tow, they brought two German-Scots girls. The younger people, including Christian, were heading off to go to some church function soon.

The two younger girls were friends of Lydia and Grace. They were ethnic Germans but had spent their childhoods in Glasgow, Scotland. At first, they just spoke German to others but switched to English soon after. Their German was impeccable and they sounded like normal Germans. Then, they switched to English and spoke in an extremely thick Scottish accent. It was disconcerting to hear such contrast.

Since everybody was now at the house, the younger folks got ready to head out. There was going to be a big bonfire, but it had apparently started to rain during dinner. Instead, they were just going to hang out at the church.

"Do you want to come?" Grace asked me. I looked at Sam, who nodded. Neither one of us was ready for bed or homework yet.

"Ok that sounds fun," I told her. We said goodbye to the family and stepped outside. Marie got into her car with Chloe to go home. Chloe had politely declined the offer. She needed to go work on her papers and, at any rate, did not think church would make for a fun evening.

Lydia, Grace, and the Scots-Germans got into one car. Sam and I rode with Christian. As I got in, I hoped it wouldn't be awkward. As an introvert, I don't like being alone with people I don't know, as I never know what to say.

As it turned out, we had nothing to worry about. Christian was a natural people-person. My first impression was correct, and Christian effortlessly provoked conversation. We were soon peppering him with questions about the German language.

Christian was an excellent teacher. I asked him endless clarifying questions about German words and grammar. He was incredibly animated when he talked, and was a big joker. He mentioned in slow patient German that it was raining out, *es geissen.*

"That's odd," I told him. "I thought *geissen* meant 'to water,' as in water a plant."

Christian laughed. "No that would be very silly. You don't say 'water the flowers' as '*geiss die Blumen!'*". He jovially shouted the last part in German and mimed pouring a jug of water onto a flowerpot.

As we sped to keep up with Lydia, we learned that 'lead foot' is also an expression in Germany. Thanks to our high speeds, we arrived at the church in no time. I was surprised to find that the church was brand new. It looked like any other Protestant church I had seen in North America. I was expecting some ancient medieval building.

Inside the modest white church, we got a brief tour as people split into groups. There were a good number of young people here. The people were great. As Sam went to hang out with Grace and Lydia, a German girl with curly red hair showed me around.

At one point she showed me a classroom for kids. "They meet here twice a week as part of their homeschooling." She looked at me and cocked her head. "You were homeschooled right?"

I smiled and told her that I wasn't.

"Oh, well you must have your own church at least?"

I nodded and said I did. It wasn't quite the truth, strictly speaking, as I had not been to it in years. But, I felt that saying I did would let me avoid any proselyting. I was vindicated as she nodded in approval.

Of the people I met that night, the majority were first-generation immigrants. They were Russian Germans, a group that had been in Russia for hundreds of years. Whereas my German ancestors colonized Hungary, these people had moved much further east. My family had moved away before the upheaval of World War One, whereas these guys had not.

Instead, they found themselves stuck in the Soviet Union and forcibly assimilated. After the Berlin Wall came down, the newly reunited Germany generously offered German citizenship to any ethnic Germans still left behind the former Iron Curtain. The parents of these people had moved here then, in the early nineties, ending their four hundred-year-old Russian sojourn.

I found talking to these guys much more natural than strangers in big cities. These folks were happy to hear me trying to speak German. They encouraged me, and even sometimes refused to let me speak English.

"*Sprechst du Deutsch?*" they would ask me, and I would reply the same answer each time.

"*Nur ein bisschen,*" only a little. They were good sports, and within a few hours of being immersed, my German was vastly improving. I had a great time with these kind Christians.

After a while, Lydia, the Scots-Germans, Sam and myself went to a nearby 'Mexican' restaurant for some drinks. We walked over the place, and the inside was yellow plaster with classic Mexican decorations. I looked at the drink menu. It was identical to any other German restaurant with nary a Negro Modello or Tecate in sight. We sat at a booth near a wooden dance floor. Colored lights spun around us as the disco lights shone over a small crowd of gyrating people.

As it turned out, it was a big holiday. The holiday celebrated the start of summer by having revelers dance all night until the sunrise. It was supposed to ensure a good and plentiful harvest. It was a surprisingly pagan holiday for such a church-y crowd.

Sam bought a Berliner Weisse, while I had a local dark beer. Most beer in Germany is relatively local. We happily chatted with Lydia and the younger girls for a while. We ended up staying for hours, stretching into the wee hours of morning.

Although very tired, I had a wonderful time. It was just so nice to connect with these family members I had never connected with before. Sam and I chatted with Lydia on the quiet drive home, aware that this might be our only one-on-one for years to come. She told us how she had just gotten a job in her profession, hairdressing, and it looked like she could at last stay in Germany. She was so happy about it, and we were delighted for her.

We got back to the house around three. It had been a good but very long day. I got ready for sleep and then went to my bed. It was my first night not in a hostel in weeks. I collapsed in bed and fell right asleep.

Bielefeld, Day Thirty-Five: 1st of May

I awoke to the sounds of conversation and cooking coming from downstairs. I opened my eyes find the room mercifully dark, despite it being half-past ten. Those automatic shades worked great. I brushed my teeth and walked down the slippery stairs.

Across from the staircase was the dining room table. The house was compact. Every room bled into the next, and the space was allocated perfectly. Leave it the Germans to not waste a single inch. A breakfast feast was being laid out on the table.

I greeted Aunt Marie. She was finishing up cooking and pointed me to where the coffee was brewing. I grabbed a cup and sat down at the table with Christian.

Christian and I had an enjoyable conversation about all sorts of things. We covered regional German accents, travel and seatbelt laws. He told me how the northern Germans thought the southern German accents sounded funny and how he had spent much time volunteering in Brazil. When we reach the topic of mandatory seatbelt laws, he shocked me by being vehemently against them.

"How can the government have a right to tell me to wear one?" he insisted. By that time Chloe was awake and had joined us. She became the devil's advocate and argued for the positive effects of the laws.

Christian adamantly refused to believe these laws could do any good. Instead, he just talked about the overreach of the government. It was such a classically Republican position to take, and I had not expected any Germans to think like that.

Before long Samie also came downstairs. Right afterward Grace arrived, having spending the night at a friends' house. It was time to eat breakfast. Marie set the last dish down on the table.

There was an incredible amount of food spread around us. There was meat, cheese, rolls, slices of bread and fresh fruit.

"It's a *Deutsches Frühstück* with an American twist," Marie said proudly.

We had a quick prayer and then began to eat. It was great as it had looked. When we finished, my family and Christian got ready to leave. There was an important church function happening soon. Although I knew this was the reason Christian was here, I never quite figured out what the big event was.

As the three of them headed out the door, my aunt politely asked us if we wanted to join them.

"I know you guys are probably busy, but if you want to join us at the church, we are going to have food and fellowship."

I nodded my thanks but let her know we were going to be busy. Sam and I had known the inevitable invitation had been coming sooner or later.

"Thanks, guys," I said, "but we have a lot of homework to do."

My aunt nodded. "You can call my cell phone if you want to get some food there later."

I jotted down her number and wished them well. The three of us cleared some space on the table and got to work. My excuse was not a lie. The three of us did nothing but type for hours.

I wrote until my eyes were red and my wrists were sore. As the time stretched well into the afternoon, the three of us began to get hungry. We ignored it long as possible to get more work done. Finally, our collective hunger was too great, and I dialed my aunt's phone number.

It was quiet for a moment, and then we heard a phone ringing. It sounded like it was coming from right outside. As if in slow motion, the three of us looked at the front door. Right then the door swung open, and my aunt came in. Perfect timing.

Aunt Marie talked with us for a little bit and then went to the kitchen to make some pasta and soup. It was an enjoyable and straightforward dish that reminded me strongly of my grandmothers cooking. I laughed to myself a little bit. Marie was my grandma's daughter after all. It is always interesting to me to notice how these little quirks got passed down.

Chloe, Samie and I went back to work as Aunt Marie went back to the church. However, soon after she left my cousins came over.

"Do you guys want to hang out with our friends?" Grace and Lydia asked us.

We looked up from the table we had been sitting at all day.

"Sure," Samie said. "That sounds fun!"

"Awesome," Grace replied, "we can show you the local castle."

That sounded like a good plan. Before we got into their car Grace grabbed a couple of bottles of beer from the refrigerator.

"You can drink in cars legally here," she told me, offering me the beer. I couldn't refuse.

The five of us got into Lydia's car and drove to downtown Bielefeld. The castle was on a hill overlooking the city. I drank the beer as we drove up the steep, narrow lanes to the castle.

We got out of the car in the parking lot. I stepped out of the cramped backseat, leaving the empty bottle of beer behind.

Truly more of a Renaissance-era fort than a castle, it had been recently renovated. From the parking lot, we crossed over a small bridge over the empty moat and walked around the fortress. A stone path ringed the perimeter of the fort. On one side of us were walls looking over Bielefeld. On the other were a few stone buildings and a large watchtower. Flowers were planted in neat little garden beds.

It was an enjoyable place. In America, this would be a big attraction. But in Europe, it was just the local castle that nobody thought too much of. We admired the view of the town. I was just happy to spend some time with my cousins.

As the sun set, we saw a man propose to his girlfriend. She squealed with delight and hugged him as he was down on one knee.

"*Könnten Sie bitte mein Foto nehmen?*" the newly engaged couple asked us. We were happy to oblige and took their pictures for them.

On the other side of the castle, we could see a nearby hospital. It was quite big and took up a lot of the skyline. We chatted among ourselves in English. A couple of middle aged German men must have overheard us and walked over. They were eager to point out some of the local sights to us.

"That is the former hospital," they said, pointing to the big nearby building. "The kids there had much dark diseases."

We thanked the man, careful to keep our faces straight and not laugh. My cousins told me that the Germans in Bielefeld did not often get the chance to practice English so they would get very excited when they heard English speakers. My cousins told us that most Germans here were not nearly as fluent in English as the Germans in bigger cities like Berlin were. They took every opportunity to practice English.

As night came on, we went back to the car. Lydia and Grace wanted to meet some friends for dinner, so we tagged along to a local pasta restaurant.

We parked and went inside. It was a Chipotle for pasta. Customers would order at a counter. Ever considerate, one of my cousin's friends came with us to order. He helped us order in German, an otherwise very difficult task.

We got our pasta and sat down at a big table. In addition to this gentleman, there were about six other people. I was seated next to a different guy. He was chubby and bearded, and I soon fell into conversation with him.

I happily spoke with him for a while. Before long, our conversation switched to German, which I was pleased with. Just as we were getting into it, Lydia's suddenly got an intense stomachache. She felt very nauseous, so we got up to leave. We paid at the cashier's stand, which was right near the exit.

As we paid our bills, I noticed a bowl of gummi bears. In American restaurants, this is where a bowl of mints would be. Gummi bears? I was surprised but grabbed a few anyway. Maybe it was just a German thing?

We got back into the car to go home. I was a little disappointed because the original plan had been to do some barhopping. Nonetheless, I enjoyed the chance to have a good talk with Grace as she drove. Just like my talk with Lydia yesterday, I knew that this might be one of the few personal conversations we would have for a long time to come.

It was refreshing to hang out with my older cousins these last two days. It had me wish I had seen them more growing up. Despite the religious differences I felt very much connected to this branch of my family after these short few days.

We got home around ten or so. Still tired from the night before, I fell asleep almost instantly.

Bielefeld, Day Thirty-Six: 2nd of May

I couldn't believe it was our last full day in Europe. Christian and Marie were busy making breakfast, so I joined Sam on the couch. She was already typing away, so I pulled out my laptop and got to work. Some of our papers were due in just two short days.

We were hard at work when suddenly there came a great crash. We looked up to see Chloe tumbling down the wooden stairs, red hair askew and limbs flailing. Christian rushed over to help her. I looked over at Sam who was trying and failing to keep a straight face. She couldn't help but laugh. After all, Marie warned us about those stairs.

Chloe was shaken up a bit but was unharmed. Well, unharmed except for her ego. Lucky for us, we had another big spread for breakfast to help ease the pain. We said a quick prayer and then dug in. There were sliced bits of meat, cheese, and some warm baked goods. It was another fantastic meal.

It was soon interrupted when Lydia came in the front door. In stark contrast to her cheerful, bubbly self, she now looked gray and downcast. She was stopping in to tell her mother that she was going to the hospital.

Naturally, this caused concern. Marie took her to the local hospital, dropped her off and came back. A friend of the family came over to speak with Marie. The friend was an older German lady, who was a nurse.

We had cleared the table while Marie had been gone. The friend and Marie now sat at one end and spoke quietly. I was back to work on my paper, but was seated nearby. I took the opportunity to eavesdrop on their conversation.

They spoke entirely in German. To my surprise and delight, I understood almost every word. It seemed that Lydia had a stomach bug. I was relieved to hear it was nothing too serious. I was also overjoyed to understand so much German.

By now we had spent six days in Germany, plus the earlier two in Austria. Being immersed in German was boosting my language skills. Just a few months ago I could barely string a sentence together, and now I could follow conversations about medical conditions. If I could spend a month here, I would probably become fluent.

The morning crept into the afternoon. Marie went back to the hospital, leaving us to work on our papers. Initially, we had planned to go zip lining with Christian, but Lydia's emergency threw our plan off. I was a little disappointed, but the three of us truly needed the time to work.

After a few hours, Marie came back again. It turned out Lydia had food poisoning and was going to be all right in a few days. Although we no longer had enough time to zip line, she asked if we wanted to see a local monument.

"It's a statue of Hermann the German," Marie told us.

Christian cocked his head at that. "Hermann the German," he said slowly. *"Hermann der Deutsche*...it sounds much better in English." He threw his head back and laughed in his infectious manner.

That sounded fun to us, so we agreed. Yet another friend of the family soon picked us up to check it out. The new guy was named Roland. He was a thirty-something German man who was serving in the German Navy. He was tall, muscular and had a shaved head. He was nice enough, but something felt a little off. I was sort of picking up 'repressed gay' vibe from him.

Not one to judge, we piled into Roland's car and drove the to the monument. The day was foggy and gray, and a light rain was coming down. As we parked, Roland told us that the view might not be too good. We were shivering in the cold rain already.

From the parking lot, we couldn't see anything around us. There were trees on either side of us, just barely visible through the thick fog. We walked up a hill along a stone path, unsure of what to expect. It felt mystical and ethereal to be in such a heavy damp fog. As we neared the crest of the hill, I looked up.

Out of nowhere, a big green sword appeared out of the mist. We took a few more steps, and the rest of the statue loomed out at us. It was a towering Teutonic warrior wearing a winged helmet and battle armor. He loomed majestically out of the fog; his colossal arm thrust up, grasping his sword. Beneath his feet, he trod upon a dead Roman eagle.

The monument was to Arminius, better known in Germany as Hermann. At the height of the Roman Empire, Hermann led tribal Germans in a massive ambush and massacre of Roman soldiers. He single-handily ended Roman expansion into Germany. During the 19th century, Hermann became a potent symbol of German nationalism. The statue had been built then, as modern Germany would certainly never construct such a nakedly militaristic monument.

The statue stood on top of a ninety-foot tall rotunda. We entered it and climbed the stairs to the foot of the figure. Usually, one could see for miles around, but the fog limited our views. Roland and Marie were apologetic about the view, but we thought the foggy forest was cool. The mist made it seem like the forest went on endlessly. The whole experience was strangely powerful. It had been foggy like this during the ambush of the Romans, so the weather only added to the mystical feeling.

As we walked around the platform next to the massive feet trampling the eagle, we noticed several bronze plaques on the stone wall. They had arrows and pointed to the nearest little town. Marie happily pointed out which town we were staying at, the town Stacy lived, and the closest local town of Detmold. Despite the chilly rain and fog, it was a cool, unique experience.

Back down at the base, Roland told us the word for monument in German is *denkmal*. "The literal translation," he said, "is 'think-more.' Statues and monuments are supposed to make you 'think-more' about the subject."

I nodded. I thought about the different monuments I had seen so far. Most of them had certainly made me 'think-more' about a lot of different subjects and events.

Roland led us on a path through the woods. Just a little ways away was the high-ropes course we had initially planned to visit. Multiple levels of wooden platforms, catwalks, zip-lines, and tightropes were strung up in the trees. There were at least three distinct levels, high above the ground. The high-ropes course looked awesome. If only we had had one more day the three of us would have loved to climb and swing around here. They told us you could see the Hermannsdenkmal by looking out over the canopy. It must be an unparalleled view.

But it was not to be. It was already late afternoon and time to go. We headed back home to Aunt Marie's. Back at the house, Christian was busy making dinner.

"*Was kochst du*? Roland said to Christian, asking him what he was cooking.

Chris laughed a little bit and responded "*Kochen? Das ist zu viel zu sprechen.*"

I smiled at that. 'Cooking? That is too much to say.' Christian was baking bread and making bruschetta. Roland left right before dinner, so it was just the five of us when we sat down to eat.

Christian led the customary prayer and then we piled our plates high with bruschetta and toasted bread. It was fresh and delicious, made with local vegetables. We ate almost as much as Chris made, which was a lot. Eventually, the three of us kids even switched from drinking pop to drinking wine.

I was still adjusting to drinking with my family. It had been wrong for so long, as I was just recently of legal age. In fact, drinking wine with Marie was the first time I had openly done so with a family member. It was a bit of a heady experience. As usual, we made great conversation with Christian and I felt a new sense of bonding with my aunt.

We cleaned off the dinner table. Marie and Christian were interested in going to Bad Salzuflen, a nearby town that had a spa. I wasn't sure if I wanted to go, as I still had papers to write. Additionally, our flight back to London was pretty early, and we needed to take a train for a few hours to get to our airport in Dortmund. However, Sam and Chloe both seemed eager to go, so I joined at the last minute.

It was already past ten as we got into Christian's car. Nevertheless, we drove out to the spa, checked in, changed into bathing suits and met on the poolside of the building. We stood overlooking a cavernous room.

Spread out around us were cold pools, hot pools, saunas and hot tubs. There were an Olympic sized pool and a salt bath. There was a wading pool that exited the building and spilled outside. It looked amazing.

As Marie went to relax in the gentler warmer pools, Christian, the girls and I went to the saunas.

"You have to do this first," he told us. The sauna was small, about ten by ten feet and made entirely of glass. The inside had two benches and a large eucalyptus plant. It smelled terrific, but we soon grew sweaty and dizzy.

"Just a little longer" Christian told us. We sweated and sweated until he finally stood up.

"Ok, now we jump into the cold pool."

We had not expected this next step. Slightly in shock, Christian opened the door and calmly strolled to the cold pool. He gestured us over and jumped in. The girls and I stood dumbly at the side of the pool. I looked at them, shrugged and jumped in as well.

The water was icy cold. It felt like daggers on my body. It was strange to be so hot and sweaty and then to be so cold so quickly. I came up for air, gasping at the intensity of the moment. I climbed out of the pool to where Christian was standing. He gave me a high five. Indeed, now that I was out of the water, I felt refreshed and renewed.

Satisfied with the sauna experience, we split up to explore the spa. I went over to Aunt Marie. She was soaking in a salt bath.

"You have to try this," she said, gesturing for me to get in. She was floating on her back, with one arm extended over her head, where she held onto a metal bar. I got in and lay back like her. The salt water suspended my body with no effort on my part. I reached back to hold the bar so that I wouldn't float away.

"Now lay your head back so that your ears are underwater."

I did so, gently relaxing my neck muscles. As the warm water closed around my head, gentle sounds of classical music enveloped me. They were playing music underwater! You could only hear it if you were submerged. I closed my eyes and floated there, suspended and listening to an underwater symphony.

Sam joined me and we floated in bliss. Satisfied, we got up to check out the outdoor pool. We walked across the tiled floor near the entrance. We stepped down into the pool. The water was room temperature and came up to our chests. The pool was long and narrow and headed into a tunnel. We floated down it. At the end of the tunnel was a thick plastic curtain. We pushed it aside and floated outside.

The pool opened up outside. It was much larger than the narrow tunnel, and nobody else was around. There were only a few streetlights visible, so we felt even more alone. The air was chilly, so we kept our bodies beneath the surface.

We looked up to see the night sky clear of clouds and fog. The atmosphere was calm and stars splayed out in all directions. Steam rose from the water and floated into the sky. The warm, gentle water embraced our tired, sore bodies. It was transcendental to be here, so far from home, bobbing gently in the waves beneath the quiet night sky. I held Samie from behind as we looked into the night sky, feeling more in love with her than ever before.

It was the perfect end to our trip. In contrast to new and exotic locales and cheap hostels, our trip ended with a familiar homecoming, clean beds, and a relaxing spa. We had gotten used to being dirty and disheveled during our travels, so the cleansing waters of Bad Salzuflen felt even better than they would have otherwise.

Samie and I floated out there, happy and in one of those eternal moments one rarely gets to experience. It seemed like, for a moment, time didn't move. I floated in the warm waters forever, happy and at peace.

I felt like this was truly the end of my journey. I looked up at the stars. I was so happy my trip would end on such a high note. I was floating in warm water with my partner next to me. Nearby were new friends I had made and old family members I had reconnected with. I couldn't have planned it to be this good.

The lights in the pool began to flash. They were closing down for the night. We left the pool reluctantly, showered and got dressed. We were feeling joyful from our experience. We got into Christian's car and left the parking lot.

We came to a stop sign. There was a pedestrian walking across the intersection. Christian rolled down his window and shouted to the stranger.

"Kennen Sie wo Eis man kaufen können?" He was asking the man if he knew where to buy some ice cream.

"McDonalds" the man replied, pointing to familiar golden arches just down the block. Christian thanked him, we went inside and ordered some ice cream.

"Ein McFlurry, bitte" we each said, one at a time. We got our ice cream and found a booth. Chloe, Sam, Christian, my aunt and I crammed in a booth and happily ate ice cream. It was past midnight, and we could not have had a better time.

The car ride back was quick, and I struggled to stay awake. At the house, I gave Christian a goodbye hug. I thanked him for a wonderful time. I was sad to see him go. People like Christian and Marie are examples of the best kinds of religious folks. They practiced a lifestyle of true Christian fellowship. They never preached at me one time. If more people could be like them, we would live in a better world.

I went to bed happy. I was fortunate to have my friends, my family, and Samie. I was grateful for and content with my marvelous journey. I happily fell asleep.

Leicester, Day Thirty-Seven: 3rd of May.

My alarm woke me up bright and early at six in the morning. I stumbled downstairs groggily, having only gotten five hours of sleep. I was joined at the table by Sam and Chloe, both equally exhausted.

It was quiet as we drove to the Bielefeld train station. We saw the sunrise over fields of wheat. The sunlight was like liquid gold as it reflected on the amber fields. There were small farmhouses and clumps of leafy green trees. I had seen the sunrise from a boat in Amsterdam, a ghetto in Madrid and a campsite outside of Venice. I admired it one last time. I had found a real community here in Bielefeld and was sad to see it go.

We pulled into the train station parking lot. Marie helped us unload our bags, and then hugged me. Our first hug had been awkward and without intimacy. Our last hug was full of it.

"Now that you've been here, let the other family know it's not so bad here," she asked me. I told her I would.

Aunt Marie hugged the girl's goodbye and drove away as we entered the train station. We had a few minutes before our train came, so we poked around the small station. We bought some pastries for the ride. I was even lucky enough to find a postcard of Bielefeld, completing my collection.

The train to Dusseldorf arrived precisely on time. We found some seats, opened our Eurail passes and filled out the prerequisite lines. We wrote in 'Bielefeld to Dusseldorf' in the blank spaces. A ticket inspector soon came by to check them. These passes expired in just a day or two. As the man handed them back, I felt satisfied that we had gotten so much use out of them.

The rest of the ride was uneventful. Conveniently, the train went directly to the airport, where we found our gate easily. The airport was medium sized, clean and bland. All airports strike me as more or less the same and Dusseldorf was no exception. We had a few hours before our flight, so we killed time by spending the last of our euros. We bought snacks and cheap souvenirs. I spent my very last euro coin on a coffee. I left Europe with only three euro cents in my pockets.

Before we flew, I had to use the bathroom. I walked into the bathroom and walked past the sinks to where the stalls were. There were only two stalls, both occupied. I could see feet clad in leather shoes underneath the stall doors.

I walked past the two stalls, looking for a third one. There was no more stalls, so I walked back out of the room. As I passed the stalls again, I heard a voice call out a goodbye, "*Tschüss.*"

Immediately the other man called out "*Auf wiedersehen.*" Who said Germans don't have a sense of humor?

I joined sat back down at the gate. Our adventure had come nearly full circle. We were only fifty miles away from the Dutch border, and about hundred miles from Amsterdam. We had almost made a complete geographical circle.

Happy with our journey, we boarded the British Airways flight. We were overjoyed to hear the crisp English voices over the loudspeaker. Before we knew it, we were back at the familiar Heathrow Airport.

Heathrow was massive. It took us a few minutes to just orientate ourselves. We took time to check out some tourist shops, happy to finally be surrounded by British flags and things like that again. We felt like we were home.

We went towards the trains but soon halted. We realized we had no British pounds or pence, and so we stopped by an

ATM. There we had a painful shock and readjustment to the exchange rate.

The euro was only slightly stronger than the dollar. One euro was worth about a dollar and fifteen cents. The pound was utterly different. One pound, at the time, was nearly two whole dollars. The two-to-one exchange rate was brutal on our bank accounts. I have since kept an eye on the exchange rate. In the next several years I never saw the pound as strong as it was then.

When Chloe withdrew her money, the machine issued her a bunch of pound coins. They came rolling out of the machine. Chloe, unprepared, saw them spill out on the ground. She bent to pick them up while Sam and I stood by impassively. The three of us were tired of each other. We had spent all day with each other for the last thirty-six days straight. We sorely needed some time apart.

After some much needed time apart, the three of us stayed friends. Not all travel buddies can say the same. Several other friend groups had splintered during that spring break, never to come back together. I am happy to report that Samie, Chloe and myself are still good friends today. A few years later, Chloe would be a bridesmaid during Samie and I's joyous marriage.

We gathered our British money and went to the ticket counter. We bought the next available train tickets to Leicester. Our town was only an hour or so away, so trains ran pretty frequently. In no time at all, we were settling into our seats. The train felt like home. Sam had the window seat, and I sat next to her. The train was packed to the gills. It was so crowded Chloe couldn't even sit near us. Instead, she was up near the other end of the car.

I started to write in my journal to pass the time. I was several days behind, so I was just writing about Berlin. I wrote for a little, then impulsively looked across the aisle. My eyes settled on a young Filipino man sitting across me. I was deep in thought about Berlin, so I did not immediately recognize why the man looked familiar.

"Phil?" I asked, incredulously.

The man looked at me and smiled. "Hi Nate, how's it going mate?"

My jaw dropped. Of all the trains to running to Leicester, of all the cars and seats on the train I ended up sitting next to my good friend Phil.

Phil and I happily spoke the rest of the way. I am American, and he is Australian so to the English it must have seemed like we were screaming. They kept giving us dirty looks, but I couldn't care less. They should have said something out loud if they had something to say.

Phil filled me on his adventures. After leaving Venice, he had gone to Rome. There, Phil snuck into the Vatican at the end of a big mass, by entering through the exits. He was hanging out in a nearly empty St Peter's square, when the Pope unexpectedly drove by, waving at people. Only Phil would be able to infiltrate the Vatican and see the Pope by accident.

When the train arrived, we found Chloe. The platform felt as familiar and comfortable as home. Chloe hugged Phil, and we were feeling good. Not sure of what to do next, we walked over to Oksana's apartment. The walk was short, and we were excited to see the curry shops and fish and chip joints.

We reached the asphalt car park where the student apartments stood. It was as ugly as any other massive blocks of student housing I'd ever seen. Our journey had begun here on a rainy day five weeks ago. It felt like a lifetime had passed.

As we crossed over the lot, we spotted Oksana's window high on the top floor. As we got near the base of the building, her window slid open, and Oksana leaned out.

She had a broad smile on her face. Her straight black hair pointed down to the ground as she waved at us. We waved back and jogged over to the door. It felt like a scene in a movie.

Oksana let us in and we set down our packs in her room. It was a tiny one-room studio, about the size of a dorm room. With five of us in there, it was intensely claustrophobic. As soon as we set our stuff down, we walked back into the hallway.

"How about Nando's?" Phil asked.

"Nando's sounds amazing!" Chloe said, and the rest of us agreed. We had not seen a Nando's in all of our European adventures. Lucky for us, there was one just around the block from the apartment.

We walked over and ordered the spicy peri-peri chicken Nando's is famous for. It was my favorite fast food place in England. The spicy, cheap chicken never disappointed.

Oksana, Phil, Samie, Chloe and myself crammed into a round booth, ate spicy chicken and told each other stories. We had all had misadventures, near misses, a few scares and lots of unforgettable experiences. Being back in Leicester we all simultaneously felt much older and also like nothing had changed.

The sun was starting to go down and we needed to grab our dorm room keys. The student office was closing soon, so we left Nando's to find a bus stop. We hugged goodbye to Oksana and told her we would meet up with her later.

At the stop, we hopped on the bus when it arrived and flashed our expired Leicester bus passes at the driver. The bus was a blue double-decker. We walked up to the second floor and took our seats. Sam and I sat together while Chloe and Phil were in front of us. They twisted around in their seats to keep up the conversation with us.

While the bus didn't take us directly to the campus, it got within a few blocks. We were concerned we might get lost trying to find the dorms, but the quiet suburban streets came back instantly. I could go back and navigate it today. We walked past the wooden fences and tall hedgerows that are so common in England.

We got to the student office just a few minutes before it closed. We were handed our keys as they were shutting off the lights and locking the door. If we had missed them, we would have had to pay for a hotel and our budgets were dangerously low.

We split up to go to our respective dorms. The four of us lived in separate places. We agreed on a time to meet back up, then headed off.

I approached my dorm, the Shirley House. The lovely Downton Abbey-era house looked empty, which very much suited me. I unlocked one of the many side doors and stepped inside. The smell of the unwashed English lads greeted me. I sighed and trudged up the stairs. Some things never changed. But, the house was mercifully quiet, as nobody seemed to be home.

I got to my room, put the key in and swung the door open, delighted to have it to myself.

Inside, I found my erstwhile roommate sitting on the two beds he had pushed together. His girlfriend was sitting with him. He looked shocked at my stubborn tendency to keep existing.

"I'm so sorry, I thought you were gone for good," he stammered hurriedly as he hopped up to push the beds apart.

"Still here," I said with a wry smirk. "Just glad I didn't interrupt anything."

They both blushed deeply. The English are very uptight about these kinds of things. "Yeah, I just got back from the holiday."

I unbuckled my backpack and set it on my bed.

"Is that all you had with you?" his girlfriend asked me meekly. Like a lot of English girls, she was petite and tiny.

"Well, it's all you really need," I replied before heading for the door. I wanted to head out before they had a whispered argument about whether to stay or not. I knew they would decide that it would be improper for her to stay, and that would set off a whole another round of whispered angry planning. This would, of course, be considered the polite way of handling my unexpected arrival.

"I'll be back tomorrow," I said as I stepped out of the door. I would spend the night with Samie, as her roommate was still gone. I would spare my roommate this time. We didn't get along very well, and it was just my luck that he was the only student back in the house besides me.

A few hours later, Phil, Samie, Chloe, Oksana and I met up at the Firebug, our favorite pub in Leicester. It was a low-key hipster student bar. There was always a thumping indie rock playlist blasting out of the speakers. It was just dive-y enough without being a total shithole. It was my kind of place.

We got our favorite drinks and snagged a table. My drink of choice was always a nice cold, creamy Guinness. Guinness in the British Isles tastes much better than back home. In America, they brew it on the East Coast, but here we got it straight from Dublin. I never tasted Guinness this good elsewhere. It felt great to be back.

Marx & Engels & Chloe

Epilogue: Last Days in Leicester & Going Home

The following night, back in my dorm room, I had a hard time falling asleep. I stared up at the white plaster ceiling. As I laid there, it felt like I never left in the first place, like maybe the last five weeks had never happened at all. I knew when I was back in Ohio the sense would be thousand times stronger.

In the coming days, Leicester would feel different somehow. It felt a little more colorless and hollow. One by one my friends left to go home. Some, like Maxime, had simply never come back from holiday. As some left, I knew I would probably never see them again. Each day more students turned in their final essays, completed their last tests, and packed their bags to fly home.

We knew that the incredible experience of living aboard was coming to an end, and we knew that we soon had to return to reality. Most of us had less than two weeks from the day we returned to our final departures. Still, I was able to make some of my best memories of my time abroad from that short interim period.

Each meal with friends was more heartfelt than the last. We savored each drink just a little bit more. I got up early a few times to watch the sun come up over the misty English hedgerows. Even walking to the local Asda already felt nostalgic.

After we turned in our final papers, our professors brought us out to the pub. They spent all night buying beers for Chloe, Samie and I. By the time the pubs closed, we were all well knackered, including the professors.

Leicester is the curry capital of the world, outside of India. Several times during the semester a big group of us went out at the same restaurant. In those last few days, the remaining members of my friends went out there one last time and ate a spicy, delicious Indian meal.

Samie went on day hikes across the rural parts of the East Midlands. She and her friend Jackie jumped over quaint little wooden fences and crossed fields of sheep. The English countryside, although perpetually damp and misty, has a magical quality.

And yet, in the blink of an eye, it was the last day in Leicester. Oksana hosted a goodbye party in her tiny apartment complex. We squeezed into her communal kitchen and drank ourselves silly. After playing drinking games, we walked over to the on-campus nightclub and danced all night. I got a little too drunk and ended up losing my trusty leather jacket. I had worn it across the U.K., Ireland and the rest of Europe. Although I was disappointed, it somehow felt right for it to stay on the European side of the ocean.

The next morning we left Leicester nursing a nasty hangover. It was a beautiful sunny day. Phil and Oksana joined us on our way to London. When we had arrived in the United Kingdom in January, we had spent a few days there and so it was very fitting to end our journey back there.

In London, we toured the incredible British Museum, shopped in the flea markets of Camden and ate dinner in a pub between the Thames and the London Eye. During our very last night before our flight home the five us of crammed onto a single hotel bed and watched, most appropriately, *Euro Trip*.

Our flight was quite early, so Chloe, Sam, Oksana and myself left the hotel at the crack of dawn. We hugged a very groggy Phil goodbye. I knew we would meet again, and indeed we did. Years later, during our rehearsal dinner in rural Wyoming, the day before our wedding, I looked up to see Phil, Jess and a few other Leicester friends running over to embrace us.

That was in the future, as we rode with Oksana to the airport. With our backpacks strapped on and suitcases in hand, we each embraced Oksana. We'd be seeing her again within a year and would later attend her beautiful wedding in Fairfax, Virginia. I am so grateful to count people like Chloe, Oksana and Phil as my good friends.

We printed out our boarding passes. Sam and I had an unfortunate error, where our second ticket, from Dublin to DC, didn't print. When we went to board our second flight in Dublin, the flight attendants made us leave and then re-enter the airport, going through the whole process again. We had barely twenty minutes to get new tickets, check our luggage and go through security. I was so nervous that it must have shown in my body language, for I was pulled out of security and searched.

In the end, we made it through security and were greeted by a friendly Texan who was working American Customs in the Dublin airport. "Howdy y'all, how was y'alls trip?" he asked.

My adventure flashed before my eyes. I saw myself in Amsterdam's Red Light District, lounging beneath the Eiffel Tower at night, standing inside an ancient Spanish mosque, wandering the streets of Florence, touching the Berlin Wall and sipping beer in the Old Town Square. I saw myself fumbling in the dark hostel bathrooms with the broken showers, eating endless Nutella sandwiches for breakfast, drinking black coffee at train stations and running to catch my connecting rides. I felt the freezing Mediterranean, the hot Tuscan sun, the chilly night air on the English Chanel and the warm salt-water baths of Bad Salzuflen. I thought about the fights in Italy, the tensions in Lavapiés, the laughter in Prague and all the other adventures the we had shared.

I smiled.

"It was great."

The man nodded politely, and we finished going through Customs. We boarded our plane with only minutes to spare.

After a long transatlantic flight, we arrived in Washington. We had one last flight to Cleveland from there. As soon as we got off the plane, my senses were assaulted. TV's were playing everywhere. The talking heads were spewing out fear and hate. Commercials were blaring about how to sue some company for something or other. I was instantly reacquainted with our insane media.

I went to bathrooms and was surprised at just how exposed American public toilets are. The gaps and spaces in the door seemed ridiculous. Getting some cash from an ATM, I noticed for the first time in my life that American money was all the same size and color.

I had one more moment of culture shock, one that brought my mental state back to America. On the plane from DC to Cleveland, a flight attendant came by and asked Samie and I if we wanted anything. I politely asked for a coffee, and then went back to staring straight ahead.

"Uh uh uh," the lady said rearing back and wagging her finger at me "I was asking the lady first. Where are your manners, young man?"

She shook her head. "Young people don't have no manners, isn't that right young lady," she asked Sam rhetorically.

I stared at the attendant in shock. I was stunned. I had no idea what to say. In Europe, nobody would ever say anything like that in a million years.

Seeing my confusion, she handed me my coffee and gave my shoulder a light squeeze. "Just joking honey" she said and walked to the next row.

Samie laughed at me as the attendant walked away. She leaned over, smiling, and said, "welcome home."

We'll meet again: Samie, Phil, Oksana and Chloe in London

Made in the USA
Coppell, TX
05 January 2023

10510206R00225